Japan Society

An organization of Americans formed in May, 1907, "for the promotion of friendly relations between the United States and Japan and the diffusion among the American people of a more accurate knowledge of the people of Japan, their aims, ideals, arts, sciences, industries, and economic conditions."

It endeavors to interpret Japan to America and America to Japan, and to educate public opinion in America by giving accurate and reliable information about the land of the Rising Sun.

Facilities

Monthly News Bulletin
Monthly Trade Bulletin
Lecture Bureau
Bureau of Information
Hospitality Committee
Travel Information Bureau
Book Publishing Department

Address: 165 Broadway, New York.

The Japanese Nation

Its Land, Its People, and Its Life

With Special Consideration to Its Relations with
the United States

By

Inazo Nitobé,

A.M., Ph.D., LL.D.

President of the First National College, Japan
Professor in the Imperial University of Tokyo
Exchange Professor from Japan to American Universities
Author of " Bushido, the Soul of Japan," etc.

With a Map

Published for
The Japan Society of New York
by
G. P. Putnam's Sons
New York and London

The Knickerbocker Press, New York

To

THE UNIVERSITIES OF

BROWN

COLUMBIA

JOHNS HOPKINS

VIRGINIA

ILLINOIS

MINNESOTA

UNDER WHOSE AUSPICES WERE DELIVERED THE LECTURES WHICH

GAVE IT BIRTH

I DEDICATE THIS BOOK

IN GRATEFUL REMEMBRANCE

PREFACE

THE present work is the outcome of my labours as Japanese exchange professor in this country, during the academic year of 1911–12, and I take this opportunity of explaining how my work began and ended.

The idea of sending public men of note unofficially from this country to Japan and from Japan to the United States, owes its inception to Mr. Hamilton Holt of New York City. When his plan had been developed to a certain degree of feasibility, the task of carrying it into effect was accepted by President Nicholas Murray Butler of Columbia University, in whose hands the idea took the more practical if the less ambitious form of an exchange professorship, and he interested certain typical universities to join in putting it into effect. After the enterprise was fairly launched, the responsibility for its continuance was passed on to, and made a part of, the work of the Carnegie Peace Endowment. My labours commenced after the project had reached its second stage of development—namely, while the Universities concerned had the matter in their immediate charge.

In the spring of last year, the six American Universities of Brown, Columbia, Johns Hopkins, Virginia, Illinois, and Minnesota—representing the Eastern, Southern, and Middle-Western portions of the Continent—united in instituting an exchange of lecturers with Japan. The object of the scheme—as I take it—is the interchange of right views and sentiments between the two peoples, rather than a mutual giving and taking of strictly academic knowledge. The appointees, whether men of science or men of affairs or of literary reputation, are expected to be convoys of warm human feeling rather than of cold scientific truth.

Through President Butler and our Embassy in Washington, negotiations were started between the said Universities and the Japanese Government. The latter expressed its readiness to meet the proposal; whereupon the association formed of those business men who visited this country a few years ago, entered into the spirit of the undertaking by assuming the financial responsibility, provided the Government would help by recommending a man for the task.

Late in June, I was unexpectedly asked to come to the United States on this delightful, though arduous, mission, the Government releasing me for a year from the duties of my official posts as President of the First National College, as Professor of Colonial Policy in the Imperial University of Tokyo, and as Adviser to the Formosan

Government. I accepted the honour with sincere pleasure and yet with trepidation. Is it necessary to explain why the appointment gave me pleasure? Reasons which will naturally suggest themselves to everyone—an enjoyable trip, meeting with congenial people, renewing old acquaintance, taking my wife to her native home, the honour of being the first exchange professor from my country—all had their due share in my willingness to come. But there was a particular reason which made the proposal singularly attractive to me. Allow me to relate a personal incident.

Nearly thirty years ago, when applying for admission to the University in Tokyo as a student, I selected English Literature for my minor course, in addition to my major study of Economics. The Dean of the Department of Literature questioned me as to my motive for combining these two apparently unrelated branches of learning. "I wish, sir, to be a bridge across the Pacific," I replied. On being pressed for further explanation, I threw aside the metaphor and told him of my desire to be a means of transmitting the ideas of the West to the East, and of the East to the West. Though it was a fancy of youth, it was a wish that had been slowly forming during my collegiate days, and though the days of youth have long since gone by, the fancy has remained, waxing stronger with the progress of years.

To transmit a thought from one to another may not require an intellect of high order or an original cast of mind; but I am more than willing to play a second or even a third part, if I can thereby add a note—be it ever so low—toward the fuller harmony of diverse nations or of discordant notions.

Here then is my chief motive for accepting the responsibility of an untried duty which I did not enter upon boldly. No one knows better than myself how far short of its great object I have fallen, and—may I add?—how much farther I should have fallen if I had not had the constant assistance and never-failing attention of my wife. I must not omit a word of recognition for the loyal service rendered throughout my stay in the States by my friend and companion, Mr. Yusuke Tsurumi.

The regular demands of the lectureship consisted in delivering in each University a course of eight addresses. For these I chose the subjects given in Chapters I to VI inclusive, and Chapters VIII and XI. Chapter VII—on Education—is based on an address made before the Barnard Club in Providence, and before the Teachers' Club in Columbia University, also before the Pedagogical Seminary of Johns Hopkins. The chapter on *Japan as Coloniser* is an amplification of remarks made, without notes, in the Japan Conference held at Clark University, and, later, before the National Geographic Association in Washington. Chapter X is a reproduction of the paper sent to the meeting of the American Historical Association in Buffalo, December, 1911, when illness prevented me from attending in person. The final chapter, with some slight verbal changes, is a copy of the Convocation Address which I had the honour of making at the University of Chicago near the close of last year. The first address which I delivered in this country was in response to the invitation of Leland Stanford Jr. University; but, as it contains a number of local allusions, I have placed it last as an Appendix.

Should this book fall into the hands of any one of some forty thousand hearers, whom it has been my good fortune to address, in the one hundred and sixty-six lectures and speeches I have made in the course of my year's sojourn in this land, he will find that none of them is exactly like that to which he listened; but he will recognise that the general trend of thought and message is the same.

To hearer and reader I feel like apologising for not selecting more instructive subjects and for not presenting in a more interesting manner the themes chosen. It was indeed solicitude regarding the choice and treatment of subjects which caused me to embark upon this mission with trepidation. Until I faced my first audience at Brown University, I had not had the least intimation as to the character and interests of those who might favour me with their presence. While I was preparing two or three of my lectures, before leaving my country, how little did I anticipate that more than half of my lecture-halls would be graced by ladies! My original manuscripts were prepared with a

small group of students in view, and when I compare these with the book that is now presented to
the public, I am astonished at my own unsophisticated ideas of ten months ago. How in this country one comes to adjust one's thought and speech
to a broad-cultured, general public! As I have
grown more and more intimate with my audience,
I confess my regret that I did not confine the whole
field of my lectures to more specialised subjects,—
particularly to the relations between the United
States and Japan; but when that regret came—
regrets are rarely timely visitors!—it was too late
to write the course anew. I am happy to add,
however, that my regret, if late, was brief. A
month before my duties ended, a countryman of
mine—Kiyoshi Kawakami—brought forward the
result of his serious and careful study regarding
American–Japanese relations, treating the subject in a far more judicious form and attractive
style than I could ever do.

If then my regret was short-lived, what of the
misgivings with which I left Japan? It is only just
for me to admit that these had largely vanished,
ere my work was finished; but for this fact I claim
no credit to myself. Had it not been for the
patience of those who did not agree with my opinion or could not follow my imperfect delivery;
had it not been for the approval and sympathy of
those who shared my viewpoint; had it not been
for the positive encouragement and appreciation
of those who are friendlily disposed toward me and

toward my people, my original misgivings would
have been more than realised, and the first well-
meant attempt to effect a closer bond by means
of an academic bridge between the two nations
might have ended in disaster.

Let me therefore express my gratitude for, and
gratification at, the reception accorded my lectures
such as they were. Wherever I have been, be it
in a great University or in a small country school;
be it in a public entertainment in large cities or in
the midst of an informal family circle, I have
invariably enjoyed unstinted hospitality and a
gracious welcome. The newspapers, which are
not always known for their courtesy, and even
certain journals that have won a reputation for
their anti-Japanese utterances, have very often
surprised me by their friendly reports in regard
to my work. The past year has been for me a
continuous feast of mind and soul, and now, on
the eve of my departure from America, let me
cast one more glance upon the places I have
visited and the people I have met, that they
may the more indelibly stamp themselves upon
my memory, and that I may take home the
unchanged friendship of the American people
towards us, so often and everywhere expressed
to me.

It is very gratifying to learn that, by the time
I shall reach my home, there will closely fol-
low, in person, an envoy of American good-will.
I have recently been officially informed that

Dr. Hamilton Wright Mabie has been appointed as exchange lecturer to Japan. That this able thinker, eminent writer, and perfect gentleman can and will carry the message of his country to Japan with charm and erudition, there is no shadow of doubt. Should his Japanese audience be able to express half the good-will that it is sure to feel, the first span of the trans-Pacific bridge will have been constructed.

INAZO NITOBÉ.

POCONO MANOR INN,
June 20, 1912.

CONTENTS

xiii

Contents

The Japanese Nation

CHAPTER I

THE EAST AND THE WEST

AS facilities of intercommunication, and therefore points of contact, have of late rapidly increased, and as the East and the West can now see and hear each other at close range on matters of business interests, instead of merely exchanging courtesies at a polite distance, occasions have likewise more frequently arisen for misunderstanding and for doubt. The reasons for this seem manifest, and among them is Imperialism, the overpowering trend of the last century, which, causing the stronger nations to overleap their respective territorial bounds, has brought them face to face with one another in unexpected quarters distant from home. The Dutch and the English, for instance, encountered each other in an unwonted relation on the South African veldt. The Japanese and the Russians renewed acquaintance under strained circumstances on the plains of Man-

churia—somewhat after the manner of America
and Spain in Cuba and the Philippines, or, more
recently, the Italians and the Turks in Tripoli.
Though I do not desire a rupture of friendship
between the United States and her friends, she may
yet face some of them in unamiable converse on
the pampas of South America.

Upon the frontiers of empires has been witnessed the impingement of one people upon another
during the last two decades. When one calls at
a neighbour's front door, one is usually received
with courtesy; on the other hand, one may possibly
be considered an intruder in the backyard, no
matter how innocent. Just as the marginal utility
of commodities fixes their value, as economists
teach us, so it is in the margins of civilisations that
the power of expansive nationalities seems to be
tried and determined. America has extended her
borders to the Philippines, and Japan the edge of
her dominions to Formosa. Here they almost
meet. American trade, increasing in China, is
brought into competition with Japanese, and as in
these outskirts of commercial territory, inhabited
by alien races, each nation tries to demonstrate
and assert its own superiority, the timid are afraid
that we may come to know each other in ways not
always agreeable.

With the growth of Imperialism the stronger
nations look upon each other with suspicion and
jealousy, and, unlike the more innocent intercourse
of former days, when men delighted in the ex-

change of the ideas and arts of peace, modern Imperialism, impelled by feverish megalomania and zest for commercial supremacy, has come to regard all competitors, not only as rivals, but as potential enemies, whose existence jeopardises their own and whose fate must therefore be decided at the point of the sword. Nor is Imperialism alone to blame; for it is nowadays quite the proper thing for dilettante ethnologists and amateur sociologists to put forward their incomplete theories and insufficient data only to make the imagined abyss between the East and the West appear more hopeless. How little Blumenbach and Cuvier fancied that their classification of the human race by the colour of the skin would be taken so seriously as to become a cause of animosity among the nations of the earth! Under these circumstances it is the duty of every lover of humanity and of peace to be an interpreter, a go-between in the supposed clash of national interests and racial sentiments.

Am I greatly mistaken in believing that, as far as the race question is concerned, we are now at a comparatively early stage of generalisation, having but just begun to perceive aggregate differences? Will not the next stage be a fuller recognition of spiritual affinity, of psychological unity—a realisation that "mankind is one in spirit" and the whole world kin?

I doubt whether in the earlier centuries of the Christian era Europe was intelligently aware of its own unity, as against the multitudinous

principalities and powers of Asia, any more
than these are at present conscious of their mutual
ties.

The political unity forced upon Europe by the
Carlovingians proved a premature *coup*, but religious unity survived the imperial fiasco, and
brought about social unity within the boundaries
of Europe. Then followed the Crusades to renew
and reinforce the feeling of oneness among the
warring nations. The term Christendom was then
invented,—its first appearance in the English
language being in 1389; but it long remained a
vague, sentimental denomination. With the Reformation and the Renaissance the glamour of the
Civitas Dei receded more and more into the privacy
of each pious soul, while the *civitas terrena*,
largely freed of the evil import imposed upon it
by St. Augustine, was upheld by necessity, learning, and custom.

The term Christendom, which had been steadily
losing its prestige as a communion of saints, God's
kingdom on earth, assumed the new sense of the
community of culture and the comity of nations.
Its religious significance grew fainter and fainter,
until it was at last displaced by the secular term,
West, first used by Monsieur Comte. The selection of this term involved the thesis confirming
the unity and uniformity of European civilisation,
and the antithesis as to its diversity from and
superiority to Oriental civilisation.

Discrimination of differences between the East

and the West certainly marks an advance in the differentiation of ideas upon the age when the nations of Europe were blind to their collective interests and indicates at the same time a step toward a larger synthesis, whereby Europe becomes conscious of a common bond. But the ancients seem to have made little distinction between Europe and Asia. Probably differences were not then so glaring, trade passing unencumbered to and fro, learning and peaceful arts being freely exchanged. In the borderland between Asia and Europe mingle Aryans, Semites, and Turanians. The marvellous civilisation of Babylon was not autochthonous, nor was that of ancient Crete. Indeed, how much of Greek art and thought is strictly Occidental, I should like to know. Or, how much of the arts and philosophy of Persia and India are strictly Oriental, I fain would ask. Until the Middle Ages the world was more homogeneous than now—at least in feeling and ideas.

Take the early history of art, and it seems that Greece and India and China were in pretty close contact. Compare ancient Hindoo sculpture with Greek, and it is amazing to observe how closely allied they are, with the Bactrian as a link between them. Place by their side the old Chinese images, until lately almost unknown and only recently unearthed, and we feel that the lands of Plato and of Confucius were not irreconcilably opposed in culture. The victories of Alexander, somehow, do not strike me as the descent of an army of civilisation into a region of a very inferior grade of culture. The Jews served for a long time as cosmopolitan mediators between Europe and Asia through their commercial agencies; then, later, the Arabs, not yet turned hostile to Christianity, became the intermediaries of Occidental and Oriental science and art.   But as the Saracens and afterwards the Ottomans—or shall we say Moslems?—interposed an almost insuperable barrier between Europe and Asia, the world was practically rent in twain. Then each began to pursue its own course, irrespective of the other's movements, so that when Europe awoke from its sleep of the Dark Ages, Asia still continued to slumber; but by the time they met again after the lapse of centuries they could hardly recognise each other's features.   Rejuvenated Europe, fresh and strong, armed with science and trained in liberty—how could it own a friend of "Auld Lang Syne" in decrepit Asia, worn with age and torn with discord!   Sluggard Asia had lost all consciousness of unity of any kind.   You cannot call it a Buddhaland, because unlike Christ in Europe, Buddha has rivals claiming dominion with him; nor was there any unity of race, literature, or language.   If there was then any East that could be named in juxtaposition to the West, it expressed chaos as against order, a crowd of Kings who reigned without governing, a nondescript mass of beings who simply existed without living.   Who would not then prefer "fifty years of Europe to a cycle of Cathay"?

But the question in my mind is whether this difference between the East and the West is strictly scientific or of lasting value? It is said that Leibnitz divided the human family into those who could read Latin and those who could not; and Mr. Kipling mildly hints the classification of the same family into those who wear trousers and those who wear something else—to which I may suggest adding those who wear nothing. The division of mankind into East and West is more convenient but no more scientific than that of Leibnitz or Kipling; for with Alexander Pope, we may

"Ask where 's the North? At York, 't is on the Tweed;
In Scotland, at the Orcades; and there
At Greenland, Zembla, or the Lord knows where."

The meridian that divides the globe into East and West is the line which passes through the place where the observer stands and through the two poles. Hence there are as many meridians as there are observers and what is East to one may be West to the other. The Arabs were called by the Hebrews the children of the East, and by the Babylonians the dwellers of the West; and they denominated themselves by either of these names. As there is no absolute meridian, East and West are merely relative terms. If the meridian at Greenwich was selected by the convention of 1884 in Washington as the basis of calculation for the world, that meridian itself was only conventional, in more senses than one, for the little English village has no other claim than its observatory to be the centre of the world. The line which there divides East from West also serves to unite them. Hence we may improve upon the rhetoric of the psalmist and say, "As near as the east is to the west"; and hence, too, it is not only when two strong men, "coming from the ends of the earth, stand face to face," but when the weakest man, fixing his eyes upon the polar star, stretches out his arms, that the two hemispheres are united, and that "there is neither East nor West, border nor breed, nor birth." Without being untrue to the land of one's birth or of one's adoption, one may say with Henry Clay, "I know no South, no North, no East, no West, to which I owe any allegiance."

No small pains are taken to discover points of difference between East and West, and of these there are many, especially of the superficial sort; but the very fact that attempts are made to discover differences, takes points of resemblance for granted. When I listen to the analysis of Japanese character and institutions by a hypercritical foreigner—and *vice versa* for that matter—I am reminded of an anatomist who dissects a woman's corpse and eruditely arrays all the points wherein she differs from man, and would lead us to the inevitable conclusion that man and woman are so irreconcilably opposed in every single respect that the two can never be one. If he were so minded, a nursery psychologist could easily bring out evidence tending to show that a parent and a child are of such different mental constitution that their natural relations are unreasonable and must end in disaster. A mere description without an explanation is likely to lead to a wrong inference. Not much better are the method and attitude of zoilists who write on Japan. Every oddity in manners, every idiosyncrasy in thought is magnified into a distinguishing characteristic of the East or the West, as the case may be; either way, most often for the Pharisaical purpose of self-exaltation. The very faults that are common to both, are deemed particularly blameworthy when committed by the other race. The atmosphere of the Pacific seems to possess the obnoxious power of throwing above the horizon on either side not only an inverted but a perverted mirage. For instance, a clever author of a recent book dwells in some detail on the immorality of the Japanese, which he proves by statistics—appalling figures indeed—but which will stand comparison with similar statistics of the city of New York or of Chicago, if he had only given these. The same gentleman casts a suspicion upon our public men—of course in contrast to the purity and invulnerability of American politicians, who never violate one commandment of the Decalogue—the more so as the ten commandments made no mention of graft!

It is not by mutual fault-finding or by exaggerating each other's peculiarities that we can arrive at understanding or appreciation. Not by antipathy but sympathy; not by hostility but by hospitality; not by enmity but by amity, does one race come to know the heart of another. I have already intimated that the line of division is also the line of union, and "What God hath joined, let no man put asunder."

There is something grand and graceful in the old belief or beliefs as to the locality of paradise. In the early Christian Church, on the occasion of his baptism, a new convert was made first to face the West in abjuring the devil and his work, because the West was, according to Cyril, the region of darkness; and then he turned toward the East in receiving ablution, because in that quarter of the heavens was shown God's peculiar favour. In strange contrast to this, did the Buddhists place the abode of the blest in the West, whither the sun itself makes its daily pilgrimage.

Not in the Occident and not in the Orient, but in the union of both, will be revealed many of the secrets of Divine dispensation as yet hidden from our sight. A few days before I left Japan, Seiho, the greatest painter of Modern Japan, said to me: "Though I do not profess any familiarity with European masters, I have great hopes in that region of art where the East and West come together—not the neutral land that lies barren between the two, but where Western art fades into Eastern, or where the Eastern lapses into the Western, or where the two domains overlap, as it were." As I listened to him, I thought to myself that this remark of his may be applied to other activities and walks of human life as well as to art. May we not say that some of the greatest discoveries of biology have been made in the borderland where the animal and vegetable kingdoms meet? Some of the most fertile principles have been found in the newly cultivated field which joins chemistry with physics; and as for psycho-physics, delving as it does in a realm not yet named, between the territories of mind and of matter, it has struck rich veins of precious knowledge. We may expect the greatest fertility in the virgin soil where apparently contrary natures meet and wed.

It is said that the genius of the East is spiritual, mystical, psychical, and that of the West is materialistic, actual, physical; it is said that the forte as well as the fault of the East is religion and sentiment, and that of the West, science and reason; it is said that the East delights in generalisation and universal concepts, and the West in particulars and special knowledge; that the one leans to philosophy and ideas, and the other to practice and facts; that Oriental logic is deductive and negative, and Occidental logic inductive and positive. It is also said that in political and social life, solidarity and socialism characterise the East, and individualism and liberty, the West; it is said again that the Asiatic mind is impersonal and rejects the world, whereas the European mind is personal and accepts the world. The strength of

Europe lies in the mastery of man over nature, and the weakness of Asia in the mastery of nature over man. In the land of the morning, man looks for beauty first and writes his flighty thoughts in numbers; in the land of the evening, man's first thought is for utility, and he jots down his observations in numerals. He who watches the setting sun, pursues whither it marches, and his watchword is Progress and his religion is the cult of the future. He who greets the effulgent dawn is therewith content and cares not for its further course, but rather turns in wonderment to the source whence it came, hence his religion is the cult of the past. The matin disposes man to contemplation, the vesper hour to reflection. In the East man lives for the sake of life; in the West man lives for the means of living.

On the whole there is food for thought in this contrast of race peculiarities; but such general characterisation is of little practical use in diplomacy or in commerce, for the individuals with whom we deal do not always conform to a type, and the wider the scope allowed to individual activity, the greater is the divergence from the type. This is distinctly so in Japan, where the thought and the influence of the East and of the West find their meeting ground. It is well known that the sea which surrounds my country is the richest in varieties of fish, because the various currents of the ocean which wash our shores and the rivers which flow into its waters meet and mingle and offer favourable conditions to various forms of animal life. It is along the line which unites the East and the West that we should look for a higher and a richer successor to our present civilisation.

But instructive and interesting as is fishing on the high seas of speculation, there is a more pressing and utilitarian demand for the study of the regions where Europe and Asia come in direct contact. Or—to put the case more concisely— there is, at present, urgent and practical need for America to understand Japan. As long as our planet is round, a segmental or hemispheric progress, however deep, can only remain fragmentary and falls short of perfect culture. Only in a mutual understanding between the opposite points of the compass, can man read the final destiny of the race, whereas without comprehending the antipodal soul, he can never discover his own shortcomings or his peculiar gifts. Very truly says Bailey:

" 'T is light translateth night; 't is inspiration expounds experience; 't is the West explains the East ";

and it is only tautological to add that 't is the East explains the West.

Of late years, most unfortunately and most unexpectedly have darksome clouds been lowering across the Pacific Ocean, sometimes reaching gigantic proportions and assuming threatening appearances—so much so that some Americans have imagined they saw among the clouds a dragon spitting fire, as in the cartoon drawn by no less distinguished a personage than Kaiser Wilhelm. There is a custom in our country whereby literary men who have composed a stanza ask their artist friends to make suitable pictures to bring out the meaning the better, and, conversely, artists ask poets to write some lines to elucidate their pictures. When I first had the honour of beholding this celebrated drawing of the Kaiser, there came to my mind an ancient Japanese ode:

> "Clouds on the distant hills
>   Of far Cathay—
> Smoke which from our own hearthstones
>   Rose to-day!"[1]

May we not say that the clouds which hang over the Pacific, if there really are any, are but the accumulation of fancies which have emanated from beclouded brains amongst us and amongst you? They are largely the creations of Yellow Journalism, for which, as it enjoys no legal patent right, the public pays in fright and anxiety. Then some unscrupulous individuals make a regular trade of spreading thrilling news of the imminent danger of war. Naturally, to satisfy a general craving for excitement, writers of fiction wield their busy pen, and already on the book-stands are

[1] For this translation I am indebted to Judge Duke of Charlottesville, Va.

arrayed a number of their products bearing popular titles.　There is no lack of authors who pander
to depraved or bloodthirsty lovers of the fantastic.　There are, too, not a few military and naval
men who honestly believe that they can maintain
their profession in high repute, or their trust in
high efficiency, by constantly keeping possible
warfare before the eyes of the public.　Then,
again, there are important business concerns to
which a war scare is a source of large orders and of
profit.　Not seldom does it happen that an order
for building a Dreadnaught is preceded by loud
talk about complications with a foreign country.
When we learn that an order for a single gunboat
means business to the amount of six million dollars
and employment for five thousand men for two
and a half years, it is not surprising that a Japanese
bogy should periodically appear.　Of all forms and
methods of argumentation, none is more convin-
cing, though text-books on rhetoric refuse with
lofty scorn to take note of it, than *argumentum ad
crumenam* or *ad hominem;* and the deeper the
pocket, the more keenly is the force of such logic
appreciated.　I have heard that a scare-crow in
a melon patch does some good by frightening
away innocent birds, but that it offers at the same
time a convenient cover for a thief!　"We seek and
offer ourselves to be gulled," says Montaigne.
The ancient Romans had an adage, "The populace
like to be deceived" (*Populus vult decipi*)—and
the populace have not changed much since then,

despite all the changes they have witnessed.   The
gullibility of the human mind seems recently to
have assumed most appalling dimensions; and
when it does so, it is easily taken advantage of.
It is then that false prophets and soothsayers ply
their craft; and many, too many, have already
made their appearance.   Some of their voices were
heard but lately in high places.   It is deeply to be
regretted that cheap prophecies are going to prove
very dear to believing peoples.

Doleful prophets there have been in all ages and
in all places;—for instance, in 1895, a young navy
officer uttered at Annapolis a prophecy that in the
year of our Lord 1896 or 1897 a great cataclysm
would involve the whole of Europe, and that Russia
would make irresistible march westward, while
England would dwindle into a third-rate power.
The time that was allotted for the fulfilment of
this prophecy has long passed, and poor mortals
with limited vision still fail to discern the signs of
its near realisation.   Captain Hobson started out
as a war prophet at the early age of twenty-five,
and he still continues to exercise the same gift of
foresight, only with this difference—that now the
field of his prediction is the East instead of the
West, and instead of counting the period of its
fulfilment in years he calculates it in months.   In
February, 1911, he declared that a rupture would
take place between the United States and Japan
within ten months—a per od of time which, after
further consideration, he stretched to twenty

months and which, I hope, he will be further inspired to prolong to eternity.

Nor is Captain Hobson the only alarmist; for only last summer there appeared a rival prophet who pretended to give a "mathematical analysis of the astrological evidence of war with Japan," in which the author points out that "When California was admitted to the Union Uranus was in Aries and when Washington was admitted Saturn and Neptune were cavorting together in an unholy alliance—conclusive evidence that both these States show themselves to be a sometime battlefield of the nation!"

Whatever honour these prophets may enjoy here in their own country, they have none in ours. We are too light-hearted to take them seriously. It is not childish heedlessness that makes us feel light of heart. With our eyes wide open and our minds eager for national safety, we still fail to detect any ground for going to war with any country, least of all with America. Should anything so improbable occur, you may rest assured that the initiative will not be taken by Japan.

The simple fact that Japan, during the past two decades, has engaged in two great conflicts—or three, if you include her share in the suppression of the Boxer movement—may give an erroneous idea that we are a nation wantonly fond of fighting, a dangerously cantankerous character for a neighbour to have. But is there any other nation that can boast of two hundred and thirty years of con-

tinuous peace? I do not wish to brag; but I
should like to know for the sake of information
whether any other country has broken that record,
—and yet such is the absurdity of fame, that we
figure to the world as a race of Myrmidons.

I have often seen suspicion cast upon Japan
because of her great armament; that she must be
drilling her army and building Dreadnaughts for
the ulterior purpose of territorial expansion. I
personally am opposed to such armament; but
even as it is, it is not for aggression. You know
the Scotch proverb, "Nae one can live in peace
unless his neighbours let him." Or, to put it
in more high-sounding phraseology, we have to
bring ourselves into selective accommodation or
organic adjustment to the bellicose environment
of the twentieth century. If we need an army or
navy, we need it for self-defence, self-preservation.
With the acquisition of Korea and Saghalien, our
coast line has increased, but not our navy in the
same proportion.

We do not forget some unkind comments and
hard treatment from certain countries; but we are
morally prepared to bear them, if not like martyrs,
at least like gentlemen. Like our fabled dragon,
we do not stir while maidens play with our beard
or children ride upon our back. But let a rude
hand touch his throat, the dragon will rise in all
his native fury. You understand this spirit. It
is not a warlike or aggressive spirit. Is it not the
spirit of '76, as you call it? When the Thirteen

Colonies, the "three millions of people armed in the holy cause of liberty," rose up, like one man, "invincible by any force," who called them an aggressive people? There is a wide margin between an unconquerable spirit and a spirit of conquest. "The vigilant, the active, and the brave" are not on that account the warlike. The unconquerable spirit is the spirit of peace and not of war. No people will understand the distinction better than the American.

"Westward the course of Empire holds its way," has been true in one hemisphere, while eastward has been the march of human mind in the other, and now America in the foremost files of Western time and Japan as the heir of all the Asian ages, are met to complete the world's electric circle. I would not liken you to sentinels of Occidental culture and ourselves to guards of Oriental traditions, as do some. Neither of us stands on the Pacific coast to ward off the other from the treasures of his heritage. Are we not more than willing —even eager—mutually to share our ancestral gifts?

If your country and mine should come to a better knowledge each of the other—to a fuller and deeper understanding of each other's mission and aspirations—a long stride will have been taken toward the general advancement of human happiness, a great step toward the fulfilment of the prophecy, not of a sensational soothsayer, but of a great seer and thinker, who dipped into the future, far as human eye could see, and saw the time

"When the war drum throbb'd no longer, and the
    battle-flags were furled
In the Parliament of man, the Federation of the
    world."

And to this great consummation, devoutly to be
wished for, it is a privilege to contribute a widow's
mite.

CHAPTER II

THE LAND OR GEOGRAPHICAL FEATURES IN THEIR RELATION TO THE INHABITANTS

GEOGRAPHICALLY defined, Japan is a series of long and narrow volcanic islands in the Pacific Ocean, lying off the north-eastern coast of the Asiatic continent in the shape of a longitudinal curve.

This simple definition would require a detailed explanation were we to exhaust its full meaning —a task for which we have now no space at command. All we can do is to take up one by one the salient points of the definition and treat them from the standpoint of anthropo-geography. In the present discourse, I wish to amplify the following points: 1st, that Japan is an island country; 2d, that it is volcanic; 3d, that it is narrow; 4th, that it is long; 5th, that it lies off the coast of the Asiatic continent; 6th, that it lies in the Pacific Ocean.

I. First of all, Japan Is a Series of Islands. The whole country consists of no less than five hundred and eighteen islands.

The question what dimensions raise a piece of

land in the sea from a mere rock to the dignity of an island, is not yet scientifically or unanimously decided. The statement is sometimes made that the Empire of Japan consists of more than one million islands, and the *Tribune Almanac* for 1912 gives the number of islands composing the Empire as 4223. In our official returns, however, we exclude all those whose circumference is less than one *ri* (two and a half miles), unless inhabited or unless they serve as sea-marks of some importance.

Of these hundreds of isles, we will name only the most important:

Names of Islands	Number of Dependencies	Area
Honshu	166	81,843.88 sq.mi.
Hokkaido	13	30,299.87 " "
Kyushu	150	15,600.54 " "
Taiwan (Formosa)	7	13,851.99 " "
Shikoku	7	7,036.48 " "
Chishima (31 Kurile islands)	—	6,028.48 " "
Ryukyu (55 Loochoo islands)	—	935.78 " "
Sado	—	335.73 " "
Tsushima	5	266.53 " "
Awaji	1	218.67 " "
Oki	1	130.46 " "
Hokoto (Pescadores)	12	47.62 " "
Iki	1	51.43 " "
Ogasawara (20 Bonin islands)	—	26.82 " "
	Total	156,674.28 sq. mi.

If we exclude from this list Taiwan or Formosa and the Pescadores, we shall have over 142,000 square miles, which constitute what may be called

Old Japan, or Japan Proper. This is quite a respectable area for any nation to possess. We can compare favourably with the United Kingdom of Great Britain and Ireland or with Italy. In relation to the United States, however, the comparison will not redound to our glory, for our whole area is only equal in expanse to the State of Montana, is smaller than California or Texas, and is about three times the size of the State of New York or Virginia or Pennsylvania.

Owing to the insular formation of the country, the coast line, in proportion to the area, is naturally considerable, bearing an average of one mile to every eight square miles.

The coast bordering the Pacific Ocean, or, as we call it, Outer Japan, is very much more diversified than Inner Japan, or the shores along the Sea of Japan; hence the coast line of the former measures over 10,300 miles as against 2800 miles of the latter. Many of the indentations furnish excellent anchorage.

The insular nature of our country implies that a large number of our population are born and bred within sight of the sea, and, thus destined by nature to wield its craft, breathe its winds, and fight its billows, are inured from infancy to a seafaring life. There were times when our people ploughed the Pacific Ocean in their barks as traders, adventurers, colonists, and pirates, and started settlements along the shores of Asia or in different islands of the Southern Pacific, wandering "on from island unto island at the gateways of the day." Only by a strong governmental measure was this enterprising spirit kept in abeyance for two or three centuries, during which time the insular character of the country, far from arousing an adventurous spirit, cramped it within the precincts of its native land; so that the people, instead of looking out upon the great waters which surround them, turned their back upon the sea and strenuously confined their attention to the little valleys and restricted plains of Dai-Nippon. Insularity need not spell narrowness of ideas. It ought to mean breadth of vision. Whether it does the one or the other, will depend upon the attitude which the people take in regard to the sea. The Phœnicians and the Jews dwelt side by side on the same coast, but the Jews became exclusively a land folk, while the Phœnicians filled the farthest end of the then known sea with their ships of exploration and commerce,—truly, as Gibbon says, "The winds and waves are always on the side of the ablest navigators." It is said that the love of the sea and the enjoyment of its perils are confined to people of the Norse blood, but a little closer study will reveal the same characteristic in the Malays; and here I touch upon the subject of race.

Among the manifold effects of insularity, I may mention, first of all, the homogeneity of our people.

In spite of differences of blood and origin, the races which in time past drifted to our shores— the southern peoples from the tropics, the western from the Asiatic continent—have all mixed and amalgamated on our soil, and have been politically and socially moulded together until they have formed one homogeneous nation with one language, one tradition, one history, one literature. The diverse ancestors of the constituent races have gradually disappeared beyond the veil of obscurity and oblivion; so that our people now trace their ancestry to a common stock and pride themselves upon the name of the Yamato race.

This uniformity explains the strong patriotic sentiment which with us rises to an almost religious ardour. It is also this same consciousness which forms the basis of our loyalty to our ruler, upon whom we look as the personal representative of that ethnic unity—that strong sense of solidarity which defies any uninvited intrusion from without. During the Russo-Japanese War it was often repeated that if Russia were successful, she could never land her army on Japanese soil, or, if she did, it would be after the land was entirely bereft of inhabitants; for to the last survivor the Japanese, women as well as men, would fight for its defence. Intensity is a characteristic of island life. Ratzel, in speaking of "the exclusive personality" of an insular people, says that England reaches the maximum intensity of the civilisation of her neighbouring continent, and I believe that this remark is no less applicable to the only other insular nation which is independent in the strict sense of the term; for I dare say that our compact, intense nationality is the product of the waters which surround us.

To the insularity of our country, again, is due our freedom from foreign invasions and foreign complications. Were it not for the sea, we would not have escaped the catastrophes which so often befell the Korean and Chinese Empires. Only twice in the history of twenty centuries have hostile demonstrations taken place near our shores,— once at the close of the thirteenth century, when Kublai Khan, flushed with his conquests in China, despatched what was then considered an invincible armada; then, again, early in this century, when a hostile fleet under Admiral Rozhdestvensky approached our shores. But in neither case did Japan suffer in honour or in arms. These events only served to strengthen the confidence that we are "compass'd by the inviolate sea," and that our shores are guarded by waves and winds which love our land no less than do our captains and sailors.

Not only in respect to freedom from foreign invasion, but in respect to civil liberty, has Japan been fortunately located. It is true she did not develop that idea to a degree in any way approximating its development by the English or the Swiss. But compare her political career with that of China or India—countries whose examples she usually followed—and we cannot help wondering how her children have escaped the devastation of tyranny and despotism which overtook them. If she did not rise in the cause of liberty, neither did she sink into utter thraldom such as theirs. Singing of Swiss liberty, Wordsworth wrote:

> "Two voices are there; one is of the sea,
> One of mountains; each a mighty voice."

If liberty loves the heights and the deep, nowhere will it find a more congenial home than in Japan, which is only sea and mountains. It is worth noting here that Japan is the first country in Asia where parliamentary rule, the surest guarantee of liberty, has been adopted.

It is not only in respect to ethnic unity and solidarity, to loyalty, liberty, and patriotism, that our geographic insularity tells; but also in our every-day mode of living. Fishery supplies an important source of employment and of diet. It furnishes yearly an amount of food valued at about fifty million dollars, and employs the vast number of nearly two million people. Though our people are practically vegetarians, fish and fowl are freely consumed. No less than four hundred and fifty kinds of fish are caught in our waters, many of which are edible. I shall not go into conjecture as to how far a diet of fish affects the size of our brain! but it explains at least in part why stock-farming did not attain an important place in our economy. Cattle were never abundant, swine less so, and sheep unknown until recent years. It has been thought that our climate does not favour the growth of grass; but the discouragement given by Buddhism and Shinto to the slaughter of animals, on the one hand, and the rich harvest of the sea, on the other, were reasons more potent than climate for our poverty in live stock.

Islands naturally possess a maritime climate, the distinctive features of which are equability, relative humidity, and great cloudiness. One curious effect of our moist atmosphere is the frequent use of very warm baths, which are taken at a temperature as high as 120° Fahrenheit. Newcomers to Japan regard such a practice as highly unhygienic, but a few years' residence demonstrates to them that the custom is dictated by climatic demands. Our people are not happy unless they bathe frequently, and this habit of daily ablution is perhaps due to atmospheric humidity.

We have throughout the year an average of 150 days of snow or rain, and 215 days of fair weather; that is, for every three days of rain or snow, we have four fine days. As to quantity, the rainfall ranges, according to locality, from twenty to thirty inches a year.

The best medical authorities believe that our climate is particularly excellent for children. By Americans resident in Japan, its moisture is felt to be rather hard to bear, and I have often heard them complain of what they call "Japan head," by which they mean incapacity to work—in fact a species of nervous prostration, the same ailment which Germans name Americanitis, but which American residents prefer to ascribe to the Japanese climate.

I may state in passing, however, that Japan has a modified continental, rather than a strictly maritime, climate; but, lying in the monsoon region, the comparatively regular rains have made rice-culture the basis of agriculture. Though we cannot accept Buckle's conclusion in regard to the physiological effect of rice upon the brain, we can believe with Crawfurd that rice-culture and its indispensable condition, irrigation, exercised a vast influence on the economic, social, and political institutions of our people.

As for the indirect effect of the sea upon nutrition, there is good reason to believe that it is worthy of special study. According to the researches of Schindler, wheat grown in a maritime climate contains less protein, and, to supply its deficiency, crops rich in nitrogen, notably leguminous plants, are cultivated. This accounts for the prominent part played by legumes in our farming, and for their abundant use in our dietary system. The soy bean, crushed and made into what may be called vegetable cheese, or fermented and made into a paste, or simply cooked somewhat like the famous baked beans of New England, shares with rice the honour of being the staff of life among our people.

While I am on the subject of climate, I may be allowed to call your attention to a theory lately advanced by Professor Kullmer of Syracuse and Professor Huntington of Yale, as to the secret of national greatness. Briefly stated, they claim, to use Mr. Huntington's words, that "mankind is most progressive in places where there is not only a marked difference between summer and winter, but also where there are frequent variations from day to day." To substantiate their theory, the cyclonic storms of temperate regions are taken as a measure of atmospheric changes, and they find that "the area included within the line of ten storms, embraces all the leading countries of the world"—the United States, Great Britain, France, the Netherlands, Scandinavia, Switzerland, Germany, Austria, Northern Italy, Western Russia—and, strange to say, the only Asiatic country subject to similar cyclonic storms happens to be Japan. Thus anemology serves to bind where ethnology attempts to sever. The world is an Æolian harp and nations are but its strings, athwart which the stronger blows the wind, the fuller and finer the note.

There is always a strong temptation to exaggerate the effect of geographic environment. Not a clover plant blooms but is held to sway the destinies of the British Empire. Not a few writers have tried to explain our mode of living, our mental habits, literature, and religion, as corollaries of the volcanic character of the country—the second item of our definition of geographical Japan.

II. The Volcanic Character of our Topography.
That most of our islands are volcanic in their
formation is not to be disputed. If Egypt is the
gift of the Nile, Japan is the legacy of primeval
fire.

Three principal volcanic ranges, containing
about two hundred volcanoes, fifty of which are
active, run lengthwise and crosswise through
Japan. To the fact that their mischievous spirits
hold rendezvous in the proximity of Fuji, we owe
the exquisite form of our "peerless mountain"
and many an occasion of terror at their antics.
Volcanoes, both extinct and active, abounding,
seismic phenomena are frequent. Observations
for the twenty-five years between 1885–1909 show
that Japan was subject, during this period, to no
less than 37,642 earthquakes, not to take into
account minor vibrations which are felt only by
delicate instruments. This gives a yearly average
of 1506 shocks, or about four per day. Four
shocks a day certainly represent an alarmingly
frequent occurrence of the phenomenon, and would
be unendurable if they were not scattered over a
very large area. Then, too, there is some comfort
in the assurance that minor shocks bind the strata
by removing weaker cleavages and will thus prevent the occurrence of severer ones. From records
of earthquakes for over three hundred years, one
learns to expect a shock of ordinary severity once
in about thirty months and a disastrous upheaval
once in a life-time.

Any one the least familiar with Japanese art must have observed how our Mount Fuji forms the favourite *motif* for artists, and a hasty illation is drawn therefrom that volcanoes must exert a strong influence upon the æsthetic sense and upon art. Our low, wooden style of architecture is generally considered to be due to frequent earthquakes, and the study of seismic disturbances convinces us that low, wooden structures suffer decidedly less than high, stone or brick buildings; the last mentioned suffering most.

I am not in a position to prove the effect of earthquakes upon our fine art; but that they strongly influence our architecture is so patent that it needs no demonstration. Specially worthy of mention in this connection is the curvature given to the old stone castle walls. It approximates that theoretical curve known in geometry as the parabolic, which gives the greatest stability against earthquakes, and which at the same time conforms most nearly to the line of beauty. As another illustration of how earthquakes stimulate architectural ingenuity, I may mention the way in which the five-storied pagodas, some of them over a hundred feet high, are built to endure the severest shocks. These high structures have never been known to fall. The principle on which they are built is the combination of an inverted pendulum with an ordinary pendulum, which is said to minimise the effect of any tremor. The principle is embodied in a heavy, massive piece of timber, suspended somewhat freely from the top and resting on a pivot below, so that in case the ground shakes, the whole structure sways in such a manner as to maintain its equilibrium.

Aristotle, in remarking that insensibility to fear does not necessarily argue true courage, gives earthquakes and waves as instances of forces which man may fear without losing self-respect. The Semites looked with pious awe and dread upon the earthquake as theophany, and in their language the term for it, *ra'ash*, was poetically employed for the harmonious choral song of angels. We, too, do not omit earthquakes from the list of things to fear, among which the vulgar populace count three others—the thunderbolt, conflagration, and, last but not least, daddy's frown! It is curious that the external attitude, if I may so say, of the popular mind, in regard to this really terror-inspiring convulsion, is of a humorous nature. Is the underlying idea that of defying the power of the alarming phenomenon? Or is it because, being too awful to think of, human understanding, like Hamlet in the presence of a ghost, revolts against its own weakness and pelts impotent jeers at it? The very origin of earthquakes is ascribed rather jocosely to the movement of a huge, phlegmatic cat-fish, *namazu*, living in mud beneath the crust of the earth. When its barbels twitch, seismology makes record of fresh shocks; but should the hideous monster feel inclined to raise its broad, glum head in its dozing on the muddy

3

bottom, then woe to civilisation and all its achievements! Nobody takes this creature seriously. When it is mentioned, it is always in a humorous vein. Among the eighty myriad gods of the Shinto pantheon, there is only one solitary mention of a god of earthquakes, and he has no homage paid him such as Poseidon, the Earth-Shaker, enjoyed at the hands of the Hellenes. Then among hundreds of nature-myths, to which one listens with more or less religious reverence, one looks in vain for the story of an earth-shaker.

So, of the mental influence of telluric outbursts we can say little that is definite, and as far as their physical effects are concerned, it is doubtful that the ozone produced could furnish material for nitrogenous fertiliser in any appreciable quantity. Equally doubtful is the production by earthquakes of enough ozone to show a stimulating effect on man or beast.

As a permanent compensation for the disquieting earthquake, terrestrial fire has studded the country with some four hundred and thirty mineral springs, hot and cold, and of diverse medicinal virtues.

Our mountains, not necessarily of igneous origin but as a matter of fact largely so, in conjunction with the damp climate, give rise to many cascades and cataracts, which are valuable assets in the production of water and electric power. The wealth of picturesque scenery is the price Vulcan pays for his sports.

There is a certain feature of the volcanic formation of our islands which has a far-reaching and dire economic effect. I mean the comparatively small extent of land fit for tillage. Under the present mode of husbandry, it is generally admitted that the use of the plough or of the spade is economically possible on fairly level plains, but where farms have a slope exceeding fifteen degrees, cultivation does not repay the toil of the peasant. It is estimated that in Japan tillable plains amount only to 26½ per cent. of the whole area, and even these do not exist in large complexes, being scattered here and there in small bits, sometimes along river-courses and sometimes among the mountains. Out of this limited level area, a moiety only is under actual cultivation. In other words, the arable land of Japan forms only 14.6 per cent. of the entire extent of her territory—a remarkably small proportion, when we remember that fifty million souls find their subsistence here.

Owing, too, to rugged topography and to the absence of extensive plains, large cities have not developed in any number. Tokyo, situated in the most extensive plain—that of Musashi—is at present a city of some two million inhabitants, the size of Chicago—and is still steadily growing, as a result of which the value of land increases at the rate of ten per cent. a year. Osaka, being a harbour and located in the basin of the Yodo River, has now a population approaching one million, and Nagoya (300,000) is fast outgrowing the ancient capital of Kyoto (400,000). Not for geographical but for economic reasons, as in the rest of the world, our larger cities are developing at the expense of the country—so much so that some provinces are suffering from the increase of "abandoned farms."

The smallness of the arable area will be made clearer by considering the third item in our definition;—namely, the narrowness of the country.

III. The Width of the Country. If we include recent territorial acquisitions, the Japanese Empire extends in length from the middle of Saghalien (50° N. Lat.) to the southern extremity of Formosa (21° 45′ N. Lat.), covering about twenty-eight degrees of latitude—equal to the distance from the mouth of the St. Lawrence or the Islands of Vancouver, as far south as Cuba or the southernmost promontory of Lower California. The width, on the contrary, is quite out of proportion to the length, being in many places no more than fifty miles, as the crow flies, and in no place exceeding two hundred miles. Still, having a long chain of mountains running like a rib through its central part, the country is well-nigh impassable from the eastern to the western coast, except by a few narrow valleys. A curious economic effect of this topographical formation is the nationalisation of railways; for, as the railroads must run through mountains and along precipitous valleys—much of the way across ravines and torrents—the cost of construction is very great, and even after construction, the frequent rains, with their consequent floods and washouts and landslides, necessitate continual outlay for the maintenance of the lines.

These considerations, especially the narrowness of many valleys, forbid the building of more than one good trunk line. As long as there is to be but one line, is it not wiser for the government to possess and control it than that such far-reaching public service be left to the monopoly of a private company?

Though the country has not great width, the eastern and western sides offer many points of difference. The western shores are washed by heavy seas, being exposed to the strong and cold north-westerly winds coming from the Siberian plains. Outer Japan is milder in climate, owing to the Black Current; it has more bright days; it abounds in gulfs and bays, harbours and ports. We may say that Japan faces the Pacific and turns her back upon the sea which separates her from China, and the social and political import of this simple fact may be inferred by comparing it with Italy, where harbours of any consequence are all located on the western coast; or with Greece, which turns its face towards Asia Minor.

Since the islands are narrow and mountain ranges divide them lengthwise, the rivers are inevitably short and rapid. There are only fifteen rivers more than a hundred miles long, and only three of these boast double that length. Under drier skies our streams would be insignificant; but

the general atmospheric humidity of our climate
and our two rainy seasons keep them supplied at
all times with water, which is, however, liberally
drawn off for purposes of irrigation, thus rendering
the main current less serviceable than ever for
navigation. On account of reckless denudation
of wooded area, every rain washes sand and gravel
down the naked slopes of the hills, filling the river-
beds with silt and working havoc upon the sur-
rounding regions. But I must add, to redeem the
reputation of our rivers, that many of them afford
an excellent source of hydro-electric power.

IV. The Length of the Empire. I have thus
far dwelt exclusively on the narrowness of the
country. In considering the length, however,
special attention must be paid to the fourth item—
that the islands lie obliquely within twenty-eight
degrees of latitude. This fact allows a wide range
of temperature and a great variety of vegetation,
and finally—variation in the character and temperament of the inhabitants. The temperature
of Tokyo may be taken as an average of that of
the whole country. The mean temperature for
twenty years shows 36.7° Fahrenheit in January,
and 78° in August, the average for the whole year
being nearly 57°. In Tokyo snow falls three or
four times during the winter, sometimes to a depth
of several inches. In the northern island of Hokkaido, we have snow from the end of November
to the beginning of April, and there the tempera-

ture falls 10, 20, and even 30 degrees below zero.

To Japan's humidity and its prevailing winds, we have incidentally referred. All these factors combined explain in part the wealth of our flora, which Savatier in his *Enumeratio* gives as 2750 species of plants indigenous to Japan.

Each month of the year has its favourite flower. January has its pine, the symbol of evergreen old age, which, with the bamboo and the plum, form in our language of flowers a triad used on all propitious occasions. February has its plum, the *umé*—botanically different from your plum—which is the first tree to bloom in the spring, unfolding its pink, white, or yellow buds while the snow still continues to fall. Under such adverse circumstances does it bloom, that the plum has won a reputation for courage among flowers, and when you see its pink blossoms covered with snow-flakes, its delicate perfume lending further charm to the song of the warbler which delights to make its abode among its branches, you will not wonder at our infatuation over it. The fruit of the *umé* has an economic value, for it is not only edible in itself, but makes the juice with which our best silk is dyed red. The plum is succeeded in March by the peach, a flower that typifies beauty, and, like beauty, quickly fades to give place to another no less ephemeral but the most exquisite of all—the cherry. April is sacred to the *sakura*, the cherry, the most popular child of all our floral world. It is cultivated not for its fruit, nor for its wood, but

for its flowers, that bloom for half a week, and if a
more material motive for its cultivation is looked
for, it lies in the use of the flower as a dainty
beverage when pickled in salt and steeped in hot
water.   Thus we quaff this vernal essence of our
clime in as literal a sense as we inhale its breath.
No wonder we look upon it as the national flower,
embodying the spirit of the race, as an old poet
has sung,—

"Should strangers ask what the spirit of Yamato is,
   Point to the cherry blowing fragrant in the morning
      sun."

But the short-lived cherry is succeeded in May
by the Wistaria, which was introduced into this
country by Dr. Wistar; hence the name.   This
is followed in June by the iris, and as the heat of
summer rises in July, the morning-glory refreshes
our eyes with its many tints, and while it is still
at the height of its glory, the lotus, dear to the
religion of Buddha as lilies are to Christians, takes
up its turn in August.   The lotus, of various
dainty hues, grows in water; and many a lover of
flowers leaves his bed before dawn to hasten to a
pond that he may hear the bursting of its buds.
The lotus adds to its spiritual meaning a tangible
quality; for its seeds are edible and its long rhi-
zomes are used as a vegetable.   When the summer
heat is gone, and with September the thermometer
begins to take a downward course, the so-called

"seven plants of autumn" (including the graceful Eulalia, the chaste Campanella, the rough-leaved Patrinia, which we call the maiden-flower, etc.) gladden the hearts which are sobered by the fall of leaves and mellowed by the saddening moon, which shines particularly clear in the drier autumn nights. When these rather delicate and tender plants begin to fade one by one in quick succession, robbing the wayside of its glowing tints, then in the month of October bloom in luxuriance chrysanthemums of every imaginable hue. Amateurs and professionals then vie with each other in exhibiting their best plants, and the Emperor opens his garden to his invited guests to show the chrysanthemum—this flower, painted with sixteen petals, being the crest of his family. The chrysanthemum has long outgrown its Greek etymon— the blossom of gold. It boasts of innumerable shades of colour, and gives promise through its fecund power to produce newer varieties. You certainly have worked marvels in the chrysanthemum in this country; but I wonder if you raise two or three edible varieties of this plant, using, as we do, the petals for salad and the leaves as well as the flowers for fritters. But I have no time now to linger in the kitchen; for, when November comes with its bright sunshine, it is time for every lover of nature to sally forth among hills and dales "a-maple-hunting," as we call it. As in the spring multitudes wend their way to certain localities famed for the *sakura*, so now they make their excursion to feast their eyes upon the brocade of foliage. Japan, I understand, is richest in varieties of maple, but when the branches are shorn of their gorgeous drapery by the chilly breeze of December, this month makes compensation by bringing among the deep verdure of the camellia a profuse display of colours—white, scarlet, pink, and red.

I have loitered too long—a whole year—among the flowers of my land, but will now retrace my steps to take up a more serious discussion of the fifth item of my definition, which refers to the fact that Japan lies off the coast of China, at considerable distance from the rest of the world.

V. Japan's Location off the Asiatic Coast. This distance from the continent as well as from the southern seas is not too great for a daring people to cross, but it was too far to enable large numbers to make an expedition with weapons and provisions in days when steam was unknown. Hence, peaceful immigrants came from time to time to settle here, to merge with those who had occupied the land before them, while invading troops could not make inroads upon these shores.

Being located where they are, the Japanese islands are farthest removed from the centre or centres of world politics,—from European capitals or from the Atlantic coast of this continent. It is over seven thousand miles from New York to Yokohama. It has become a fashion in these latter days to speak rather disrespectfully of distance, as though electricity and steam have practically annihilated it. We brag of the recent achievement, whereby a wireless message was sent and received across the Pacific Ocean. This is all very remarkable and we are justified in congratulating ourselves, but the element of space exists just the same, the actual distance not shrinking a mile or an inch. It is as impossible to subtract a cubit from space as it is to add it to our stature.

To the artistic, distance may serve the purpose of lending enchantment to the view, but for more utilitarian purposes, it is too real an element to be lightly trifled with. As applied to our case, this distance brought in its train at least two important psychological consequences, viz.; the sense of isolation and of discontinuity. In spite of all the recent improvements in transportation, it is still no easy undertaking, financially or physically, for most people to go back and forth across a space "where half the convex world intrudes between." Such remoteness is enough to create apartness or to estrange sympathy. Hence Japan has to bear the disadvantage of a certain degree of isolation, until the centres of the world are moved elsewhere or until easier means of transportation come in vogue.

Then, too, the sense of discontinuity engendered by the presence of vast deserts, lofty mountain chains, and unfathomed ocean, gives one an impression that there must be a wide and deep chasm that cannot be bridged over between the mental habits and moral notions of the denizens of the antipodes.

In connection with the distance factor, I may here refer to an idea advanced by Professor Davis of Harvard, who in speaking of a remote colony, says that the most enterprising and aggressive new-comers press to the frontier where gentleness, considerateness, forbearance in their dealings with others, especially with inferiors, are less common on the part of the invaders than the contrasted qualities of roughness, dominance, and intolerance. The hasty acts of the isolated frontiersman are seldom restrained by a tempered public sentiment in favour of patience and conciliation, for at the outposts of civilisation there is no public to have a sentiment.   In the case of the United States, California being on its frontier, that State has once or twice given an illustration of this effect of the distance factor in its attitude toward Japanese immigration.   That brilliant French writer, Maurice Leblanc, has recently shown in the form of a novel, *The Frontier*, how trivial deeds of unfriendliness, when enacted near national boundaries, may assume a gigantic magnitude.

Now, let me proceed to my sixth and last article of definition.

VI. Japan's Position in the Pacific Ocean.
Japan lies in the Pacific, with her face toward the morning sun and her gates open to the east. Before her spreads the illimitable expanse of the Pacific,

where the bravest of folks, nurtured in the salt air and in the daring crafts of the sea, can find ample space for action. They can ride on the wings of the storm or plunge into the billows for the treasures of the deep, realising here the widest scope of action, fulfilling their highest calling and prepared for whatever awaits them. Here will be solved many a world problem that has puzzled philosophers and perplexed statesmen. We believe that it will be in the island realm of ours, lying between the two continents, that the world's contradictions will be solved.

Japan is aware that her mission is to mediate between the old and the new civilisations. We believe that it is in us and through us that the East and the West should meet. Our history of the last fifty years is a proof of our assertion.

On the Asiatic continent there are crude manifestations of impatience of European control; of fear and hatred of the White Peril. There are also evidences of the awakening of self-consciousness; of a feeling that an organised Asia can turn back the flood of European aggression. For all these recent signs of an inimical attitude that the East takes towards the West, Japan is held directly or indirectly responsible. She is in the exceedingly delicate and unenviable position of a scapegoat for the whole of Asia. If a white power snatches a piece of property on the continent, be it in China, India, Siam, or Persia, and the victim raises a hue and cry, Japan is suspected of supplying the air to his windpipe! But he reads these signs of the times amiss who sees bloody conflicts as their final and inevitable issues. Japan feels it her own responsibility to set the world's ideas right on this momentous point. She interprets her geographical position not in a negative, hostile spirit; but in a positive, friendly attitude of service to mankind, by bringing together nations that have long trodden different ways and establishing between them bonds of mutual understanding, unity, and respect.

The meaning of the Pacific Ocean seems to have dawned with sudden luminosity upon the eyes of the Occident. Twenty years ago, a British statesman of first rank could hardly be induced to annex part of an island near Australia; but now, were there discovered a fragment of a coral reef in the remotest part of this ocean, the great powers would rush with their gun-boats to plant their flag. Spain and Portugal have practically receded from the stage where they played their best and their worst, and in their stead Russia and America have made their appearance. Holland and England still maintain their prestige, and France and Germany are ambitious to have their share in the interests of the Pacific. To China and Japan this ocean presents a question of life and death. When we remember that in the Asiatic countries bordering it, swarms of mankind numbering some six hundred million souls, or one-third of the whole human family, live and have their being, it is no wonder that the world's chief interest during the twentieth century will be centred here. Should concerns of such magnitude be decided by one or two powers for their selfish ends? Whatever suspicion other nations may maintain, it is not the ambition of Japan to control all these vast masses of humanity or to make the Pacific Ocean her lake. As to a breach between America and Japan, that mighty sea may well rest peacefully true to its name. It is interesting to note that, while some people on this side of the Pacific speak of the completion of the Panama Canal as a signal for the outbreak of war, the Japanese are looking forward to it with utmost complacency and the hope of increased trade.

When the Suez Canal was about to be opened, many anticipated the event with consternation— among them no less a statesman than Sir Robert Peel,—fearing that the new waterway might serve the purposes of war rather than those of peace; but with us who have seen the working of this canal, should there not be a rational belief that its history may be repeated in that of Panama, and that through this great new artery will throb the life blood of the East and the West in ever swelling and rhythmic pulsations of vigour and health?

CHAPTER III

THE PAST IN ITS SIGNIFICANCE TO THE PRESENT

IN compressing into the space of a few pages the history of Japan, which covers a period of twenty centuries, I shall try to make you acquainted with those larger landmarks in the genetic development of my people which may be of general interest to students of *Culturgeschichte*. Though I shall try to be chronological in my presentation, I despair of any narration of concrete events in successive order. I shall endeavour to make a continuous story of our political and social evolution, but I shall not afflict you with long, outlandish names, however great and glorious they may sound in our own ears, unless they stand for something that is still concerned with living issues. I may have to recount some anecdotes which, trifling in themselves, typify the spirit of an age. My idea is to cast a cursory glance at the past in its vital relations with the present, and with this end in view I must beg of my audience to borrow the hat of Fortunatus, or the more fashionable cap of Monsieur Maeterlinck's Tyltyl and turn its diamond, so that time and space may be shortened at our discretion. Only, I shall ask you not to turn it too far, for then there will be nothing left for me to say.

Our history may be roughly divided into five periods, namely:

1. The Ancient—(including the legendary age, which is strictly pre-historic) from the founding of the Empire down to the middle of the seventh century, and including the introduction of Buddhism.

2. The Early Mediæval—beginning with the radical political reforms of the seventh century and ending with the close of the twelfth century, covering epochs specially important in the history of art.

3. The Late Mediæval—beginning with the rise of the military clans at the end of the twelfth century and concluding with the sixteenth century—an essentially heroic age under militant feudalism.

4. The Modern—which was the age of the Tokugawa Shogun, characterised by peaceful feudalism and by encouragement of art and learning.

5. The Present—beginning with the coronation of the present Emperor in 1868 and covering the period of occidentalisation.

1. The history of Japan, like the history of every people, has, before daylight clearness, its age of dusky twilight, when all its forms are obscure. This is the age of myths, of the legends of deities,

and of the achievements of demi-gods, whose actions are not to be reckoned by a mortal's standard of time or space. Disjointed narratives of exceedingly commonplace personages, anecdotes of heroic deeds, tales of impossible characters —in some particulars too accurate and revoltingly realistic—fill the first few pages of our annals. Animistic stories that would rejoice the heart of a child or that may complement the *Metamorphosis* of Ovid, are told in our book of Genesis. The beings of this dusky period furnish no end of material whereby the fanciful may work out theories in anthropology, sociology, and folk-lore.

The account of this early age has been handed down as oral tradition in more or less metrical relation, and was first put into writing under the title of *Kojiki* (*Records of Ancient Things*), in the early part of the eighth century. The work of compilation was an intellectual feat of an extraordinary character, because the compiler had to use Chinese letters or ideographs to convey the sound of the Japanese language. This feat has been aptly compared by Captain Brinckley to the task of a man who has set himself to commit Shakespeare's plays to writing by the aid of the cuneiform characters of Babylon.

Within a decade of this compilation, another was undertaken and called *Nihongi* (*Chronicles of Japan*), and this was written in genuine Chinese style. These two works, together with a third *Koga-Shu* (*Ancient Records*), of much lesser re-

nown, form our earliest historical documents.
The narrators never claimed Divine inspiration,
plenary or otherwise, when they recounted the
story of creation;—how the Creator and the Creat-
rix, Isanagi and Isanami, (or in English translation
the Male-that-invites and the Female-that-invites)
met on the Floating Bridge of Heaven;—how
when they thrust the gem-headed spear into the
abyss of the sea and took it out, the drops which
fell from its point congealed and formed the first
of our islands. The historiographer continues to
relate the birth of other islands, of the children
born of the twin deities, and a long tale is told of
the Sun-goddess, the chief of the native pantheon.
Whether she was a real being of flesh and blood,
or whether she was an embodiment of a solar myth
or whether she was symbolic of a benignant and
light-bringing government; whether the dominion
over which she ruled was an actual geographical
locality or whether it was an aërial region, science
has not decided any more definitely than it has
some other questions—such as, whether the so-
called deities, the culture heroes, were colonists,
some from the continent and others from the
Southern isles, or whether they were representa-
tions of earthly and heavenly powers, or whether
the gem-pointed spear was the javelin of a primitive folk, or whether it meant, as Dr. Warren
in his *Paradise Found* suggests, the axis of the
earth; whether the so-called Floating Bridge of
Heaven was a canoe in which the daring couple

found their way to Japan, or whether it implied a grander conception which connects this little planet of ours with the heavenly bodies above; —these queries and others, yes, even the form of the Sun-goddess herself, we leave behind in the shade for Imagination and Science to decipher, while we now move forward to the time when the crepuscular dawn brightens into daylight, and when we can discern figures somewhat more plainly.

Before proceeding further, I may intercalate a remark or two on the subject of the name of our country. The land now called Japan was in its earliest, legendary days, called by a long poetical name, "The Country in the Midst of Luxuriant Reed-Plains," owing perhaps to the prevalence of marshes. After its conquest by Jimmu, the appellation "Yamato" (Mountain Portal?) was used to designate the country under his sway. In the Middle Ages, in official correspondence with China, the name "Hi-no-moto," "The Source of the Sun," was adopted. At one time "East" was used as against "West," by which China was meant; but the poetical designation, "The Land of the Rising Sun," best describes its location. The Chinese characters which were used in spelling Hi-no-moto gradually came, for brevity's sake, to be pronounced—*à la chinois*—Nippon. The later Chinese pronunciation of these characters was perverted by Marco Polo, who spelled it Jipangu, from which all the European names for Nippon are derived. This sinified form certainly is a time-saving improvement upon the first august title—"Toyo ashi hara no Nakatsu Kuni!" But from the marshland—*revenons à nos moutons!*

The fantastic episodes to which I have only slightly alluded by way of suggestion, have for their background the province of Izumo, which is situated on the south-western coast of Japan, just opposite the coast of Korea, and the legends may well be of Korean origin, preserved by the first settlers in Japan. As history begins to be less mythical, the scene shifts from that part of the main island to the southern part of Kyushu, where we meet a people claiming descent from the Sun-goddess rising to prominence. It is not unreasonable to conjecture that they were a band of immigrants of Malay blood from the southern islands.

In its advance eastward and northward, and in the course of fifteen years of fighting, this brave band brought the different tribes along its route under one government, at the head of which appears the founder of our royal dynasty—given the posthumous, honorific name of Jimmu Tenno, "the Emperor of Godlike Valour."

The date of his ascension to the throne is fixed upon the eleventh of February, 660 B.C., and the day is still observed as the anniversary of the foundation of our Empire, and is with us a time of universal rejoicing, such as the Fourth of July is with you, excepting that we are not advanced enough to express our jubilation and patriotism with the help of fire-crackers.　To the Emperor it is a solemn occasion, when he worships before the shrine of his ancestors, to thank them for the heritage they have left him, and for their constant protection.

For several centuries after the death of the first Emperor, there is not one among his successors who distinguished himself in any way.　Like some tedious chapters in the Bible, history barely mentions their names and their diuturnal reigns. So strangely devoid of events, right after the subjugation of the savage tribes, are these reigns, that some historians have cast a doubt upon their very existence.　An hypothesis has been advanced that, in those early ages, a year was counted from equinox to equinox, and hence its duration was only six months.　It is also thought quite probable that, in editing and inditing ancient records, there was a miscalculation in the sexagenary cycle (a form of calendar in vogue in the East, according to which twelve years make one course and five courses, or sixty years, make a cycle), and until historical criticism establishes a more certain date, an error of about ten cycles—that is of six hundred years—may be suggested as a solution of these unnaturally long, uneventful reigns.　This would bring the inauguration of our Empire almost within a half-century before Christ, and the demise of our first founder within a year of the

Christian era. It is also believed by some annal-
ists and ethnologists that this curtailment of six
centuries brings our history into better accord
with some records of China and Korea, as well as
with some anthropological discoveries of recent
date. India, China, and Korea were then already
at the height of their civilisation.

At whatever date the reign of Jimmu Tenno
may be fixed, be it 660 B.C. or only 60 B.C., it is
not unlikely that in his time, as well as in the
reigns succeeding his, constant exchange in trade
and in thought went on between Japan and the
continent on the one hand, and with the Southern
Seas on the other. Peaceful communication was
now and then interrupted by warlike demonstrations, as in the case of the invasion of Korea about
200 A.D., by our more or less mythical Amazonian
Empress Jingu. If diplomatic courtesies were but
seldom exchanged, private individuals must have
passed to and fro. The first official communication with China took place in the latter part of the
third century (285 A.D.), when a Korean envoy
brought with him a copy of the *Analects* of Confucius. This first introduction of letters marks an
epoch in our history. Until this time the Japanese
had not possessed any mode of writing. Under
Korean teachers, eager students soon mastered
the Chinese ideographs and the sciences that
China had to teach us.

The intellectual enlightenment, as well as the
material progress which followed in the train of

Chinese studies, was overwhelmingly great. The
Court adopted Chinese customs and costumes;
the learned and the rich strove in imitating celestial
manners. Chinese art was bodily accepted, and
its canons blindly followed. Upon Chinese models
radical reforms were made in the laws. A new
partition and distribution of land were even enforced. A student at leisure might amuse himself
by drawing parallels between the inflow of Chinese
traditions into Japan and of Greek traditions into
Italy—even comparing the coincident geographical circumstance of Japan's turning her back to
the continent of Asia, as does the Apennine
peninsula to Hellas.

While the Chinese leaven was thus vigorously
working among us, by the middle of the sixth
century, another, and perhaps a stronger germ of
fermentation, of Hindu origin, found its way
into our Court, whence it soon spread far and
wide and deep; but as I shall speak of Buddhism
again in my lecture on religions in Japan, I shall
not devote much time to it here, but will proceed to the second epoch of our history.

2. The adoption of Buddhism as a state and
popular religion is synchronous with what is known
in our history as the Nara period, corresponding
to the eighth century of the Christian era (710–785
A.D.). It was the first great epoch of our authentic
history and is so called because—whereas the seat
of government, or what amounts to the same
thing, the residence of the sovereign, used to

move from place to place with the beginning of
each new reign—early in this century, Nara, in
Central Japan, was selected as a permanent place
for the capitol, and the physical stability of the
Government, if I may so term it, was for the first
time secured. If the Government and the Court
were not as yet sharply distinguished, a nucleus
of that germain distinction was now introduced.
The ancient identification of state and religion—
our word *matsurigoto*, meaning either the art of
government or the observance of religious rites—
still continued, and was, in fact, endorsed by the
teaching of Confucius, who taught kingship by
divine right or, perhaps more properly, kingship
as divine duty. The Court, the Government, and
the Church were all collected at Nara, the city
itself being laid out in regular squares after the
approved Chinese fashion, with gates and seques-
tered quarters for different social ranks. It is
even surmised by modern philologists that the
very name "Nara" is an ancient Korean term for
capital. Here were fostered with tender care and
displayed in lavish splendour all the arts learned
from the continent. Buddhist images of all descriptions were cast in precious metals and bronze;
magnificent temples, still standing and said to be
the oldest wooden edifices in the world, were built
with an elegance of decoration that now is the
wonder of the art-world. Schools and universities
were also started during this age. I have often
wondered whether the effect of Korean culture

upon ancient Japan was not analogous to Etrus-
can influence upon Rome; while the part played
by China was comparable to what Greece did for
Italy.

Japan afforded an asylum for the continentals
who sought refuge from the misgovernment and
wars of their own home lands. Colonies of
Koreans were given land in different parts of the
country. Artisans were invited and settled
in the towns. About the middle of the seventh
century, the ruling sovereign wrote of the amal-
gamation of different races in this stanza:—

"Oranges on separate branches grown,
When plucked are in one basket thrown."

In 815 A.D. a census was taken in Kyoto, which
showed the distribution of population according
to classes: (1) the royal; (2) the divine; (3) the
barbarian,—meaning respectively those connected
by blood with the reigning family, the Japanese
(or rather those who were in the train of the first
Emperor), and the immigrants from the continent,
as well as the pre-Japanese occupants of the soil.
The returns showed that one-third of the population belonged to the last category.

Thanks to Buddhism, the manners of our people
were greatly softened. We do not hear of the
soldiers of that time. We hear only of monks and
nobles. Instead of war-drums stirring us to imitate the actions of the tiger, were heard the tran-

quil tones of temple bells.   In place of steel armour
and weapons, rustled Chinese silks and brocades.
Literature, though it retained some traces of
rugged, pristine vigour, began to show signs of
feminine fastidiousness.   Priests and nobles vied in
writing love-poems and amatory epistles.   It was
indeed a golden age of poetry, and if it lacked
manly vigour, it certainly showed elegant finesse,
both in sentiment and in diction.   This period is
conspicuous, too, for having a number of women
who distinguished themselves in belles-lettres.
That the fair sex enjoyed great social freedom is
evident from contemporary records, though they
strangely enough omitted to claim the right of
suffrage!

Not a few European students of history have
observed that the predominance of the gentle sex
in intellectual pursuits has proved a precursor of
social decadence.   Though America may reverse
this verdict of historians, the Nara period confirmed it only too well.   With all its refinement,
or rather because of this very refinement, in art
and literature, the manly tasks of government and
warfare came to be sadly neglected.   The Emperor
had for some time ceased to take a direct personal
part in the government, this onerous and terri-
bly terrestrial labour being left to his subjects,
especially to the family of the Fujiwaras, who—
as all mortals under similar conditions are tempted
to do—exercised this delegated power to the
aggrandisement of their own house.   In their

hands the imperial throne was elevated in reverence "above the shelf of blue clouds,"—an expression which anticipates the modern English phrase "to be shelved"—so that the person of the Emperor was believed too sacred for profane eyes to behold.

Needless to add, the royal power was reduced to a mere name—nay, to the shadow of a name. Not infrequently pressure was brought to bear upon emperors to abdicate at an early age. One babe was crowned at the age of two, only to abdicate at the age of four. Nor was he a lone example of august infancy. There was an instance of the throne being occupied by a child of five, and in several cases boys of ten years were placed upon it. Adult rulers, who might prove troublesome by asking questions about their rights and duties, were speedily persuaded to retire into monasteries. By dexterous manipulation did the regent family—first the Fujiwaras and subsequently the Tairas—manage to concentrate all political power in their own hands; but as these families abused this power for selfish gratification, their real influence grew weaker and weaker, so much so that it was not seriously heeded in the provinces, where powerful men and influential families took slight cognisance of the central authority, and practically dominated villages and counties, attaching to their persons guards of soldiers—very much as did the robber barons of the Rhine, or the manorial lords of England. These local magnates were the men who afterwards became feudal lords, or *daimyos*, and their retainers developed into the samurai of later days.

A nation fallen into the silken languor and gilded euphemism of the Nara period, however delectable to the Epicurean, cannot escape political reaction, and such a reaction was brought about by the Emperor Kwammu, who, in order to effect a radical change, not only in administration but in the very spirit of the people, removed the capital, late in the eighth century, from Nara to the present site of Kyoto. That period of our history, during which the government had its seat here for nearly four hundred years (794–1196 A.D.), is known as the period of Heian, literally "Peace and Ease"—"Sans souci"—the name by which the capital was called. The reforms instituted by the heroic sovereign Kwammu included the separation of religion from politics—a task which sounds very modern in its conception and phraseology. He removed priests from posts of administration and restricted the number of religious ceremonies and rites performed in the Court. The building of temples was also prohibited, without special license from the authorities. New laws, savouring more of Confucian doctrines than of Buddhist precepts, were now the order of the day; but after the death of this Emperor the course of events fell very much into the old lines. If anything, moral degeneration and political corruption went farther than they had done during the previous epoch. We know how it was in England in the time of Charles the First, and especially how it was after the Restoration. Virility was sapped in the ruling classes and manly stamina undermined among the people. Society as a whole was steeped in sensual and sensuous amusements, and of this City of Peace it may be said that if war slaughtered its thousands, peace slew its tens of thousands. The hold which Buddhism had on the people was as great as ever, and there was untrammelled indulgence in learning and art. Superstitions, which curiously enough so often accompany luxury (is not superstition itself a sort of mental luxury?), brought the clergy more and more into prominence. And as religion was not rigidly concerned with morality, a dissolute clergy could exercise power without relinquishing pleasure.

They learned art primarily for outward embellishment, but also necessarily for the expression of their inner self; they trifled with learning chiefly for social entertainment but did not study in search of truth. Is it any wonder that art survived learning? Altogether it was an age of laxity of morals, of effeminacy of manners, of imbecility of religious faith. It was, however, this period that gave to Japanese civilisation many of those features which still remain objects of admiration. Its architecture, or what there is of it after the devastation of many conflagrations, its works of art, the gentle and graceful manners and customs of the people, our

landscape-gardening, and painting and poetry—
these are the greatest legacies left by this sybaritic
age. Herein lie the present charms of Kyoto.
We should have had more of these art-gifts, had
they not been destroyed by the vandalism of the
latter part of this period, when the military power
of the Minamoto clan, which had been slowly
forming in distant provinces, especially in the
eastern part of the country, succeeded in putting
a stop to the exercise of an effete authority on the
part of the Court. The leader of this clan, Yori-
tomo, organised a system of feudalism and established his government in the town of Kamakura, not
indeed as the usurper of royal power, but under the
name of Shogun, the maréchal of His Majesty, as
the vice-regent and the majordomo of the Emperor.

3. This ushers in the third era of our history,—
namely, the militant age of feudalism, lasting for
some four centuries, the early part of which is
known as the Kamakura period and the latter as
the Ashikaga. It is one of the most stirring and
romantic epochs of our history. It is an epic age
of heroism, of daring, of action and achievement.
If literature is the mirror of the age, the writings
of this period certainly reflect a spirit very different from that of those preceding it. We meet
with very few of those debonair romances which
in former times called forth sighs and blushes
from ladies and nobles. We meet instead tales of
adventure, combat, and battle—such as enliven
the pages of Froissart and Scott.

The traditions of culture had not entirely died away. On the contrary, the samurai patronised and fostered different arts, and so we find in the fifteenth and sixteenth centuries the beginnings of the tea ceremony, and of flower arrangement. The artists of this age of hero-worship and of romantic adventures, naturally delight to paint portraits and the spirit of motion. Sculpture created statues of heroic size and character. This age bequeathed some few works of art and of literature which may claim immortality; but the best product of this period was men, and these of the type of Nietzsche's *Uebermenschen*—men of strong masculine calibre, who could wield a sword and govern a kingdom; a type of men who have become household names for terror and strength, as well as for generosity and tenderness. If history is, as Carlyle says, the biography of great men, the history of this militant age is beyond doubt the most eventful in our annals of feudalism. It has certainly left a marked impress upon the moral ideas of our people.

This age naturally brought into strong relief the figure of the warrior, the samurai. We speak of it as one of constant fighting and of horrible bloodshed; but warfare itself developed a cast of character, daring in deed, patient in endurance, subdued by a sense of the vanity of life and of the mutability of earthly things—a sense that Buddhism helped in large measure to encourage. To know the sadness of things was a characteristic of the true samurai. Hence the consummate product of this age is not a fierce fighter, but a strong personality, with the tenderest of emotions; a man who has under control all violent passions, whose tears are kept back by sheer force of will.

Have you not seen a picture of a Japanese warrior on his steed, pausing under a blooming cherry tree? Every Japanese child is familiar with the leader of a great army, who, in the course of his march, had to advance over a path strewn with the wind-blown petals of the cherry. Here he halted, deeming it desecration to trample upon the carpet of blossoms.

The samurai of those days looked upon the profession of arms, not as a matter of slaughter but as a means of mental and spiritual training. He went to battle, and he prepared for combat, not so much to gain a victory as to try his skill with his peer. Fair play and the square deal were the chief attractions of warfare.

We read of a young warrior of the sixteenth century, Kato by name, engaged in a duel with Suwoden. When the latter's sword broke, the former threw away his own weapon; for it was not fair to take advantage of the misfortune of one's enemy. In the grapple that followed, Suwoden got the better of Kato, but as Suwoden had his hand upon his enemy's throat, he said;—"It is not samurai-like for me, sir, to strangle you, who did not slash me when my sword was broken. Now I pay you back; we are on equal terms. This is only a skirmish, let us meet each other again in full battle array." They parted, and in a few days they confronted each other again at the head of their armies. While the battle was raging and the forces of both were in disorder, the two heroes came forth and were soon engaged in single combat. They both knew that Suwoden's was a losing cause. He himself felt that he came to die at the hand of one who had once saved his life; Kato on his part had come to the field with the determination to give a ray of hope by his own death, to his falling enemy, who likewise had spared his life. It was a strange conflict. Neither party seemed to make the right stroke. Both showed ridiculous weakness, as though they were ready to fall at the first thrust. And when through a mishap a slight touch of Kato's sword inflicted on Suwoden a shallow wound, he fell, exclaiming, "I am beaten, sir! Take my head to thy general as an addition to thy many trophies." Then Kato raised him up quickly, assuring him that the cut was not fatal; but the wounded warrior begged that his head be taken by one so worthy of it. According to the etiquette of war, this was done, and after his triumphal return, Kato interred, with due ceremony and with many hot tears, the mortal remains of his friend and opponent.

What do you think of a mode of warfare during the hottest engagements of which poetical tournaments took place or repartee was exchanged

between the belligerent parties? The same ideals
held sway even in the siege of Port Arthur. It so
often happened in that siege that, when Japanese
soldiers had occupied a trench, they left behind
them a sad or comical letter in broken Russian
or else a droll picture, for the Russians who might
next take possession of it. Then the Russians
would leave behind them some well-meaning
memento for the next Japanese party that
might retake the trench.

"War is hell";—but in mediæval warfare the
sense of honour often robbed it of its horrors, its
stigmata, and its subterfuges.

Women, too, imbibed in those militant times
those virtues which we still admire in Spartan and
Roman matrons. They did not as a rule advance
to the front. It was their duty to stay at home,
and attend to the training of their children.
Naijo, the inner or interior help, was their avoca-
tion. So, to keep one's family intact and in good
order, while the master was in the field, was what
was expected of woman. But if for some reason
or other she found that she was a hindrance, how
unflinchingly she sacrificed herself! We read of
a young man infatuated by a girl. When she
found that her beauty kept him from marching to
the front, she disfigured her face with a red-hot
iron. We read of another young warrior who,
soon after he left the threshold of his home, where
he reluctantly bade his last farewell to his wife,
received a note, a few lines of which will show her

decision;—"Since we were joined in ties of eternal
wedlock, now two short years ago, my heart has
followed thee, even as its shadow follows an object,
inseparably bound soul to soul, loving and being
loved." Then she goes on to say, "Why should
I, to whom earth no longer offers hope or joy, why
should I detain thee or thy thoughts by living?
Why should I not rather await thee on the road
which all mortal kind must sometime tread?"

This again is only the prototype of what repeatedly happened during the Russo-Japanese
War, when aged mothers were known to stab
themselves in order to encourage their sons to
go forth and not to have their thoughts drawn
backward.

I have caused you to linger among our mediæval
warriors perhaps longer than you care; for without
understanding them, their ideas in regard to life,
to duty, to right and to wrong, modern Japan
will remain unintelligible. If you can grasp their
view-point, many things which seem so queer and
paradoxical in Japanese life will become clearer.
That life may strike you at first sight as very
un-christian; but, strange to say, it was just at
the time when the power and honour of the
samurai were at their height, that Christianity
reached Japan and found a field white unto harvest
—and this not among the down-trodden masses
only, but among the bravest of the gentry and the
most genteel dames.

It is indeed a remarkable feature of the missionary enterprise of this time, that it permeated the highest social classes as well as the lowest. Only in recent years, is it becoming clear what a deep and far-reaching spiritual influence it exercised on the new converts. Some of our historical personages (inclusive of women) noted for purity or strength of character, whose religious profession was not generally known, are now found to have been followers of Jesus. One can very easily imagine new religionists, in zeal for their faith, sometimes taking an imprudent course that would offend the more conservative of their countrymen. If history repeats itself, it seems to me that no history does so more frequently than ecclesiastical. A study of its earliest days and of those following the Reformation, will give a clue to the right understanding of the experience through which the Roman Catholic Church in Japan passed in the sixteenth and seventeenth centuries. Unfortunately for the papal—not to say Christian—cause, the one respect in which our church history differed from that of Europe, lay in the fact that the blood of our martyrs did not turn out to be "the seed of the church." Does this prove that the Japanese converts were so weak as to deny their Lord at the sight of the sword and of fire? Were they traitors and apostates? On the contrary, thousands of them willingly and joyously acknowledged the cross and died for it. Martyrdom was quite in the line of Bushido teaching. Equally samurai-like, if not Christ-like, was the

step taken by a large band of believers, who rose
in arms as the last resort of their faith.   The so-
called rebellion of Shimabara (1638) was the extreme measure of the Christians' protest against
political and religious tyranny.   It ended most
disastrously for their cause, and with the summary
slaughter of the best Christian knights ended all
public profession of the religion of Christ.   Henceforth Christianity was known as *Ja-kyo*, an evil
faith, a religion that encourages treason, rebellion,
deception, assassination, poisoning, and all clandestine tricks and magical incantations.   To con-
jure the name of *Yaso*, as Jesus is pronounced in
Japanese, was to call upon all the legions of evil
spirits.   Whoever survived the rebellion alluded
to, was put to the sword.   Every nook and corner was searched lest one should escape.   A strict
census was yearly taken by the Buddhist monasteries, for the Buddhist priests of those times were
in no small measure responsible for the blood of the
Christian martyrs.

The decisive stand Japan took against Christianity affords a most fruitful theme for speculation.   If the country had been brought entirely
under the control of the Jesuits, what would have
been its fate?   It is not probable that it would
have lost its political independence and simply
succumbed to Spanish rule; but it is conceivable
that, but for the eradication of the incipient faith,
Japan would now be a second or third-rate Catholic power in the East.   If Japan had formed a part

of Christendom, sequestrated and humble, and continued as such from the seventeenth century, it is presumable that the mental affinity between the East and the West would have grown closer. On the other hand, it is likely that the Catholic Church would have proved an additional factor in the conflicting and disturbing forces at work in the country and would have prevented Japan from realising the unique peace she enjoyed, and the arts she developed, as well as the racial homogeneity and compact nationalism she maintained— all of which marked the following epoch of her history.

4. The Shogunate, which represented the actual governing power, passed, after the eleventh century, from one family to another in quite rapid succession until the beginning of the seventeenth century, when it fell to the lot of Iyeyasu, head of the Tokugawa house, in whose hand it was centralised and elaborately organised.

On the ground that all the Spaniards and Portuguese were followers of the "evil sect," they were ordered to leave forever the "sacred soil of the divine land," as we call Japan. Before the close of 1639, there was thus left neither a missionary nor a merchant of either of these nationalities, except some few who were naturalised or who apostatised.

Thus was consummated by the founder of the Tokugawa family, the *exclusive* measures so jealously maintained by his successors for two and a

half centuries.   His policy did not stop here.   It
was as *inclusive* as it was exclusive.   So rigorous
was the Edict of 1637, that not only were foreigners forbidden to land on the Japanese coast,
but the natives were prohibited from leaving it.
Ships above a certain tonnage were not allowed
to be built.   Prior to this period, the Japanese
had been free to go from and return to their country at will.   Many had been the ships that plied
between Java, Manila, Annam, Siam, Malacca,
China, Korea, and India, and there are interesting
pages regarding our colonial activity in the history
of those times.   Now all these enterprises received
a death-blow by the stroke of a pen.

Cut off from the rest of the world by this exclusive and inclusive policy, there was formed a
society impervious to ideas from without, and fostered within by every kind of paternal legislation.
Methods of education were cast in a definite
mould; press censure was vigorously exercised; no
new or alien thought was tolerated, and if any
head harboured one, it was in immediate danger
of being dissevered from the body that upheld it;
even matters of friseur, costume, and building were
strictly regulated by the State.   Social classes of the
most elaborate order were instituted.   Etiquette
of the most rigorous form was ordained.   It was
during this period that the tea ceremony, flower
arrangement, and other devices for mollifying
social manners reached a high degree of perfection.
Even the manner of committing suicide by splitting

one's bowels was minutely prescribed. Industries were forced into specified channels, thus retarding economic development. As no relations existed with foreign powers, international wars did not trouble us. Peace reigned within the Empire, but only such peace as would be possible in the slumber of the Middle Ages.

If, however, in the Middle Ages, clouds were gathering to burst amidst the thunder and lightning of the Renaissance and the Reformation, conditions in Japan were not dissimilar; for, in spite of political and economic inactivity, the Tokugawa period was pregnant with mighty forces —forces which, as we shall see, were soon to reveal themselves in the awakening life of the New Era.

Recent events in China have made us familiar with the fact that her present reigning dynasty dates back to 1644. That was the year when the capital of the former dynasty, the Ming, was captured. As two centuries previously the fall of Constantinople drove Grecian scholars into Italy, there to disseminate the seeds of the Renaissance, so the fall of Nanking made Chinese scholars seek refuge on our shores, there to spread anew the teachings of Chinese classics and ultimately to bring about the regeneration of the Island Empire.

The revival of Confucian classics reminded the scholars of Japan that their allegiance was due solely and singly to the *Tenno* (Emperor), and not to the Shogun. The simultaneous revival of pure Shinto, which inculcated the divine right and de-

scent of the Emperor, also conveyed the same political evangel. Whispers, started among priests
and savants that the Shogun must go, spread from
ear to ear, and in spite of everything his authority
could devise to stem the current, the new doctrine
took wings from one end of the country to the
other. He who ran might read the ominous signs
of the times. The abrogation of the Shogun only
awaited the slightest provocation, and this was
supplied by the coming of an American—the
appearance of Commodore Perry in our waters, in
1853. Very naturally he believed that the Shogun or Tycoon, as he was sometimes called, was the
legitimate and ultimate power in the Empire, and
opened negotiations with him. Better versed in
world-politics than the Emperor's Court, which
had not been in touch with actual affairs, the
Shogunal government accepted the Commodore's
proposals and signed a treaty of peace, commerce and navigation, in the spring of 1854.
This high-handed proceeding on the part of the
Shogun precipitated the crisis. Those who were
opposed to him and advocated that the Emperor
alone had the power to enter into foreign relations, were called Imperialists, and they demanded that the treaty be nullified and that the
Shogun forfeit the authority he so unscrupulously
abused.

Keiki, the last of the Shoguns, willingly surrendered it, because he knew well enough that he
held it only in trust. Not so the feudal lords who

had been created by his house. They naturally
desired the continuance of the old régime. Many
daimyos espoused the falling cause of the Tokugawa Shogun, but a still larger number of powerful houses arrayed themselves under the brocade
banner of the Emperor. Ever since the Shimabara
rebellion, people had not known war, and now
the whole country was rent by a commotion from
which no samurai could be free. The god of war
decided in favour of the Imperial cause and the
Tokugawas retired to private life (Prince Keiki,
still living, is a respected gentleman of seventy-
five) and the system of Shogunal government
was abolished.

5. This episode in our history is often called a
revolution; but the term is misleading, as it suggests many an event known by that name in
Europe. "Restoration" will better express the
character of this crisis, because the issue involved
was the restoration of the Emperor to his legitimate authority. This was consummated in 1868,
and marks the beginning of the present reign. It
is from this date that we count the new era, the
era of *Meiji*—"The Enlightened Reign,"—the
present year (1912) being the forty-fifth of Meiji.

Though the Imperialist party commenced its
hostility to the Tokugawas by opposing their
policy of opening the country to foreign trade, a
few bitter encounters with European gun-boats
soon convinced them of the futility of exclusivism.
It is, however, only just to state that a large num-

ber of those who publicly denounced the treaty, entertained in their hearts no hostile feeling regarding intercourse with western nations, and when they cried "Down with the western barbarians!" they used this slogan only to hide their real intention, which was the overthrow of the Shogunate. In the midst of national convulsions the Emperor died, leaving the throne to his son, the present ruler, Mutsuhito—then a lad of sixteen. Within a year of his coronation, the Imperialists gained a complete victory over the forces of the Shogun, so that by the year 1869 the country was pacified, and the duarchy, which had lasted from the twelfth century, was entirely dissolved, and an unhampered monarchy re-established. The young Emperor, fortunately of sterling character, commanding intellect, and good physique, signalised his new reign by proclaiming on oath, on the sixth of April, 1868, the five principles of his government, known as the Charter Oath of Five Articles. This proclamation was the Magna Charta of the Japanese Empire. It runs:

1. An Assembly widely convoked shall be established, and all affairs of State decided by impartial discussion.

2. All administrative matters of State shall be conducted by the co-operative efforts of the governing and the governed.

3. All the people shall be given opportunity to satisfy their legitimate desires.

4. All absurd usages shall be abandoned, and justice and righteousness shall regulate all actions.

5. Knowledge and learning shall be sought for all over the world, and thus the foundations of the imperial polity be greatly strengthened.

New Japan has been governed in accordance with this enlightened policy.

The year 1871 saw the abolition of feudalism with the voluntary surrender of their fiefs by the *daimyos* themselves. At that time there was already in the minds of a few, as is also indicated in the first article cited, the vision of a constitutional government. The more radically-minded among them would have liked to have seen it realised at once; but calmer counsel prevailed, and the most advanced statesmen estimated that it would take two or three decades to prepare the nation for a limited monarchy. Not only was education made compulsory between the years of six and twelve, but education in the wider sense of self-governing citizenship was insisted upon. For instance, a deliberative body was formed, consisting of old and tried public servants, and soon after an annual assembly of provincial governors was convened. Publications relating to parliamentary forms of government were translated and disseminated. In short, every method was employed to prepare the nation for the final adoption of the constitution. I may say it took over twenty years, from the time a constitution was seriously discussed until the time when it was finally promulgated in 1889. Side by side with the preparation for civil liberty, reforms were set in motion in every social and political institution. A broad basis for intelligent democracy was to be secured by erasing social distinctions.

The time-honoured social classification of citizens into the samurai, or military and professional men, the tillers of the soil, the artisans and lastly the merchants, was abolished.

The defence of the country was entirely remodelled. The place of the samurai as defenders of the country was taken by a standing army, raised by a system of conscription. The old samurai descended, as it were, into the lower orders, and in so doing elevated the moral tone of the masses by instilling their code of honour into their hitherto despised inferiors. The populace, being now amenable to military duties, were raised, so to speak, to the ranks of the samurai.

It was a great experiment to prove whether an army or navy, necessarily consisting according to conscription laws very largely of peasantry, could be made an efficient engine of territorial defence. The test of this experiment came when, in 1877, the so-called Saigo rebellion occurred, in which the flower of the Satsuma samurai, always noted for their bravery, was met by the Imperial troops, recruited by conscription. It was soon discovered, to our amazement and satisfaction, that in our peasantry was the material for an efficient army. As for the material for the navy, the brave fisher-folk of our coasts formed a more than adequate supply.

It was not only in military institutions that reforms were introduced and bore fruit, as has been demonstrated to the world at large in the three wars in which we have since been engaged— the wars with China in 1894–5, with Russia in 1904–5, and at the time of the Boxer revolt in 1900.

The progress made in the military and naval régimes is but a small part of our national progress. In political life, the transformation was, if anything, more marvellous. When, as the result of twenty years' preparation, the nation was deemed ripe for representative government, the constitution was, in 1889, proclaimed in the name of the Emperor, and the first parliament took its seat the following year. This constitutional experiment—the first to be tried by an Asiatic people—was watched with much interest, if not curiosity, by outsiders. It is enough to state here that an experience of twenty years has deprived the constitution of the character of an experiment. It has come to stay on Asiatic soil. It even threatens to invade the continent in a far more radical form. As to party government, however, we have as yet only a feeble semblance of it; but here we feel no regret—in the face of recent examples this country has shown us.

The Gregorian calendar was adopted and the Christian Sabbath made a regular holiday. Laws were codified on the principles of the most advanced jurisprudence, yet without violating the best traditions of the people. Higher education in cultural and technical lines was encouraged and patronised. New industries were constantly introduced or old ones improved. Means of communication—shipping, railways, the telegraph and telephone—have been steadily extended. Changes in all the departments of national and commercial life are still transpiring; but an account of them would take me out of the pale of history into the story of the Present.

This statement is often repeated—that Japan has achieved in five decades what it took Europe five centuries to accomplish. The privilege of youth lies in the inheritance of the dearly-bought experience of age. We are forever indebted to our older sisters in the family of nations. Who can believe nowadays that the Western Powers at one time seriously discussed the partitioning of Japan? This was actually contemplated about forty years ago.

I have sketched in rough outline the course of our historical development to give you an idea that the institutions of modern Japan, introduced, as many of them are, from abroad, have all been the outcome of genetic growth, no great violence having ever been done to the law of continuity. It is often said that our progress is confined to our

leaders; but you do not hear that a mob of the
people destroyed a telegraph line or a railway
track, or set fire to a schoolhouse.

Psychologists and sociologists have always
looked upon the progress of Japan with no little
suspicion. Le Bon and others of his school called
the occidentalisation of Japan a thin veneer. They
thought that our army, trained and armed after
Western pattern, was only for show. They thought
that our navy was a plaything, invincible only in
peace, and probably invisible in war; for never,
they said, could an Oriental organise or manage
such an intricate machine as a modern gun-boat
in the face of actual danger. They thought that
our education in Western science and philosophy
was but apish mimicry, for, they avowed, white
philosophy and white science can never penetrate
the brown head. I do not know where Monsieur
Le Bon now stands; but the nations that have
seen our people not only in times of peace and
play, but in those dark hours which try men's
souls, have judged differently. The American
people, with their youthful optimism and broad
human sympathy, have always been the first to
recognise whatever steps we have taken in the
onward march.

When other nations tried to bar our progress or
slur our reputation, America always stood for us
and with us. Indeed American sympathy has
been a potent influence in the latest phase of
our national life.

There are many pages in our recent history which will be unintelligible, unless the reader keeps in mind the presence of hostile and friendly foreign Powers. No nation of our day and generation can live in isolation, any more than can a lower organism, and as ecology decides what a plant will be, so does foreign environment determine a nation's course. Which nation has retarded and which accelerated our growth? Which offers, or will offer, a favourable, and which a fatal, condition? We shall speak in a future lecture of the part played by America in our national development—how her Stars heralded to the world the rising of our Sun.

CHAPTER IV

RACE AND NATIONAL CHARACTERISTICS

IT is related of Napoleon that when the vexed question of his pedigree was once discussed, he cut the Gordian knot in his characteristic way by the naïve and pregnant affirmation, *"Je suis moi-même un ancetre."* To an egoist or the *nouveau riche*, this reply may be all-sufficient; to a race already possessed of a tall ancestral tree, the question of whence they came and how they came to be where they are, is a natural intellectual pursuit, replete with practical consequences, and when the cult of that race happens to consist largely in the veneration of its forebears, a knowledge of genealogy will free them from the charge of worshipping the "unknown gods."

In my last lecture, I hinted that among Asiatic peoples we are the youngest. We used to boast of a history of twenty-seven centuries, but it seems more probable that it is to be shortened to the space of twenty. This brings the birth of our nation to the time of the beginning of the Christian era, but even for four or five centuries after this, our history can hardly be called strictly authentic.

When documents so accurately compiled as that of the Hebrews, claiming moreover divine inspiration, are still constantly being improved and reconstructed, we may well expect no slight alterations in the rendering of our chronicles from the hand of future investigators.

Whatever the exact dates in the early records of Japan, this much is certain—that compared with Korea, China, or India, we are a young nation, and stand to these hoary peoples, as far as age is concerned, as did the Germanic folk to the Romans, or, more aptly, to the Phœnicians and Egyptians, and are thus the heir of all the ages of Asiatic tradition.

When our forefathers lived by the hunt or by crude agriculture—which can scarcely be called agriculture in the modern sense, being what Hahn calls *Hackbau* (hoe culture) as against *Ackerbau,*—without letters, without cities, the Koreans and the Chinese were in the enjoyment of a high civilisation. It is possible, as we have seen, that some adventurous spirits among these peoples braved the sea that separated Japan from their home. Aided by a favourable wind, a bark can cross these waters without much difficulty. Indeed, Japan is geographically quite accessible from many quarters. An intrusion—not in great hordes but in single files as it were—from the north is not impossible either from the Asiatic continent by way of Kamtchatka and Saghalien or from America by the stepping-stones of the Aleutian and Kurile

Islands. The same is true of a passage from the South Sea Islands, there being an almost continuous stretch of archipelagoes.

A group of islands under a genial sky and with enchant ng scenery may well have allured races from the torrid south or from the frigid north, or from places of corresponding latitude on the continent, whence extremes of cold and heat or whence misgovernment or overpopulation might have driven the inhabitants.

The Chinese had from of old a pretty legend of three mountainous islands in the eastern sea, where the dwellers quaff the elixir of life and enjoy immortal bliss. It was in search of this place, Horai Mountain, as it was called, that a Chinese Emperor, Shi-Houang, sent a physician in the third century B.C. It is said that the envoy set out, taking with him three hundred youths and three hundred maidens, and, landing in Japan, was loath to return and settled permanently near Mount Fuji. Jofuku, for such was the name of the physician, did not pretend to be the discoverer of Japan, much less the founder of a rew nation.

I give this legend as an instance of old-time intercourse between the continent and our islands, and as an illustration how our people may easily have come under Mongolian influence. Only there seems as yet little philological affinity established between the continental peoples and the Japanese. In this respect a relationship with the Malay races promises to be closer, though as yet no definite conclusion is reached.

But before the Malays or the Chinese reached the shore of Japan, a hairy race of Northern blood, large in numbers and known as the Ainu, seem to have held the entire country in possession.

Were the Ainu, then, the original inhabitants of the Japanese islands? According to their own tradition, when they came they found a people settled there, a description of whom suggests a race akin to the Lapps. Tradition and archæological remains are responsible for the hypothesis that the autochthons of our land were this pigmy race, fair of skin, gentle in spirit, and nocturnal in habits. It is said that they never made their appearance in the day-time. They were known as Korupo-unguri—*Korupo* being the name of a plant, the *Nadosmia Japonica*, and *Unguri*, like Ungarn (Hungary) meaning a man—so called because, according to their legend, they lived under the large, round leaves of this plant. They were superseded by the hirsute Ainu, but whence these came we do not know; though this much is certain, that they were once in possession of the whole of the islands, as is shown by the geographical names they left behind them. In the course of time the Ainu themselves were gradually driven northward, and only a handful of them, amounting to about eighteen thousand, still live in the northern island of Hokkaido (Yezo). As they are now found, they have not yet emerged from the Stone

Age, possessing no art beyond a primitive form of horticulture, being ignorant even of the rudest pottery. Their fate resembles that of your American Indians, though they are much more docile in character. Who drove away these Ainu, is a question not clearly answered; but it is probable that tribes allied to the Koreans crossed the Sea of Japan and, being much more advanced in civilisation, made themselves masters of Ainu territory. There is some ground to believe that it is the traditions of Korean tribes which largely formed the beginnings of our chronicles. The headquarters of the early Korean colonists were in the province of Idzumo, which faces Korea across the sea, and where still linger the oldest historical legends; but these people, whoever they might have been, did not multiply and replenish the entire land, much less subdue it; for another race, stronger and more robust, seems to have occupied the southern part of Japan, where they formed a community quite independent of the Idzumo people. Were they Malays? No evidence can be drawn from legends or traditions. Indeed, there were no legends or traditions of Malay immigration; but the morphological characteristics of the occupiers of Idzumo and of Kyushu show marked divergence in the form of their skulls, the colour of the skin, and the shape of the face.

Thus the farther we trace our lineage, the more entangled grow the threads which as warp and woof went to weave our nationality. We are still on

the hunt after our ancestor. With better reason
than can usually be assigned for the proverbial dis-
sensions of scholars, the latter are not yet agreed
about our ancestral trunk, some of them even
delighting in fantastic theories. To take a few
examples;—the old Dutch scholar Kaempfer believed that the primeval Japanese were a scion
of the people who built the Tower of Babel. Hyde-
Clarke identifies them with Turano-Africans who
have travelled eastward through Egypt, China,
and Japan. Macleod took them to be one of the
lost tribes of Israel. The presence of curly hair
causes Siebold to believe they were related to the
"Alfuros"—Melanesians and Caroline Islanders.
Some years ago, a young man went to infinite
pains to draw parallels between the language, customs, and institutions of the Hittites and of the
Japan se—only our knowledge of the Hittites is
not much greater than our knowledge of the canals
in Mars. Whitney and Morton, and latterly Grif-
fis, do not hesitate in tracing us to a Caucasic
ancestry.

In view of the fact that one's pedigree can be
verified in more ways than one—anatomical, philological, religious, traditional, and what not—we
may one day arrive at a solution from some
most unexpected quarter.

Just here I may be allowed to make a digression
which may throw some light on the race-affinity,
hitherto unsuspected between Japan and Europe,
whoever may have occupied the West of Europe

contemporaneously with the beginnings of Japan. Excavations and documents point to the fact that the ancient method of burial in Japan was first in barrows and later in dolmens. The barrow is simply a mound of earth, such as the Chinese heap over their dead. The dolmen is an underground chamber of stone with the earth mounded over it. Now the interesting point is that no dolmen has hitherto been found in China or Korea. In fact, dolmens like those we have in Japan have thus far not been discovered in any part of Asia east of the Caspian Sea, and Western Europe alone offers exactly analogous types. Of course, similarity of this kind may be a chance coincidence and no more; but it is, nevertheless, interesting to learn that dolmens do not date from a period anterior to the third century B.C. Can it be possible, is the next question—can it be possible that the founder of our Empire, the leader of the last and the most powerful band of settlers migrating to our shores, had his home—he or his ancestors, somewhere in remote Western Europe? A caustic querist may ask,—Did the pre-historic progenitors of modern Japanese imitate the European mode of sepulture? We shall look forward with eagerness to further revelations which science may make to us.

Some years ago, when I was in Paris, I had the pleasure of meeting Professor Hamy, one of the greatest craniologists of the day, who, as the result of his examination of several hundred Japanese skulls, told me that he had never found traces of a more extensive miscegenation than in the Japanese. When the fifty or sixty different nationalities that have come to the United States are more thoroughly amalgamated and make a more homogeneous race, his remark will more likely apply to America. To further elucidate his opinion, he added that "there is scarcely a race which has not contributed to make the Japanese nation, the Caucasian, the Mongolian, the Malay, and even, in the south, a slight tinge of Negrito from the islands of the Pacific."

A race so diversified in its origin must naturally present characteristics, physical and mental, that are widely divergent. Whether or not we can identify and call by their names our forefathers, one by one, the mere fact of a great mixture ought to be sufficient to explain the extremes of temperament, the wide range of selection, or what the biologists call the spontaneous variation, in one word plasticity, by virtue of which we adopt with ease foreign ideas and institutions,—all this in spite of the close homogeneity we have attained. It is not surprising that Japan has been dubbed topsy-turvydom. No less close an observer than Miss Scidmore calls it the land of paradoxes, in the same sense in which one of the latest and most careful students of American life, Mr. Muirhead, calls this country a "Land of Contrasts." I congratulate your country and mine on being paradoxical and inconsistent, for "consistency is," as Emerson says, "a hobgoblin of fools and little minds." Where man is given a field for the free play of his mind and body, what he does to-day can but be inconsistent, in a sense, with what he did yesterday and with what he will do to-morrow. It is no discredit to a nation to have some specimens very different from the type; on the contrary, it would argue a plentiful lack of wit, if a whole people were cast in a rigid mould of body and soul. The biogenetic law has been formulated that the individual organism, in its brief period of life, repeats the main stages of development through which the race has passed. Now, when a nation is not coterminous with a race—or, as the Germans have it, when the people do not form a strict *Nationalstaat* but only a *Staatsnation*—but embraces individuals of originally different races, one cannot expect much uniformity in physique or intellect. Composite phylogenesis will naturally allow a wide scope for recapitulation. Generalisation is risky; and I approach the subject of our race and national characteristics with fear lest I may not be just. Even as regards our somatic features, until a more exact measure of the average man, *L'homme moyen* of the statisticians, is established, we shall have to content ourselves with a more or less indefinite type.

Suppose we could obtain an average for the present generation, so unstable are human types —as Boas, Bolk, and other ethnographers have demonstrated,—that a few generations hence will show a marked difference in Japanese anatomy. From the extensive mixture and the large dynamic possibilities of anatomical qualities, it has long been, and probably still is, no easy task to assign a definite place to the Japanese in the general scheme of ethnic classification. We used to be dumped into the heap of linguistic non-conformity, under the name Turanian. A German ethnographer divides mankind into day-folk and night-folk, and finding us not conformable to the requirements for admittance to either, prepares a special seat in the gallery of the twilight folk (*Dämmerungs-menschen*). The Japanese, as they are, according to the carefully compiled table of Professor Amos W. Butler, belong to what he calls the Sibiric branch of the Asiatic race, and with the Koreans constitute the Japanic stock, quite apart from the Chinese, Mongolic, and the Tartaric. Perhaps this classification is the most concise.

The most obvious morphological traits which first strike one in a foreigner are stature and pigmentation. We are a small race—five feet two inches being the general average height for men and five feet for women. Although this is the average, there are many men who outmeasure six feet. In the case of wrestlers, a height of six feet is not considered exceptional. I may remark in this connection that the average in the north is decidedly higher than that in the south. As stature is not a statical character of a race, its increase is being constantly retarded or acceler-

ated, and though eugenics is not yet a fashion
with us, there is shown a decided tendency towards increase of stature in the case of the growing generation, especially among girls. Without
doubt, this is due to gymnastic exercises in the
school, and to the fact that the use of chairs and
benches during school-hours permits fuller development of the limbs than does our national
custom of sitting with the leg folded back from
the knee.

The limbs, both upper and lower, are small and
delicately shaped. The legs are proportionately
shorter in comparison with the length of the torso
—a feature certainly not beautiful. Then, too,
they are generally more or less bowed, perhaps
from the posture in sitting, or, can it be possible
that it is a characteristic inherited from one of our
ancestors, the Mongolians, of whom Dr. Hehn
says that their legs became bent from constant
riding on the steppes of Central Asia!

The arms, too, are comparatively short, and
in spite of the fact that the most beautiful Buddhist statues have arms reaching to the knee, we
speak rather disparagingly of long arms, meaning
thereby a propensity to violate the eighth commandment. In this scant proportion of trunk and
limbs as well as in brachycephaly, Havelock Ellis
notes an approach to the infantile condition of the
human species. Lest the more sensitive of my
compatriots feel insulted by so belittling a statement as this, let it be added for their consolation

that the negroes and Australian savages are farthest removed from this infantile structure. If the hand, like the arm, is also small, the fingers are comparatively long and very often tapering. The delicacy of our hand explains the dexterity of our workmanship, a dexterity no doubt enhanced by the constant use of the brush in writing and of chopsticks in eating.

The pigmentation of the skin is typically light brown with a tinge of yellow, with variations from skins as fair as that of any Caucasian to those as dark as a red Indian. If the skin shows variation of hue, the hair is almost invariably black, and the chemical knowledge of our girls does not include the beautifying value of peroxide of hydrogen. I may remark in passing that our albino looks like an ultra type of your blonde. Our hair is straight, though quite often wavy, albeit curls are not enjoyed by the possessor. If frizzly hair is not abhorred, it is for the same reason that nobody is afraid of a snake in Ireland. Should nature play a prank on Japanese girls by covering the head with a woolly texture, I am afraid it would swell the army of female suicides. The beard and moustache of the men are as a rule not heavy. The race as a whole is the reverse of hirsute. Occasionally one meets with people who are remarkable for their hairiness, and this quality is ascribed to Ainu blood.

The head is relatively large, a fact that is attributed by some, though I am not prepared to admit the statement, to the large consumption of fish. The shape of the head is brachiocephalic, though dolicocephalic specimens are not at all rare. The eyes, as a rule black, though frequently light brown, are usually smaller than those of Europeans, and the smallness is made more conspicuous by puffy eyelids and veiled corners. The obliquity given to our eyes by artists, especially in popular colour prints, is decidedly exaggerated. A curious belief prevails among us that straight eyes and eyebrows, and, worse still, those that droop at the corners, are signs of weak character.

The nasal index is of medium degree. Greek or Roman noses are not infrequently met with, nor is the Jewish type unfamiliar. Especially among the lower classes do we find very flat and broad noses. As for the mouth and the lips, there is no one type that requires particular mention. The teeth are more often than not well-formed and sound, for which one may thank plain living, which foregoes excessive indulgence in sweets, ice-cream, and beefsteak. The cheek-bones have a decided tendency to be prominent, more conspicuously so among the peasantry.

There are two facial types, the long and the round, or the oval and the "pudding-face," as it has been termed. The aristocracy have generally the longer type of face, and this is believed by good authorities attributable to Korean blood; whereas the "pudding-face" may have been inherited from the Malays or the Ainu.

As regards our standard of beauty, naturally it is not in every respect uniform with the Greek or the Egyptian, or with the canons of the Renaissance; but only in a very few points are the different canons at direct variance; that is to say, what we deem beautiful will never be positively ugly to you and *vice versa*.

A woman, to be considered beautiful by us, need not be tall. Height may be divinely imposing, but not essential to human beauty. With us, about five feet would be considered the most desirable height, but if one must err, it is advisable to err by exceeding rather than by falling short of the mark. The figure should be slender without being bony, the waist long and the hips narrow. To secure grace, the body should be held slightly forward, not boldly erect. A very important feature is the neck, which should be long, white, slender, and gracefully curved. The hair should of course, be abundant, long, and perfectly straight, and while no deviation from black is tolerated, it should not be just black, but should be so glossy that it seems blue-black. The face should be oval and long, with a straight nose, which should also be high and narrow. As for the eyes, opinions are divided, one school of connoisseurs demanding that they should be large with a double line of the lid, while another school prefers that the eyes should be long and narrow and slightly slanting upwards at the outer corner. The colour of the eye should always be clear and deep brown; the

lashes thick, long, and curved; the eyebrows black
and distinct, their line long, and well arched; the
mouth small; lips thin, curved, and red; teeth small,
regular, and white. The ears must be evenly
curved, with no angle, and in size not too small,
for pinched lobes look poverty stricken. Large
ears, like those of the probable inhabitants of
Mars, lately described by Professor Perrier, if
not exactly beautiful, are believed to be lucky.
As for the shape of the forehead, there are four
types. By the one termed "horned," we mean
that in which the hair grows to a point in the
middle of the forehead and high at the sides after
the fashion called by the Germans *Geheimraths-
Ecke* or the "Councillor's corners." Then there
are the square and the round types; but the forehead most admired is high and narrow at the top,
and obliquely slanting at the sides, suggesting the
outline of our sacred mountain, Fuji.

As for the complexion, it should be fair, with a
tint of the rose on the cheek, only, in our parlance,
we would call it cherry-hued.

A figure combining all the points of the canon
I have enumerated—and above all softened by
eternally feminine modesty and gentleness of
expression, and heightened by faultless refinement,
and gracefulness of dress and manner—cannot fail
to strike an alien critic as pleasant, agreeable and
even charming; and as his eye gets more and more
accustomed to this type of beauty, he may pronounce it quite enchanting.

7

It has often been remarked by foreigners that there are far more beautiful women in Japan than handsome men, the latter being a rare article.

From the general description of the physical characteristics of our race, you must have discovered, if you have not previously been aware of the fact, that the Japanese are by no means a beautiful race.   To me, an ardent admirer of Greek civilisation, it has ever been a thorn in the flesh, because I have always believed that our people will in the future achieve the welding of two types of civilisation, as did the Hellenes in times past.   When I expressed this, my disappointment, in the hearing of Dr. Rein, the well-known German geographer, he remarked;—

"I have travelled around the world and studied different peoples, and I will tell you of two great disappointments.   One was in Spain, where the people are unusually handsome, but where I found them so incongruously inferior intellectually.   The other experience was in Japan, where in secluded mountain districts and among peasants living an almost primitive life, and extremely unattractive in their appearance, I found surprising signs of intelligence; so setting intelligence over against homeliness, I think you may be comforted."

I flatter myself that the observations of such experienced travellers as Dr. Rein and Professor Hart, are more favorable than the judgment of a young Frenchman of twenty years, who concluded an account of his tour in Japan with this sweeping assertion—"*Le Japonnais n'est pas intelligent.*" I know it is a flagrant breach of good form for me to say, "We are more clever than we look." Suppose for modesty's sake I reverse the proposition and say, "We look uglier than we deserve," we revert to the same idea, and I may just plainly and honestly confess that we are well aware of our own strength and weakness, and are bent upon adding, as our phraseology expresses it, "to whatever is short in us from whatever is long in others," and "to polish our gems with stones quarried in other lands."

This brings me to the subject of the mental traits of our people, and in treating of them I shall first of all give a very brief account of our language. Philologically Japanese is a forlorn and solitary orphan, that can claim no relationship, either lateral or collateral, with any other languages. Like poor little Mignon in *Wilhelm Meister*, its face is turned vaguely to the south (Malayasia?), yearning for the land where lemons bloom; but not a few scholars have traced the trails along which Japanese travelled from the foot of the Altai Mountains. A philological student went farther than that and tried to demonstrate the linguistic affinity between Japanese and Hittite; but in the present state of Hittite—perhaps it sounds more erudite to say Alarodian or Armenoid—researches, we may just as well identify our language with that in which the sons of God made

love to the daughters of men, or even with that
in which Adam wrote that wonderful diary so
faithfully translated into English by Mark Twain!

Usually Japanese is put in the group of those
agglutinative languages under the general name of
Turanian. But among them, as I have said, it
stands by itself. Still, it is not to be denied that in
the course of centuries it has appropriated words
and expressions from Korean and Chinese, much
as the English tongue has been enriched by the
free use of Norman, Latin, Greek, and what not;
and just as you pronounce words of alien origin in
your own way, or attach new meaning and value to
them, so have we also drawn heavily upon Chinese
sources for a vocabulary, pronouncing monosyl-
labic Chinese words as suits our orthography.
Moreover, we borrowed Chinese letters, which are
pictographs or ideographs, simply as signs to
express the same ideas, but pronounce them
entirely differently. To illustrate, take the first
syllable of my own name, *Ni*. In writing it, we
use a certain Chinese character which every
Chinese will pronounce *shin*, but which the Japanese will read *ni*. Linguistically there is no relation
between *shin* and *ni*, however closely they may be
related in the American vocabulary! The Chinese
character for man is written with two strokes (λ),
and we use it in the same sense, only it is pro-
pronounced in Chinese *lun*, and in Japanese
hito. This rather complicated relationship between
Japanese and Chinese may be easily exemplified

by the case of the Arabic or rather Indian numerals. All the nations of Europe and now of the world have adopted the use of figures; but each nation pronounces numbers differently. To take another illustration, the Latin abbreviation "i.e." is freely used in all European languages; but instead of pronouncing it "id est," the English read it "that is," the French "c'est-à-dire," the Germans "das heisst," &c. This last abbreviation might serve as another good illustration.

One great drawback in the use of Chinese characters is their unlimited number. A man of ordinary education must be acquainted with two or three thousand, and a dictionary in common use gives about forty to fifty thousand. There is no greater drain or strain on our school children than to learn by heart, to simply memorise, some thousands of these characters.

I must add now that the Japanese, while they make free use of Chinese ideography, have invented an alphabet of their own. It is not an alphabet in the strict sense of the term, as it does not consist of letters on the phonetic system. It is properly a syllabary, and contains forty-seven syllables (including the five vowels which are purely phonetic) called *i–ro–ha* from the first three characters. It was the invention of an ingenious Buddhist priest of the ninth century.

The forty-seven syllabic signs do not express all the sounds in our language, of which there are about seventy. By the use of diacritical marks,

certain characters are made to represent other
but allied sounds. In the synopsis of sixty-eight
sounds there are a number which one greatly
misses when one attempts to transcribe a European
word. Entirely absent are the sounds of *l*, *v*, the
English *th*, and the German *ch*. In the case of *l*,
we force *r* to do its work, and as to *v*, its burden is
borne by *b;* that is to say, only ears or lips accustomed to English can distinguish between *lime*
and *rime*, *van* and *ban*. No very serious issues
are involved in a schoolroom when a mistake is
made between *vile* and *bile*, or between *light* and
right; but the solemnity of a church service is
dangerously threatened when *hallowed* is pronounced *harrowed*, or *benison*, *venison*. Far worse
and unpardonable is it, of course, when the
errors are carried into writing and *v-a-l-e* is spelt
b-a-r-e; l-i-f-e, r-i-f-e; l-a-w, r-a-w; and *l-o-v-e,
r-o-b-e!*

With all of its deficiencies, disadvantages, and
cumbersome syntax, our language can express, if
sometimes somewhat awkwardly, all the ideas that
the human mind anywhere has conceived or human
heart has felt. We have already in our own tongue
some of the works of Plato, Schopenhauer, Dar-
win, and Carlyle. The Bible was translated long
ago, and a new version has been attempted. Of
poetry, Homer is partly translated and also several plays of Shakespeare, and quite recently
Faust. Classics are the common property of the
world. They are masterpieces in any tongue.

Japanese classics, too, may be gradually introduced into the Western world of letters.

The same patriotism which makes us proud of
our national literature, teaches us the necessity of
learning foreign languages and of introducing reforms in the written and spoken vernacular.   A
linguistic commission has been appointed by the
Government; language teaching has been improved
in the schools; English has been the principal
study in high schools; German is obligatory in
colleges and universities; transliteration societies—
whose aim is to displace the Chinese ideographs by
adopting Roman script—have been preaching the
need of radical reform for the sake of the next
generation.

The spread of foreign languages and foreign
literature is synonymous with the dissemination
of European ideas.   Can the Japanese long bear
the weight of foreign thought?   Can they really
grasp Western sentiment, not only understand but
enjoy it?

The rich variety of races and of tongues that
have come to be our heritage, explains without
further demonstration our quickness in adopting
foreign ideas and institutions, and in adapting
ourselves to changing conditions of life.   This
process of selective accommodation has been called
by various names—imitation, mimicry, love of
novelties, fickleness.

Hardly a book is written by an outsider without
mention of Japanese imitativeness,—often quali-

fied with such an adjective as blind, apish, childish, slavish. The same criticism is also expressed in another form, namely, lack of originality.

This characterization of our mental trait cannot be gainsaid. If there were only two kinds of men, the imitative and the original, the Japanese, together with the Greeks, Romans, and Normans, would certainly belong to the former. We borrowed (imitation is borrowing) Buddhism from India, Confucianism and some few other isms from China. Our much boasted arts are largely of continental origin. Our modern institutions have been learned chiefly from the West.

We take pride in our imitative faculty. When in the Charter Oath with which our Emperor opened his auspicious reign, he plainly gave out an injunction to seek knowledge all over the world, he expressed the nation's willingness to follow the Biblical command—"Prove all things and hold to that which is good."

Imitation is education, and education consists mainly in imitation. Whether it turns out to be apish mimicry or not, depends on the judicious choice of the model. Imitation is voluntary adjustment persistently followed by the use of the criterion of fitness or of utility. It is essentially a power with which one subdues all things —even one's own self. An obscure recluse named Thomas, in the small village of Kempen, made it his life-work to imitate his Master and we all know what he attained in holiness and in literature.

Moreover, is it never possible to excel one's master? What of Raphael? For whether in religions or ethics, in art or literature, though they all originally came from China and India, we have transformed them to our own taste. We have not only adopted but adapted them. Assimilation of foreign ideas is impossible unless the receptive people are prepared for them. As Monsieur Tarde enunciates in one of his laws of imitation, international, collective imitation can proceed only from within outwards, otherwise it is only apish mimicry. Thus we console ourselves in the charge of imitativeness, accepting it, first, as a sign of our plastic, mobile youth; secondly, in the hope of one day returning with interest the capital we are borrowing at present; thirdly, because we have made of it a deliberate and organized instrument of great cultural and political efficiency.

As for originality, what does it mean any way, in the face of Emerson's assertion that great genial power consists in not being original at all, but rather in being altogether receptive? If originality means inventions and discoveries, we are achieving something in these directions too. Our army is supplied with rifles of our own invention, and they have done some service; our gun-powder was invented by our compatriot, Shimosé, and it has not been altogether useless. To science, too, especially in bacteriology, we have made a few contributions and expect to make more. Grant a little time to an imitative child, and he may some day amount to something.

As for fickleness, which is closely connected with the imitative faculty—being a product of quickness of perception and alertness of action—this is a charge that can hardly be brought against a people who have lived under the same dynasty for twenty centuries. There is, however, some reason for taking as proofs of fickleness, the many experiments we have made in order to "prove all things." When Luther Burbank takes a hundred new plants, cultivates them for a season, compares and examines them, and then throws away ninety-nine as unfit for his use, he shows intelligence, judgment, and decision, but not fickleness. No one thinks of calling a lady who is always dressed *comme il faut*, a fickle ape for being modish; and yet, is not fashion every inch imitation? If so, the people among whom fashion changes oftenest must be the most fickle. This may be one of the simplest reasons why Americans and Japanese are like-minded.

In seeking the best from abroad, the mental trait which has served us most has been quickness of perception, an intuitive recognition of the fit; for the Japanese imagination can sweep a wide (I dare not say a deep or lofty) range of space, and discern at a glance all that there is within its view. This is the vision of the artist, and the soul of woman.

It seems to me that there is at the bottom of

Japanese character a feminine trait. In the up-
bringing of a child by its parents, the mother
plays a larger part by far than does the father—
much more so than in the West. As a child grows
up, the intimacy between him and his father
lessens and the relation between them assumes a
respectful and polite distance. Not so with the
mother. Between her and the child, intimacy
never stiffens into formality; she is ever the mother.
The child's soul is moulded by her influence and
her spirit, and it partakes of feminine qualities,
both good and bad. The undercurrent of sadness,
of kindliness, of tenderness, of pity, of compassion
that is moving deep down in the Japanese soul
comes from the mother's bosom, but there is
another undercurrent equally deep and equally
strong—of jealousy, envy, revenge, and vanity,
which should be traced to the same source. These
two currents, flowing from the two maternal breasts,
feed the Japanese soul, and it would be quite
feminine if the mother, in bringing up the child,
did not keep before it for admiration manly deeds
and virile virtues. The child whose soul is moulded
in womanly qualities, is made to admire masculine
strength. The result is:—in his temperament he
remains feminine, but his character grows masculine. He feels like a woman and thinks like a man;
and when he acts, his action is like a woman's,
when it is prompted by temperament, or is like a
man's, when urged to it by the force of his
character.

This will explain why sentiment obtains such a powerful dynamic inertia. Japanese heroism is more frequently actuated by sentiment than impelled by judgment and character. Where from a flash of noble emotion a hundred men may jump into fire, there will be only ten who will bear the slings and arrows of outraged fortune, and only one who will endure taunts and scorn for the sake of his principles.

In a word, the Japanese is the child of his mother, trained in the school of his father.

Modern psychology has confirmed the ancient belief that temperament is largely a matter of physiology. The great rapidity of response to external impression, and the quick transmission of nervous impulses among our people, can be explained by neurology, and will in turn explain many a so-called race trait. "The quick sympathy, the wide outlook, the rapid accomplishment," have ever been the advantages which a composite race has enjoyed over one of simpler extraction.

Susceptibility to outside influences is largely what makes the Japanese delight and excel in art; for outside influences in their surroundings cannot fail to produce in the dullest a spark of love for the beautiful. The art instinct has become the subconscious property of the race. While Europeans admire nature and love to analyse its beauty, the Japanese, in their feminine soul, feel it and enjoy it *tout ensemble*. To us nature is a complete whole in itself, and we make no attempt to force or even direct our mind above or beyond it. It distracts nature's child in his ecstacy to soar "from nature up to nature's God." Among Japanese poets the water-fowl is a favourite subject of inspiration, and they feel and sing much as Bryant, with the omission of the last stanza. I am not comparing Eastern and Western minds with a critical or didactic intent, but only to show how tastes—tastes and not minds—differ.

Professor Ladd, in his study of our national psychology, says that the Japanese temperament is that which Lotze has so happily called the "sentimental temperament," which characterises youth in all races, and is marked by great susceptibility to a variety of influences, with a tendency to a will, impulsive and alas! liable to collapse.

When I speak of the alertness with which our brains and nerves work, I do not say this altogether in praise of ourselves, for I am well aware of the shortcomings of a quick brain. I know its temptation to form hasty judgments, to become hypercritical, to be suspicious, to be affected by variations of temper. It is not now my purpose to justify or to criticise the race characteristics of my people. All that I attempt is candidly to present what I believe to be facts. Perhaps our alertness is most clearly evinced by this, that of all the foreign games that have been introduced into Japan, baseball has become the most popular sport. Not only are we quick to receive impressions from without, but we are also keen in observing things and events.

Before I leave the subject of our art and sensory acuity, I must make mention, however cursory, of our music. Years ago, a German musician of note made an interesting remark that island life is not conducive to voice or music. Whether it is upon the geographical location or upon a racial trait that we should lay the blame for the stunted growth of our music, I am in no position to say definitely. It is the branch of art which has developed least in the East. It has been cultivated assiduously by the Court for ceremony, by religion for rite, by the aristocracy for festivity, and by the populace for amusement. In the Court and the Shinto shrine, music is from the very nature of its object, open to little change, and they are, in a peculiar sense, its conservatory. But in the case of the aristocracy and more especially in the sphere of the popular ballads, dances, and recitals, one might have expected more progress. As a matter of fact, Japanese music was confined to a few stringed instruments and flutes and drums of all kinds—most of them of ancient Chinese origin. The typical Japanese instrument, invented in the seventeenth century, is the thirteen stringed *koto*, a sort of lyre, which is learned by every well-bred young lady; but the more plebeian and popular *samisen*, a banjo introduced from Manila, is a ubiquitous instrument of three strings, which produces a sound characterised by

Mr. Piggott as "a mixture between a thrumming and a tinkling," to be called "thrinkling." The fiddle, originally introduced from India, fills by no means the same position that it does in Europe, neither does the *biwa*, a kind of guitar, which was one of the earliest instruments that came into Japan, in the tenth century, and which has been the mother of several other instruments.

As far as the varieties of musical instruments are concerned, our people had—say in the fifteenth, or perhaps as late as the eighteenth century—an assortment very nearly as great as that of the Europeans. I wonder—and this is only a crude surmise of mine—whether the legal measure which made the teaching of music a monopoly, together with a few other social and economic advantages, of the blind (a piece of protective legislation for this unfortunate class), did not in the end have a disastrous effect on the progress of music, excluding, as it did, the possibility of writing music. Whenever acquired talent cannot be committed to writing, however partially and poorly, it is practically lost to future generations, and growth is arrested.

As to music proper, I confess my utter ignorance on the subject. All I can do is to repeat from the opinions of experts that our scale consists of only five notes of the harmonic minor scale, the fourth and seventh being wanting. What lends an outlandish character to our music is the introduction of a semi-tone above the tonic. Moreover, there is very little harmony. The whole effect of our music is, therefore, not at all pleasing to foreign ears, and the Japanese themselves are far from professing themselves a musical people.

Has the Japanese then no music in himself? Is he not "moved with concord of sweet sounds?" Is he not, then, "fit for treasons, stratagems, and spoils," and are "the motions of his spirit dull as night and his affections dark as Erebus"?

Whatever may be implied in this famous aphorism, the Oriental moralists from Confucius down have always insisted upon "the concord of sweet sounds" as subsidiary and subservient to the music in one's own self, the harmony of all one's thoughts and emotions with the rhythmic beat of the heart. If harmony, in the narrower technical sense, was but meagrely developed in our music, harmony of sounds on a large scale was not passed unnoticed. The frogs that croak in the pool, the birds warbling among the swaying boughs, the insects humming in the dewy grass, the zephyr blowing through groves of pine, never failed to catch a listening ear, and were translated into articulate songs.

Our poetical composition proper, the *uta*, consists of only thirty-one syllables. Our long poem is an alternating repetition of long and short lines —seven and five syllables each, or sometimes reversed in the order of five and seven. There is even a shorter form of versification, called *haiku*, consisting of but seventeen syllables. If the *uta* proper savours of aristocratic refinement, the *haiku* is the more plebeian and popular form of poetic expression. Both usually take for their theme the simplest natural object and only hint at the emotions stirred by it.

These pithy, short lines suggest more thought than they express. They leave so much unsaid. The Japanese do not accept the definition usually credited to Talleyrand but previously used by Goldsmith,[1] who himself derived it from Dr. Young, that "speech is a means of concealing thought"; but I admit that they do not wholly comply with the usual English definition that it "is a means of expressing thought"; for among us the highest use of speech is to evoke thought. *Ars est celare artem*—"True art is to conceal art": to which one ought to add—"and explicitly or implicitly to reveal truth." In our drama, for instance, a Hamlet would not take the trouble to make a long soliloquy, but would let his audience have a glimpse of his soul struggle by a few suggestive phrases.

A suspicion may have arisen in your mind that speech and language may not have developed sufficiently among us to express deepest thoughts and emotions. I have already stated that some of the greatest works in European languages have been translated into our tongue.

[1] Goldsmith's *Essay on the Use of Language:* ". . . the true use of *speech* is not so much to express our wants as to conceal them."

Yet, I admit, though with reluctance, that our thought-world — our word-world — suffers from paucity of great ideas. I have said in a former lecture that our leading ideas are importations— Buddhism from India, Confucianism from China. So it is with literature and philosophy. I do not think that we are of the stuff of which great metaphysicians and philosophers are made. Our minds are too practical and terrestrial. As for myself— and my patriotic countrymen will not thank me for my plain speaking—I doubt very much whether we shall make any notable contributions to world-literature in the next generation or two; but in the domain, the ever widening domain, of scientific researches and attainments, we may stand on equal terms with the most advanced peoples of the world.

As he is his mother's son, though disciplined by his father, so is the Japanese an Oriental, fortified in sentiment with the conviction of an Occidental. Poetry lurks within him to burst forth when feeling is stirred; but prose controls his daily round of care. He attends to the menial chores of the shrines sacred to the Muses. Have you seen those quiescent volcanoes that abound in the land, with fire hidden in their bosom; the peasants tilling the terraces and the very crater itself, to raise kitchen vegetables? How unbecoming and incongruous! If in a museum of folk-psychology, the different races were arranged in two opposing groups, of which one is theoretical, religious, emotional, communistic, and the other practical, scientific, intellectual, individual, and if the two groups were respectively labelled Eastern and Western, the Japanese should be classed with the latter, perhaps on the same shelf with the Italians and Austrians.

I believe that our plasticity is such that we can understand the West as we do the East, and can sympathise with both. Emotionally and traditionally allied to the latter, by intelligence and conviction we belong to the former. Now and then we hear of anti-foreign feelings; but if their sight and sound deceive me not, they are simply a phase of contra-imitation, which always accompanies social transformation.

The occidentalisation of Japan is a process psychological and ethological, as well as social and political. And as Monsieur Tarde has pointed out, the permeation of society by foreign ideas works from the upper to the lower classes. Before community of sentiment can become general between the East and the West, the intellectual leaders must own to a common brotherhood. The light of science and of advanced ideas, as it rises above the dim horizon, will first gild the highest peaks, and only as it illumines the plains, will the toilers in the fields recognise each other face to face. If the full dawn has not yet enlightened our peasant and your labourer, it behooves us to whom the early beams of the morning have brought clearer vision, to open the way for better understanding and a closer bond.

CHAPTER V

RELIGIOUS BELIEFS

IN view of the endless field of inquiry which the varying and conflicting definitions of religion will open, I shall start in the present lecture with my own rough notions of religion, which are put forth not for general acceptance, but solely to delimit the sphere of my discourse.

What man believes concerning his existence beyond this life, be it in the future or in the past, constitutes his faith, and what he does as corollaries of his faith—especially in the act of worship—constitutes his religion. If his belief is contradicted by positive science, it is called superstition. A man may have some faith, with which, however, he may mix more superstition. Rarely do we meet one who is wholly and only superstitious, for his superstition is usually a more or less logical inference of his faith. Superstitions do not stand on their own feet, for they have no feet of their own; hence, in order to stand at all, they must borrow the pedestal of faith. And the very reason why superstitions are so general and hard

to fight is, because they are not "a lie which is all
a lie" but "a lie which is part a truth." I have
omitted from my concept of religion the belief in
an infinite God, or in divine revelation,—doctrines
usually considered to be necessary postulates of a
religious faith.

In the sense I have above indicated, the Japanese
are by nature a highly religious people.

In a previous lecture, I dilated at some length on
the artistic temperament of our people. The
sense of beauty extended horizontally generates
art, and the same sense projected upwards paints
and carves a religion. When I speak of my people
as deeply imbued with a religious sentiment, please
note that I lay particular stress on the term *sentiment*. They are sentimental and artistic, and
among their higher sentiments and elevated tastes
are a religious taste and sentiment. This is far
from saying that they are so swayed by religion
that their very sentiments and tastes are governed
by it. Our zeal will not manifest itself in the same
manner as it does among the Jews and the Spaniards, the Hindus or the Arabs. We are too matter-
of-fact in our every-day life to become zealots;
but should persecutions arise, martyrdom would
be hailed in heroism rather than in faith, and death
courted as an honourable exit from this life rather
than as an entrance to the next.

Being largely of the nature of sentiment, the
creed of the Japanese is incapable of concise statement. There are religions, more properly religious

systems, whose articles of faith are reduced to clear-cut phrases in black and white, on vellum and bound with gilt-edge, still leaving ample room for divines to dispute about them. Can any articles of faith make up a religion? Certainly a cut-and-dried theology is not faith. Are there not in the very nature of a religious faith mystery and vagueness, or is this only so in the primitive forms of belief?

The Japanese conception of religion is clear in spots, but generally vague. It begins in instinct, gains volume by sentiment, and grows in strength by emotion. "First guessed by faint auroral flushes sent along the wavering vista of his dream," the Japanese draws nearer to his theme of the hereafter, not by power of intellect but by intensifying his emotions and calling for aid upon his personal sensibilities. The race feels deep down in its consciousness that sublunary existence is not the whole of life. Indeed, this belief is so ingrained in us that it has become a mental habit which asks for no demonstration—a subconscious faith which no materialism can destroy.

It is true we have failed to formulate the immortality of the soul in terms of philosophy or science. Nevertheless, instinctively do we believe—be it only in that impersonal way which in the Buddhist philosophy is known as *Karma*—that the dead are alive, and that the living are not mere dust destined to return to dust; but because we have not elucidated this faith into a rigid doctrine, we are said to be irreligious, and we ourselves not only admit the charge, but the so-called advanced thinkers among us rather pride themselves upon it,—hence the impression that agnosticism is the prevailing attitude of the educated Japanese mind. Ask the most advanced "agnostic" among us if he entertains no belief in a future life. His characteristic reply will be, "I do not know," by which he means, "I cannot prove it." But watch him as he stands by his parents' tomb, or as he throws the clod into the grave at the funeral of his friend; his inborn faith crops out in words or deeds, attesting that in the night "the stars shine through his cypress-trees," and that he "looks to see the breaking day across the mournful marbles play." The most scientific will not dream of peeping into the tomb of his father or "botanising upon his mother's grave." Nor is it only in hours of sorrow that his faith gleams through the darkness. At times of rejoicing his mind fondly turns to the absent from earth, and hears their glad response to his joy. He feels his life bound to all life, past, present, or future. He believes as Savage did, that he had his birth when the stars were born in the dim æons of the past, and that his cradle was rocked by cosmic forces.

Of the many religious systems which either sprouted in Japanese soil or were transplanted therein, three attained national importance. These are Shinto, Buddhism, and, later, Christianity. I exclude Confucianism from the list of religions, since it is silent on the question of life beyond this world. As to Taoism, it found only a very small following. Zoroaster and Mohammed found none.

In the present lecture, I shall occupy myself mainly—almost exclusively—with Shinto; first, because it is a cult strictly native to the race, and secondly, because it is so little known outside of Japan. As for Buddhism, I have had occasion to speak of its introduction and progress in Japan, and of its great social and political importance. As a religious system it transcends the boundaries of Japan, and I take it for granted that you are familiar with its general features; therefore I shall only call your attention to one or two phases of its doctrines which are of special interest to Westerners.

Of Christianity, too, I have had occasion to speak;—how it was first introduced and how it was practically eradicated. Between Christianity as propagated by the immediate followers of Xavier, and Christianity as taught anew by Protestant missionaries, there is no historical continuity in our land. Even at present Christianity is only tolerated in Japan, and not publicly recognised as are Shinto and Buddhism. The Imperial Constitution, however, secures religious freedom to all, and no believer in any religion is molested in the observance of his faith. At the present time, while I am giving these lectures in America, there is a significant project afloat at home. The Vice-minister of Home Affairs, by conviction a faithful Buddhist, and a man of large heart and of wide outlook, has launched the idea—which he wishes to materialise into a legal or administrative measure—of bestowing upon Christianity government recognition, and, by thus elevating its worldly status, to win for it an equal place in the respect of the nation.

The importance of Shinto is due primarily to the fact that it is in its essence strictly indigenous, and that it comprehends more than a religious faith, as this is usually understood. Shinto may be called a compact bundle of the primitive instincts of our race. All religion is conservative; but in the case of Shinto, this loyalty to the past has more truly than in the religious life of ancient Rome, so philosophically depicted by Mr. Jesse B. Carter, "developed from the status of an accidental attribute into that of an essential quality, and became by degrees almost the sum-total of religion." *Koku-fu*, the old custom of the land, has as much power as the *mos majorum* among the Romans, and Shinto is the most faithful guardian and guard of our ancient traditions, keeping intact even their defunct doctrines and effete usages—not always in the cold scientific spirit of preservation, but often enough in reactionary zeal against modern progress.

Another reason for the importance of Shinto lies in the fact of its being the religion of the reigning house. Its tenets run through all the chief rites and rituals of the Court. It was, indeed, in

earliest times the act of government itself.   To
govern and to worship are etymologically synonymous—*Matsurigoto* meaning either.   Numerically,
too, Shinto assumes vast importance, not that it
has a large following, for it is impossible to count
the number of its adherents, but because of some
sixteen thousand shrines, great and small, national
and local, and because of some fifteen thousand
ministrants distributed throughout the country
under a dozen or more sects.

The name Shinto, literally the Way of the Gods,
or the divine doctrine, is in its derivation Chinese,
and was first applied in Japan, in an historical
compilation of 720 A.D., to the native cult, in
contradistinction to Buddhism and Confucianism;
but the term itself is of a much older date.   In the
broad sense of the ways of heaven or of nature,
or in its more restricted moral significance of the
righteous path, or in the philosophical meaning of a
divine dispensation, it was used by Confucius himself thirteen centuries before its adoption amongst
us.   Prior to the introduction of this appellation,
our simple faith was known as *Kami-Nagara*, a
word which defies exact translation, since the first
of the component terms, *Kami*, commonly rendered god or deity, fails to convey the meaning
originally attached to it; and as to the second
term, *Nagara*, which literally consists of *naku* and
aru, "to be and not to be," and which can be
approximately rendered "being like gods" or
"being in a state of godhood," implies the original

innocence of man. For though human life is generally conceived as a struggle between the dual natures of good and evil, between "the good which I would and which I do not, and the evil which I would not and which I practise," as Saint Paul complained, godlike (*Kami-Nagara*) partakers of the divine nature differ from ordinary mortals in that they cannot forsake the path of wisdom and righteousness as long as they keep true to their own nature. To borrow the ancient Japanese words, men and women are *hiko* and *himé*,—literally, sons and daughters of light. The focus of the Shinto faith lies in the doctrine of *Kami*. This term has no exact equivalent in English. As far as I can translate it, it lies between super-man and superhuman being. Every creature, at the instant of departure from this life, is freed from the trammels which the flesh imposes upon the spirit, and thereupon attains an existence which is superior to that of the ordinary mortal, but which is still not quite divine. If I do not err, *Kami* is the quintessence of all being—animate or inanimate, as I shall have repeated occasion to testify. Shinto is hylozoism or rather panpsychism, *Kami*, being the psyche, which manifests itself in every form and force of nature.

Shinto has no sympathy with the doctrine of original sin and, therefore, with the fall of man. It has implicit faith in the innate purity of the human soul. Like George Fox, it believes in the existence of the inner light, the divine seed, but not going farther or deeper, it stops where Matthew Arnold stops, by teaching that sweetness and light are not only a normal but an ideal condition to strive after.   In fact, Shinto did not teach us to pray for forgiveness of sins, but for the sweet things of this life, for happiness but not for blessedness.   The Hebrew conception of sin hardly exists. Evil is identified with defilement, something foreign to the soul; for as to the soul itself, it cannot partake of evil.   Light cannot lose its native purity, however far it may be deflected in its course by an opaque barrier or refracted by a prism; but its real nature remains unchanged, intact.   So with the children of the gods—reminding us of the words of St. John: "Whoever is begotten of God, doeth no sin, because his seed abideth in him, and he cannot sin, because he is begotten of God."

Emphasise as best he may the diviner element in our nature, the most consistent Shintoist cannot be blind to its weaker side, and the deeper he probes into his own heart, the clearer grows his discovery how far short of godlike purity his thought and practice fall.   Like the old Stoic, he may mentally deny the existence of sin, but from personal experience he is forced to admit its reality.   He may refuse to dub it a sin; he may call it an impurity.   Whatever the nomenclature, he cannot escape the uncomfortable feeling of a child who has told a story.   As there is no third party,—say a wrathful god to propitiate, or a redeemer to atone,

and as the evil in his mind is only an accident, so
to speak,—the problem which lies before him is
easy of solution.   He can of his own accord blow it
off (*harai*) like dust, or wash it off (*misogi*) like a
stain, and regain purity.   A hymn says:

> "Pure be heaven,
>   Pure be earth,
>   Pure be within, without,
>   And the six roots."

By the six roots are meant the five organs of sense
and the heart as the organ of feeling.   A religion
which takes such slight cognisance of the gravity
of evil and sin, and which accepts the facts of
mortal life as divinely ordered, can easily dispense
with any elaborate theology or a stringent moral
code.   A groaning Hebraism is out of the question,
but a smiling Hellenism is in place.   There is self-
contentment in Shinto.   How can it be otherwise
when death itself is conceived of as deification,
and when nature—all its destructive forces not
excluded—is thought to be working for us?

That the dead are alive somehow and somewhere, is the strongest faith of our people, and as
long as science does not prove such a belief to be
contrary to its discoveries and teachings, ancestor-
worship is not to be deemed a superstition.
Illatively of this belief, we revere and venerate
their memory.   We do not carve their images as
idols; we do not carry their remains as charms.
Their words of wisdom we hoard in the secret

chambers of our heart; and their good deeds done in the body we bear in reverent remembrance. Maeterlinck is teaching this skeptical generation that the dead are not gone as long as we think of them, and that as oft as we remember them, they rise from their graves. Our custom of observing the anniversaries of the day upon which our dead left us, instead of their birthdays, should meet with approval from the Belgian idealist.

There are a few phases of our ancestor-worship the significance of which is little regarded by the West. Christian Europe would be scandalised to be told that its religion is ancestor-worship, and yet between Christianity and the cult of forebears, there is a strong link of human interest, which fondly traces one's existence to his parents and thence again to their progenitors, and so leads ever upward, ascending from generation to generation, only to find rest in accepting as its ultimate source the Ancient of Days.

I am far from identifying the Shinto with the Christian or Jewish faith, but the idea of ancestor-worship, if consistently practised, will approach the Christian doctrine of immortality, and the Jewish conception of monotheism. Even if Shinto fails to grasp the belief in a spiritual Father, it can be seen what a force it must have accumulated by constant recurrence to the dead and the past. To quote Schiller,—"Didst thou wish for an immortal life? Live in the Whole! And if thou stay'st long in it, it will stay." With the thought oft intent upon those who preceded us and living with them in long-past years, one attains something of past eternity and of previous existence—and so, dwelling in contemplation or veneration of the "Whole of existence," he comes to a foretaste of future immortality.

When Christ, wishing to lay stress on their duty to the living, enjoined His disciples to "Let the dead bury their dead," He did not intend to discourage a reverence for ancestors, for in His eyes there could be no dead to be buried.

Our veneration of the dead (whatever its origin) is something far removed from the primitive fear of ghosts. Neither is it a peculiar weakness of the East; for the West shares the same feeling, and however feeble an influence at present, you must admit that the ideal of Anglo-Saxon knighthood, Sir Galahad, the purest character in English literature, is represented as having his thought constantly fixed on his ancestor and the spirit of Joseph of Arimathea as ever guarding and guiding him.

There stands on the Kudan Hill in Tokyo a shrine dedicated to the memory of those who have died for the country. The living have consecrated this ground to the dead. Here are inscribed on sacred rolls the names of those who fell on the battle-field,—from the humblest foot-soldier to the greatest commander. Here they are, as it were, canonised, deified. They are immortalised and elevated in the holy of holies of the nation's memory.

Some of you may have seen and heard, as I have seen and heard, a widow leading her child there and reverentially instructing it that its father's spirit surely, though invisibly, dwells in this place. More than this!—I have heard her say, "Look well! He is there. Do you not see him?"

We may characterise Shinto as a religion of suggestion by introspection. Instead of formulating a creed, it leaves to each worshipper the formulation of his own creed and so has this advantage, that no obstacle is placed in the way of individual interpretation. From the field that lies before him, limitless and unlimited, each may cull whatever flower his fancy loves and carry it in his bosom; hence there is no danger of believing by proxy.

Shinto only furnishes a condition for worship, and displays extraordinary simplicity in the furnishings of its shrines. These are the plainest of wooden structures, of an ancient form of architecture, unpainted and undecorated, usually in the shade of cryptomeria groves—groves which as Bryant sings "were God's first temples." The silent trees at once whisper of the crowding millenniums that have flown in mutest throng. The worshipper feels his life but a moment in the endless horologue of the universe, but not the less an integral part of the vast scheme, which without him would be incomplete. A real Shintoist should feel at once his greatness and his littleness, that he is but a fleeting shadow and yet not the less a god.

Nothing is more striking or more disappointing

to the tourist in Japan than to visit the great temple at Yamada in Isé, the temple cf the sun-goddess, who is reputed to be the ancestress of our royal family. As an American tourist once said: "There is nothing to see in Yamada, and what there is to see, is not to be seen." It may be interesting in this connection to cite an English authority on the history of Greek art, who told me that without a visit to the court of a Shinto shrine one cannot clearly understand an ancient Greek temple-ground.

Teaching the worshipper not to rely upon visible objects of worship, but to place himself in surroundings conducive to contemplation, an ancient Shinto oracle says, "When the sky is clear and the wind hums in the fir trees, 't is the heart of a god who thus reveals himself." This sounds like panentheism, yet so far removed is it from panentheism that it can at best be called pantheism. An old Buddhist poet put into verse the sentiment aroused by a visit to Isé:

" I know not who dwelleth in these precincts,
But my eyes overflow with tears of gratitude."

As you enter a shrine, you see scarcely any instrument of worship, a mirror being the chief object to attract notice. "Behold thy image," the oracle seems to whisper as you stand before the shrine, "Behold thy own image as reflected in the mirror, and know for thyself how it fares with thee!"

9

Thus left to contemplate nature and to reflect upon self, one comes to a monistic conception of the universe and of life. "There are moments in life," says Schiller, "when we feel like pressing to our bosom every stone, every far-off distant star, every worm, and every conceivable higher spirit,—to embrace the entire universe like our loved one. . . . Then does the whole creation melt into a personality."

In this exalted, spiritual mood, Schiller is a Shintoist at his best; or, with a fifteenth century countryman of his, Nicholas of Cusa, he would find in all forms of existence "a divine grain of seed which carries within it the original patterns of all things." Shintoists believe with Nicholas that in all that is, God (*Kami*) is omnipresent; but I doubt whether they could follow him in the next assertion, "All that is, is in God." I doubt, indeed, whether they could even say, "All that is, is God." In the cosmogonic myth of Shinto, which I casually mentioned when speaking of the early times of our history, you must have noticed that it owns no creator—no *creatio ex nihilo;* for whatever was produced, be it an island or a plant, a worm or a star, it was generated. All things are begotten of gods, not made. The world and all therein is, partakes, therefore, of the same nature as the procreator. Not only the flower but the crannied wall, not only the sea but its denizens, and the pebbles on its beach, are our brothers and sisters, and therefore equally *Kami*. In this hylopathic plan, little distinction is recognised between *natura naturata* and *natura naturens*.

Shinto is a religion without a founder, without theology, and without scriptures. The absence of the first deprives it of that ardent, personal affection and fidelity found in the great religions, though the deficiency is made up in a measure, as in Greek and Roman mythologies, by distributing reverence among a host of deities and by including our own ancestors among them. We speak of the eighty myriad deities of the Shinto pantheon, and they range from the most insignificant gods whom pious spinsters respect as the spirits of sewing-needles or those to whom kitchen maids do homage as residing in the furnace, up to those that roar in thunder or shine in lightning or ride upon the whirlwind; from those who make love in the budding flower or in the tender evening star, up to those who illumine the world in the moon and the sun. Thus Shinto is the most polytheistic of polytheisms and its popular pantheon is filled with gods that dwell in or preside over every object and phenomenon of which you can think, and is farther replenished by additions of apotheosised men. The Shinto heaven is peopled with all the personified forces of nature; the Shinto shrine is a repository of every sacred memory. A remarkable feature of these *Kami* is that only a few of them have any definite shape ascribed to them. I have spoken above of the god of the hearth; but it (the sex being uncertain, I use the neuter pro-

noun) is possessed of no form, animate or inanimate, animal or anthropomorphic. The hearth
itself is not for one moment considered divine. It
is not a fetich. O-Kamado-san, like Vesta, repre-
sents the power and action of the fireplace. The
god's existence is made manifest only through what
the hearth does. It is a power but not a thing, any
more than is the thing "hearth" the power "god."

The absence of theology deprives Shinto of any
discussion concerning the hypostasis of belief. It
gives no clue to a rational interpretation of the
universe.

The absence of scriptures deprives Shinto of
final authority regarding ethical mandates. In a
meagre way compensation is made for this by
myths, legends, and tales, not always instinct
with a moral—very often gross and sometimes
more obscene than the baldest stories of the
Old Testament.

For want of a creed its votaries have no moral
code to follow. Yet, as I said at the beginning of
the present lecture, in the definition of religion, a
faith does not deserve the name of religion unless
it manifests itself in conduct conformable to that
faith, and particularly in the act of worship. In
the case of Shinto, minute rites and ritual are
dictated, the chief burden of which is purification
by one means or another.

Concerning the daily conduct of private individuals little is taught. Scarcely any form of
prayer is prescribed. In fact, even upon the

occasion of festivals, so-called prayers (*norito*) contain little supplication, consisting largely of adoration and thanksgiving. Very rightly has Mr. Aston called Shinto a religion of gratitude and love. If supplication is made, it is not for our own daily bread, but for an abundant harvest for the nation, or, if it is for forgiveness of trespasses, it is not for our individual wrong-doing, but for the sins of the people. Thus without a visible communion of saints, the consciousness of national coherence is ever kept prominent. As to the individual, the sum and substance of moral injunction amount to this: "Be pure in heart and body!" In other words, be true and genuine in heart, and clean in body. Harbour no thought of evil and thou art a god, and keep thy body as a temple meet for him to dwell in. Says a famous poem of the saintly Michizane:

> " The god blesseth
> Not him who prayeth,
> But him whose heart strayeth
> Not from the way of *Makoto*."

The peculiarly Japanese term *Makoto*, usually translated "truth" or "faithfulness," covers the whole ground or the very essence of morals, literally meaning the thing itself, reminding one of the Kantian *das Ding an sich*. *Makoto* signifies reality or truth, which implies that the real is the true and the true is the real, a proposition almost Hegelian.

The subjectivity of Shinto morality finds frequent expression in the oracles of many gods, for instance, the god of Fujiyama enjoins upon his worshippers the following:

"Ye men of mine shun desire. If you shun desire you will ascend to a level with the gods. Every little yielding to anxiety is a step away from the natural heart of man. If one leaves the natural heart of man he becomes a beast. That men should be made so, is to me intolerable pain and unending sorrow."[1]

Here is another oracle, given in a dream to an emperor:—"It is the upright heart of all men which is identical with the highest of the high and therefore the god of gods. There is no room in heaven and earth for the false and crooked person."[1]

Still another:—"If we keep unperverted the human heart, which is like unto heaven and received from earth, that is God. The gods have their abode in the heart."[1]

As long as we shut our eyes by deliberate exercise of will or by self-deception to that persistent fact of evil so stubbornly present with us, the complete identification of human nature with divine may be accepted as indisputable, and pregnant with highest moral consequences. With Goethe, a Shintoist could say, "The more thou feelest to be a man, the nearer thou art to the gods."

[1] These translations are from Mr. Aston's *Shinto*.

But herein lies the weakness inherent in Shinto. If the real and the true are identified or, at least, convertible terms, there is no room left for ideals. Whatever is, is true, and therefore right. A life, however gross, if only real, is a true life, and there is in it no condemnation. So Shinto could not escape the weakness common to all forms of naturalism, and nowhere is this more manifest, to my mind, than in its alliance with principalities and powers that be. Because it glorifies the real, it deifies mortals, and by so doing, helps to excuse and even to exalt their frailties.

Moses, lifted high above his people and invested with authority almost divine, still points above and warns them to refrain from idolatry. If we turn from the grim height of Sinai and the desert of Arabia, to the City of the Seven Hills on the smiling banks of the Tiber, we see Augustus, the sole lord of the world, making himself a divine object for supreme reverence. Then, later on in history, we come across another similar contrast. Cromwell, seated upon the throne previously occupied by the Stuarts, the absolute ruler of the British realm, still points upward and tells his countrymen to worship not him, the Huntington squire, but Him before whom he himself is but a worm of the dust. Iyeyasu, a contemporary of Cromwell, with powers unbounded, has divine homage paid to his person and his corpse. Neither Moses nor Cromwell dared usurp the divine throne. Augustus and Iyeyasu robbed their god of his thunder.

The people whose gods are inferior to mortal sovereigns can never aspire high. To the last they are of the earth earthy. As long as they cling to earth, however high they may lift their head for a time in the struggle for life or for space, they cannot win in the higher spiritual race, which after all decides the fate of nations.

Naturalism teaches us to be true to nature. No endeavour is exacted to conquer natural impulses unless they are followed to an extent subversive of their purpose. Whatever restraint we have put upon vices, or whatever encouragement we have given to virtues, has largely come from sources other than Shinto.

Whether or not you adopt the epi-phenomenon theory of consciousness, you cannot deny the fact of Belial in our nature, so intertwined with the very fibre of our being as to set at defiance any effort to separate it as mere dust or stain. It seems to me that the weakness of Shinto as a religion lies in the non-recognition of human frailty, of sin. The awful sense of condemnation which torment Bunyan's Christian and all other seekers with the soul-rending cry, "How can I flee from the wrath to come?" assumes with the Shintoist a far lighter strain, "Is this good to be preferred to that good?" The dilemma in the one case lies between eternal salvation and eternal damnation, between heaven and hell; whereas in the other it is a choice between two benefactions of different degrees, between this and that sunny spot in the groves of paradise.

The mental and spiritual pendulum of Shinto does not swing wide. The fact that Shinto fails to take lofty spiritual flight has resulted in its forming close relations with temporal concerns, and its teachings are almost altogether practical, all of the sects enforcing personal cleanliness and diligence in daily occupation, and some of them requiring as religious duties mountain-climbing and abdominal respiration.

As to the reverence it inculcates for whatever is above ourselves,—the love of the land where our gods abide and forefathers repose, the veneration of whatever is old, and respect and affection for nature and all its single objects,—no religion surpasses ours. Its animism has endowed the very stones with sentient life, drawing from us a feeling of affection. Its pantheism and polytheism have peopled the air, land, and water, with beings that call forth our respect. This attitude toward nature instils into our mind the love of the land, the instinct of patriotism. Thus from being a worship of nature, Shinto becomes an ethnic religion. It is national in its concepts and precepts. Its patriotism, therefore, may easily fall into Chauvinism. Its loyalty can degenerate into servile obedience. It can readily be made a political engine in the hands of the unscrupulous;—as such it can indeed be made a powerful one; but, as I have intimated, as a moral or a religious factor, it is and has been but a feeble motive force.

Its child-like naïveté, its very jejuneness, its easy-going ethics, verging on moral indifference, handicapped Shinto in coping with Buddhism and Confucianism, when they entered our country in the early centuries of our history. The backing of the Court and its claim to nativity could not brook the overwhelming tide of these alien teachings. "After terrible struggles," says Professor Kumé, one of our foremost historical critics, "between the three systems of teaching, especially between Shinto and Buddhism, peace was finally established, whereby the sphere was virtually divided among the three. Shinto received the dominion of public ceremonies, Buddhism of religion, and Confucianism of ethics."

The yearnings, intellectual and spiritual, which Shinto could not meet, were more fully satisfied by Confucianism and Buddhism. You may remember that Chinese studies were introduced into Japan in the middle of the third century A.D., and that the seed, falling upon fertile ground, was sprouting and growing with unusual rapidity and vitality when Buddhism reached the land.

The introduction of Buddhism into Japan dates back to the middle of the sixth century. Its missionary operations ever since the time of King Asoka (250 B.C.) had been reaping considerable fruit in the southern part of Asia, and extended by way of Bactria as far as Syria and Egypt, and even into Greece and Macedonia. By 67 A.D. it found its way to China, being brought thither by Chinese emissaries, who had been despatched westward in search of a new religion which, prophecy had declared, would be started about that time,—a prophecy which might have referred to Christianity, as far as time was concerned.

It is well to bear in mind that Buddhism is divided into two great branches, the Northern and the Southern, more divergent than the Protestant and the Roman Catholic faiths. The Southern branch, called also the "Lesser Vehicle," accepted in Ceylon and Siam, is a purer form and simpler in doctrine. The Northern, called the "Greater Vehicle" (*Mahā Yāna* in Sanskrit or *Daijo* in Japanese), has deviated widely from the original teachings of Sakya Muni, the founder. It has gained not only in intellectual volume, in theology and philosophy, but also in accretions of foreign matter, absorbing the teachings and legends and gods of alien and hostile religions. It was this Northern form of Buddhism that passed from China to Japan via Korea. It came just at the time when the country was eager to learn from abroad. On its arrival, it found the ground already occupied by Confucianism, which counted among its adherents the members of the Court and the learned of the land. Naturally it was met by opposition from them; but, at the same time, it was among them that the new tenets won their first votaries.

The Chinese ideograms, which were made familiar through Confucianism, were a ready instrument in the hands of Buddhists for the extension of their doctrines, and, endowed with erudition and deep insight and large experience in propagandism, they may well be said to have created a new era in the history of the Sunrise Kingdom. The metaphysical queries with which Shinto could ill cope and which were stimulated by Confucianism could now be answered. The educational value of Buddhism in Japan cannot be overestimated. It did not stop in its activities with things spiritual. Its influence penetrated and permeated all the ramifications of our national life. It touched the very fountains of thought and set a-flowing new currents of ideas. It sobered the light-hearted nature-worshippers. It furnished a deeper interpretation of ancestor-worship. It created new notions of nature and life. It invented a new vocabulary. It gave rise to new arts, trades, and crafts. It initiated a new polity of government. It changed the whole social structure. Indeed, there was nothing that was not impregnated with the doctrines of Gautama.

All this astonishing work was primarily due to the conquest made by Buddhism in the conversion, during the latter part of the sixth century, of the Prince Imperial and Regent of the Crown. A man of the highest character and of unlimited ability, who combined in his person all the sagacity of a statesman and all the virtues of a saint—a savant and an artist—Shotoku Daishi took under his patronage the native followers and foreign teachers of the new faith. A unique figure in the annals of our country, his contributions to our civilisation were incalculable. Upon the principles of Gautama's teaching, yet without infraction to the traditions of his race, he framed a constitution —the so-called Constitution of Seventeen Articles —for the governance of the nation. He established different institutions of charity, such as monasteries, orphanages, dispensaries, hospitals; he built many temples, some of which are still standing as marvellous monuments of architecture, having weathered the storms of time for well-nigh fifteen centuries.

Under his Imperial patronage the new religion steadily gained in numbers and influence, contributing, as it made its own progress, to that of culture in general. But, very soon after the death of this Prince, it began to be disturbed by sectarian differences of opinion.

Among the founders of sects, two names are worthy of special mention, Saicho (otherwise Dengyo) and Kukai (canonised as Kobo Daishi), founders respectively of the two strong sects of Tendai (Heavenly Command), and Shingon (True Word). Both belonged to the early part of the ninth century.

Though both of these saints studied in China and the fundamentals of their sects were brought thence, they not only admitted the incult into their faith but absorbed Shinto gods into their pantheon. That is to say, they "Buddhified" the old *Kami*.

The goddess of the sun, for instance, who occupied the highest position in the Shinto pantheon, was interpreted as an avatar of Buddhist existence, and the lesser gods shared the same fate of adoption.   There was not a legend, not a rite of Shinto origin, which could not find its counterpart or parallel in the all-embracing system of Buddhism.

In short, Shinto was swallowed up in the new faith, though it has never admitted that it lost its own identity, but has always claimed a nominal independence side by side with Buddhism.   It has kept, as it were, the names of its gods and the framework of its ritual, yet without power or life. It has barely continued its hold upon the people by its traditions and prestige.   Like the condominium of England and Egypt in the Sudan, the two faiths were allied in the spiritual domination of Japan; allied—but how unequally! The alliance lasted throughout centuries with a separate field allotted to each, as I have said before.   Adjustment was made between them, so as to leave little cause for quarrel.   Each had its own temples—the Buddhists delighting in grand and ornate architecture of Hindu origin, gaudy in colour and filled with mystic symbols of worship.

Very few Shinto shrines retained their original integrity; for the greater part the two religions mixed and mingled.   Buddhist deities found lodgment side by side with Shinto gods under the same shelter.   In private households you still see a miniature Buddhist shrine, and close by it a shelf provided with a few instruments of Shinto cult. When a birth occurs in the family, the babe is taken to a Shinto shrine for consecration and blessing; but when there is a death, the funeral is often conducted by a Buddhist priest. Shinto festivals are occasions of joy and rejoicing, of thanksgiving and merry-making. Buddhist festivals are usually suggestive of sin and of sorrow, of sober thoughts and sombre musings.

The final and practical identity of all religions has been expressed in a well-known verse:—

> "Be it crystal of snow-flake frail,
> Be it globule of hoary hail,
>   Be it the form of thick-ribbed ice,—
> If but the sun's warm rays upon them fall,
> They melt and merge in one element all."

Thus in closest ties united, the two faiths had spent centuries together, when, with the Restoration of the Imperial power in 1868, Shinto resumed its ancient dignity, and, like a prodigal suddenly awakened to the consciousness that he had been joined to an unworthy mate, the native faith left the spouse of alien origin; but the separation is still largely on legal paper only. The offspring of a long union is not easily to be disowned and the populace continue to worship the *Kami* and the Buddha with equal reverence and fervour. As ecclesiastical institutions they are both equally recognised by the Government.

The fact that there are only about 72,000

Buddhist temples, as against some 162,000 Shinto shrines, might seem to place Buddhism in a subordinate position; but the former are, on the average, much larger and more costly, and they accommodate a far larger priesthood, the Buddhist clergy numbering over fifty thousand and the Shinto priests only fifteen thousand. In erudition and in character, the Buddhist priests are decidedly superior to their Shinto compeers. Concerning the number of their respective followers, in neither case can any statistics be given. Both may reckon the whole Japanese population as their constituency; but as far as open confession and earnest attendance to religious duties are concerned, the Buddhists excel the Shintoists. For instance, no Shinto sect can vie with the Hokkei, or the followers of that commanding figure of religious history, Nichiren, in keeping alive the fire of enthusiasm; or with the Shin sect, which, of the twelve main sects of Japan, is numerically the strongest. The popularity of the Shin and some other sects is due chiefly to their tact and talent in adapting their teachings to the mental capacity of the populace. "Look at the people and preach accordingly," is a guiding principle of their homiletics. Not only the sermons but the doctrines, and, I dare say, the preachers themselves, have come to stoop down to the level of the masses. Hence, modern Buddhism, at least in Japan, has two aspects. In one it caters to the men of the street; in the other, it illuminates a saint and a

scholar. While it demonstrates to the instructed
the vanity of belief in personal immortality, it
depicts in glaring colours for the ignorant a gory
hell. While it expounds to the learned that there
is no supernatural being, it paints for the canaille
a land peopled with every conceivable form of
existence. While for the vulgar it indulges in
"pious frauds and holy shifts," it opens to the
enlightened all the resources of intellect. Buddhism for the populace has in too many instances
deteriorated into nonsense, barely kept up by
cheap incense. But Buddhism for the initiated,
Higher Buddhism, is something vastly different.
To convey its main beliefs in terms of Occidental
philosophy or theology, is a task of surpassing
difficulty, as a great many of its concepts hardly
fit into Western categories.

The most original and authentic exposition of
the teaching of Sakya Muni is embodied in the
following sentences, which he uttered as he came
down from a mount of meditation:

"There are two extremes which he who has renounced
the world ought not to follow,—habitual devotion,
on the one hand, to sensual pleasures, which is degrad-
ing, vulgar, ignoble, unprofitable, fit only for the
worldly-minded; and habitual devotion, on the other
hand, to self-mortification, which is painful, ignoble,
unprofitable. There is a middle path discovered by
the Tathagata (Buddha), a path which opens the
eyes and bestows understanding, which leads to peace,
to insight, to the higher wisdom, to Nirvana. Verily!

it is this noble (Aryan) Eight-fold Path (*ariyo attangiko maggo*); that is to say, Right Views, Right Aspirations (or Resolves), Right Speech, Right Conduct (or Work), Right Livelihood, Right Effort (or Training), Right Mindfulness, and Right Rapture."

This first public utterance of Gautama, delivered in Pali to his five former associates in Benares, is known as the *Bana*, and sounds simple enough at first hearing. The instant we inquire what is meant by the noble Eight-fold Path, we are struck at once by the recondite meanings attached to each of these categories. Indeed, the use of the mere adjective "Aryan," or "noble," as applied to wisdom, calls forth our admiration for the grandeur of his thought. It is not an ethnic distinction but indicates a grade of wisdom—not man's wisdom, not his intellect, but a wisdom prolific of more wisdom. The term "right" (*samma*), which modifies all the Eight-fold Path, may be interpreted in a narrow, bigoted sense or in a broad, loving sense. For instance, Right Views may be interpreted, as Sir Monier Williams seems inclined to do, as belief in Buddha and his doctrine; Right Resolve, according to him, means abandoning one's wife and family, and Right Speech, mere recitation of Buddha's doctrine; Right Livelihood, living by alms; Right Work, the exercise of a monk. Sir Monier's book is often misleading, always bent upon depreciation of Buddhism, and cannot be trusted as a fair presenta-

tion. The Right Views (*samma ditthi*) include
Right Views regarding existence, whether it is
permanent or transient, whether it is a being or
a becoming, and other like searching questions. Of
Right Mindedness (*sati*), four sublime states are
recounted; namely, those of Love, of Sorrow at the
sorrow of others, of Joy with those who rejoice,
and of calm Equanimity in one's own joys and
sorrows.

Under Right Conduct (*kammanto*) the power of
love is portrayed and its exercise enjoined, forming
a fit parallel to the thirteenth chapter of the first
Epistle to the Corinthians.   It says[1]:

" All the means that can be used as bases for doing
right are not worth the sixteenth part of the emancipa-
tion of heart through love. Love takes them all up
into itself, outshining them in radiance and glory.

Just as whatsoever stars there be, their radiance
avails not the sixteenth part of the radiance of the
moon, Love takes them all up into itself, outshining
them in radiance and glory.

Just as in the last month of the rains, at harvest
time, the sun, mounting up on high into the clear and
cloudless sky, overwhelms all darkness in the realms
of space, and shines forth in radiance and glory;—
just as in the night, when the dawn is breaking, the
Morning Star shines out in radiance and glory;—
just so all the means that can be used as helps towards
doing right avail not the sixteenth part of the emanci-
pation of heart through love! "

[1] I follow the translation of Rhys-Davids.

Or, under the head of Right Rapture (*samahdi*), is described the beatitude of one who has attained to Nirvana—that state of spiritual exaltation where no evil can touch or harm him. It is a state of rapture and joy, and not of unfeeling indifference, as it is sometimes supposed to be.

"Blessed are we who hate not those who hate us;
Who among men full of hate, continue void of hate.
Blessed are we who dwell in health among the ailing;
Who among men weary and sick, continue well.
Blessed are we who dwell free from care among the
    care-worn;
Who among men full of worries, continue calm.
Blessed indeed are we who have no hindrances;
Who shall become feeders on joy, like the gods in
    their shining splendour."

Were we to search among the voluminous literature of Buddhism, we should often come across words and thoughts, parables and incidents, with which the Gospels have made us familiar,—so much so, that not a few suspect a strong influence of Buddhism upon early Christianity.

But this is too large a theme for me to take up now. Whether the origins of the two religions— now called the religion of the East and the religion of the West—be one or two, if we divest both of their wrappage, we shall come to know how nearly allied in many particulars they are. Though at the foot of the hill the ways are far apart, as we ascend higher and higher, the nearer approach our paths, until they meet at the summit, to share the view of the plains below from the height of the same divine wisdom. On this height in the fulness of time may be brought into common brotherhood, the philosophers of the North and the seers of the South, the thinkers of the West, and the wise men of the East,—and God shall be glorified by all His children. The hour is coming when neither on the mountains of Samaria nor in the city of Jerusalem,—not alone in the Orient, neither in the Occident,—but in spirit and in truth, wherever men come together in brotherly love, shall they worship the same Father.

CHAPTER VI

MORALS AND MORAL IDEALS

UNDER various names—characterology, sophiology, ethology, race psychology—the study of alien character has been cultivated to discover some traits peculiar to different races, and this has given rise to the so-called *Völkergedanken* theory, which takes for granted without demonstration that every race must be possessed of some mental and moral features not shared by others. He will indeed be a great discoverer who can find in any ethnic group a new capacity of the mind unknown to other groups!

No phase of national life is more difficult to grasp than the moral. To interpret it intelligently one must often change one's viewpoint in looking at the apparent singularities of a people's manners and customs. Above all, not to draw conclusions without first inquiring into the proper bounds and the underlying motive of unfamiliar usages and the moral habits of a race, is indispensable to right judgment; for these are usually the product of national history and geography. A thoughtful observer can soon reduce them to a common denominator or what Bastian calls the *Elementargedanken* of the human race.

It may seem a startling theme; but nothing will illustrate my meaning better than the kiss. In the West—well, you know how it is regarded; in the East, in Japan in particular, the word is not so much as mentioned without a blush. The West may say: "No kiss? How cold the Oriental heart must be!" The East will say: "Kissing in public! What bad taste!" The West may say: "How strange! Because it is something so natural." The East says: "How strange! It is too natural." In the West, it is elevated to a proper moral act; in the East it is degraded to the sphere of the improper.

We read in ecclesiastical history that in early times Christian worshippers adopted the practice of promiscuous kissing, under the name of the "kiss of peace." The practice had not continued very long before the graver Fathers found that this pious act was too zealously followed by the younger brethren and sisters to be spiritually edifying. It was soon restricted to the kissing of man by man, and woman by woman.

I have often wondered about the kissing-margin of the West, and I understand that it does not go beyond first cousins, and that, if carried farther, it is fraught with some danger—from which I infer, some kind of infection is feared! I have also wondered about the marginal kiss—that is to say, the different gradations of kissing. A kiss on the cheek is certainly of a grade different from that on the forehead or on the lips, and very different from that on the hand or on the toe. I might go on asking a thousand questions about this extraordinary Western custom, which I confess I have never ceased to regard with some amazement; but I have said enough to hint a doubt as to the appropriate limit of the practice. Even the Japanese do not hesitate to kiss children on the cheek.

Now it is just the proper bounds—fitly named the Golden Mean—that determine the approval or the condemnation of a social usage, and these proper bounds are usually so delicate as to elude any definition. In other words, an Oriental who may adopt a custom he does not understand, is not likely to know how far to go. Just the same thing happens in Japan. I have more than once seen American men at Japanese banquets or in Japanese inns taking far greater liberty with the girls who wait upon them than our national customs consider allowable, and yet it is just these men who throw a shade upon the morals of our women and whose false interpretations have had such wide hearing; therefore I make bold to mention this subject here.

Again, a Japanese in an American ball-room sees ladies exposing their shoulders. An American notices that the dress of Japanese women flaps in the wind, and forthwith a Puritanic frown appears on his forehead and he calls the dress and the wearer immoral. Or he sometimes sees in the country a peasant woman bathing by the roadside. He infers that these women must be utterly depraved—a conclusion as hasty and as irrational as would be a suspicion on the part of the Japanese that the ladies at the ball are not modest, or that the occupants of a house adorned with nude pictures and statues can have no sense of decorum. *Non sequitur*, as the logicians say. It is true that our people do not hesitate to lay bare the body to the extent of what may be termed a utilitarian marginal nudity, when convenience requires this, whereas the European custom is for women to exhibit charm of person when there is least reason for it. With us it is no shame to tuck one's *kimono* high on a rainy day, whereas it is a breach of etiquette to let the foot, even though clad in spotless *tabi*, protrude unnecessarily in the parlour.

No two parties can ever come to a mutual understanding as long as either of them arrogates the attitude of superiority, and refuses to divest itself of what von der Steinen calls *Culturbrille*— the coloured spectacles of one's own civilisation. Satisfied with his own righteousness, a Pharisee can never comprehend the beauty—not to say the superiority—in the teachings of other sects.

> "That way
> Over the mountain which who stands upon,
> Is apt to doubt if it be indeed a road;

While if he views it from the waste itself,
Up goes the line there, plain from base to brow,
Not vague, mistakable!   What 's a break or two
Seen from the unbroken desert either side?
And then (to bring in fresh philosophy),
What if the breaks themselves should prove at last
The most consummate of contrivances
To train a man's eyes, teach him what is faith?"

Many others than Browning have felt the same,
and only the most thoughtless are denied the sight
of a road threading the apparent waste.

It is a remark too often made by foreign tourists
that Japanese life is as singularly devoid of morals
as Japanese flowers are of scent—a sad confession
of the moral and intellectual limitations of the
accusers themselves!   When Pierre Loti gives an
account of Madame Chrysanthème, he does not
portray a typical Japanese woman, but only furnishes a clue as to the kind of company he keeps.

Those who associate fragrance with roses only,
or morality with conventional Christianity, are
sure to be disappointed in finding but little of
either in Japan; but that is no proof that the
umé blossoms are not fragrant, or that chivalry
does not teach pragmatism.   There is, however,
good reason why the busy West knows so little of
the Far East, especially regarding things which
cannot be bought or sold with cash, for we have
neither bottled the essence of the *umé* in flasks,
like attar of roses, nor bound the precepts of
knighthood in a gilt-edged pocket edition.

The age of chivalry is said to have passed away. As an institution it has disappeared, but sad will be the day when the virtues it has taught shall likewise have disappeared! Fortunately for us, like a disembodied spirit, they still live on, somewhat modified, but retaining their essential qualities.

This ethical and spiritual legacy we call *Bushido*, which literally signifies Fighting-Knight-Ways, or better translated, Teachings of Knightly Behaviour. It was the moral code of the samurai—the class of knights whose badge and privilege it was to wear two swords.   Do not imagine that they were only swaggering, blood-thirsty youths.   The sword was called the soul of the samurai.   Like "The Sword of Robert Lee," it flashed from its scabbard for the purpose of

"Shielding the feeble, smiting the strong,
    Guarding the right, avenging the wrong."

As a separate class, the samurai no longer exists except in name; but the *noblesse oblige* which distinguished it still remains.   In his palmiest days —that is during the feudal ages—the samurai was the man.   In popular ballad it was sung, "As among flowers the cherry is queen, so among men the samurai is lord."   His ideals filtered down to the lower classes and his moral code became the standard for the nation.

The strength and perhaps also the weakness of *Bushido* lay in this, that it possessed no written creed. It was sufficient for its followers only to feel that there was something in their mind—the mysteries of which they little cared to analyse—always active with admonitions, which, when disobeyed, heaped upon the transgressors fiery coals of shame, and which could be appeased only by implicit obedience.   In the absence of any written commandments, the *Ren-chi-shin* (consciousness of shame) was the last and highest court of appeal. A man who had lost his sense of shame forfeited his human claims.

He is the best man who has no cause to be ashamed, who so masters himself that his thoughts and his person are his willing servants. A great warrior of the eleventh century left a verse behind him, which, roughly translated, runs:

> " Subdue first of all thy own self,
>   Next thy friends, and last thy foes;
>   Three victories are these of him
>   That would a conqueror's name attain."

Self-mastery—the maintenance of equanimity of temper under conditions the most trying, whether in war or in peace, of composure and presence of mind in sudden danger, self-possession under calamity and reverses—was inculcated as one of the primary virtues of man; it was even drilled into youths by genuine Spartan methods.

Strange as it may seem at first appearance, this strong fortification of self against external causes of surprise was but one side of self-abnegation.

One of the terms of highest praise was "a man without a me." The complete effacement of self meant one's identification with some higher cause. The very duties which man performs are, according to our idea, not to buy salvation for himself; he has no prospect of a "reward in heaven" offered him, if he does this or does not abstain from that. The voice of conscience, "Thou good and faithful servant," is the only and sufficient reward.

Conscience, called among us by the comprehensive term *Kokoro* (which may mean mind, spirit, or heart), was the only criterion of right and wrong. But conscience, being a power of perception, and the whole tenor of *Bushido* being action, the harmonious working of the two was taught in the Socratic doctrine—though Socrates was as unknown to us as X-rays—that thought and action are one and the same.

He who pursues virtuous conduct for the sake of virtue is, in our estimation, the noblest of men. He asks not for worldly reward. He who knows, and lives up to the knowledge, that honour and shame rise from no condition of life, but solely from acting or not acting one's own part—such a conscientious man is rare anywhere. Mediocrity must be fed on a more diluted diet, and with us this is found in an inferior grade of the honour-sense—namely, in the fear of personal disgrace or in the maintenance of family pride. "You will be laughed at," is the usual dose of sedative advice administered to an unruly child. Brought up in constant fear of disgracing oneself if one but strays from the path trodden by others, a child grows into a law-abiding or rather custom-abiding citizen, though he becomes so at the expense of freedom of thought and initiative of action. When, in spite of social control, he is inclined to be too independent, all the weight of a long line of ancestry is brought to bear on his proper behaviour. With a large majority of our people there is no higher appeal to morality than family pride—a kind of pride which, instead of going before destruction, avoids it. You will understand its significance better when I speak of filial love. To elevate the name of one's family becomes a spur to virtue and a curb to vice, and attains the dignity of a religious duty. We owe our being to our parents, and through them to our ancestors, and we can repay them only by gratitude and by showing forth their glory; hence nothing is more humiliating to one's self-respect than to bring into disrepute one's cognomen.

Confucius teaches that the highest act of filial affection is to make manifest the name of one's parent. Nothing so honours parents as that their son should add lustre to their memory; *Decori decus addit avito.* In this connection I may be allowed to make a moment's digression regarding the charge, so often made in Japan, that Christianity does not sufficiently emphasise filial affection. It is only fair to state that Jesus fulfilled the highest ideal of Confucian ethics; for did he not make illustrious his family, when, astonished at his mighty works, the multitude began to ask: "Is this the carpenter's son? Is not his mother called Mary?"

The sense of family solidarity not only delivers individual members from destruction but contributes toward their legal and moral cohesion. How many youths check their ardent desire for self-aggrandisement and hopes for larger life or higher calling, in order that they may attend to small matters of family interest! How many maidens sacrifice their aspirations for the welfare of their home! How many mothers slave and drudge to keep up ancestral reputation! Individuals are, figuratively speaking, made victims at the shrine of family-worship; their very personality is nipped in the bud at the same altar. I am sure family-honour obtains in America, too; but the conception of the family is somewhat different.

Our family is based on vertical relations, on successive, superimposed generations, from parents to children. Your system is, I think, based on a lateral or contemporary alliance, on the relations between persons of the same generation—namely, on husband and wife. The conjugal system is claimed to be Christian and ordained from on high—that is, as long as the parties are in favour of it. If conjugality is divinely ordered, what sanction has divorce? Or is the latter, in contrast to the former, the work of the evil one? Or does God change His mind now and then according as the two persons interested desire union or separation? To a Christian novice like myself it sounds like taking the name of the Lord in vain, when it is dragged into transactions where man's free will should be held responsible. I have no objection to thanking God for union in marriage; but if one is disappointed in wedlock, God should not be blamed for it. Marriage is a human institution, and in a sense less divinely ordered than parentage. Our heathen conception is that the relation between parent and child is more divinely ordered and ordained. These cannot be divorced by a minister or by law. Christians claim that Adam and Eve were the first human beings, and therefore conjugal relations take precedence of all other moral obligations. The heathen, at least the Japanese, contend that filial duty was the first moral conception, even antedating the parental.

There was a time in Eden when Eve was an utter stranger. Before this long-haired creature appeared, Adam had already often communed with his Maker, Creator, Father. So, even according to the Biblical narrative, a moral relation had existed between Father and son before that between husband and wife; in other words, filiality anteceded conjugality in the evolution of ethics. Well-nigh unknown among the lower animals, it was the first to be felt by man.

In all conservative countries, reverence towards parents is scrupulously taught and observed. "Honour thy father and thy mother, that thy days may be long upon the land which the Lord thy God giveth thee." Long-lived nations have been those obedient to this commandment.

Honouring parents is, of course, by no means confined solely to mere obedience, or to looking after their physical wants. These are trivialities in honouring. To distinguish oneself in good works, as Confucius has taught, redounds to the glory of one's family and is the great filial duty. Science will, I presume, explain more and more the mysterious laws of heredity, and the practical application of eugenics and breeding will reveal the underlying principles of ancestor-worship and family integrity. I am far from deprecating the place of personality in the scheme of moral economy; but Western individualism will, I am afraid, prove itself inadequate to cope with all the pending problems of life. As among plants and animals none can live alone, and each can live only by being associated in close relations to other animals and plants in its proximity, so the study of human ecology—of immediate milieu, of family environment—will demonstrate in a fresh light the wisdom of the older civilisations of the East. Balzac once bewailed the disintegration of the family in Europe on the ground that it was at the root of modern social diseases. But I am not here to preach. If I were to preach, I would rather do so to my own countrymen from the text, "Say not among yourselves, We have Abraham for our father!" . . .

In discussing the institution of the family, the status of woman must needs occupy a considerable part. Nowhere is this more true than in the case of the Japanese woman. She exists primarily for and in the family. We still adhere to the old way of thinking that her natural habitat is the home, and that her appearance at the polls is as unnatural as on the battle-field. Somehow an idea—perhaps obsolete in America—prevails among us,—an idea once voiced by Euripides—namely, that "a woman should be good for everything at home, but abroad good for nothing." Let it be far from me to give an impression already too prevalent abroad and at home, that we look upon women only as cogs in the machinery of the kitchen or as mere puppets and ornaments in the parlour. The personality of the fair sex is not as clearly recognised among us as it ought to be; but I am confident that it will come with more general enlightenment of public conscience. As it is at present, the aim of female education is to make "a good wife and a wise mother,"—a stereotyped shibboleth on the lips of all educators and of the nation, circumscribing the end and aim of woman's life. According to this doctrine it is not as person, but as wife and as mother, that woman is to be educated.

I doubt if this dogmatic allegation concerning the vocation of woman, without spiritual significance attached to it, can really be the last word to be said concerning her sex." A Nora Helmer is not native to Norway only: she is born everywhere, wherever similar conditions exist. Her words—"I believe that before all else I am a human being, just as much as you are"—can and will be uttered in other languages than Scandinavian. Consistently with our apotheosis of mothercraft, there are few unmarried women among us. Generally girls marry between the ages of eighteen and twenty-two. They seldom choose their own partners, but still more seldom are they forced to marry those to whom they object. Most entertaining things are written by foreigners about marriages forced upon unwilling brides, and even of marriages by purchase. I may just as truly amuse and instruct my own people with stories about ambitious American parents practically selling their daughters to European nobles, or of the sorrows of *mariage de convénance* in Europe. But the comparative study of each other's shortcomings is not edifying—muck-raking never is. There are certainly more opportunities for American girls to marry the men whom they most love, and, *vice versa*, for men to take to wife girls whom they like best; but I doubt whether the proportion of happy unions is very different in the two countries.

Should the choice lie wholly with the parties immediately concerned, would they not in most cases profit by the mature judgment of their parents, instead of rushing uncounselled into relations which may prove a life-long bondage, on the slender experience and in the blindness of youthful love? I am not at all surprised at the number of

divorces in this country; rather am I surprised
that the ultimate causes which lead to them, are
accepted as a matter of course.

Is then the lot of Japanese wives better? Far
from it! The number of divorces is appalling,
and is indeed a disgrace to our family system.
Japan and America head the world's list in numbers
of divorces. I have purposely said that this is
a disgrace to our family system, avoiding the term
marriage system; for in a large proportion of our
divorces, the cause is to be found not in the
rupture of conjugal relations, but in the custom of
a married son living under the same roof with his
parents; in short, in the universally notorious relationship between a wife and a mother-in-law! It
argues a marvellous amount of fortitude and sweetness in the women of Japan that they bear the
burden of wifehood and motherhood under conditions so exacting. Without a deep sense of family
pride and self-abnegation, it would be impossible
for any woman of whatever race or nationality, to
keep up the courage and equanimity of temper
that our women do. I may add in passing that
it is becoming more and more the custom for
young married couples to have separate establish-
ments of their own—a custom which is destined to
affect divorce. It is a remark heard quite often
among foreigners that some of our old women
(*obāsan*) have faces of spiritual maturity, wearing
an expression of attainment—the countenance of
one who has fought a hard fight and won it. For,

together with man, our woman shares the Spartan teaching of patience and heroism. Especially is this true of the samurai woman. She has been trained to inure her nerves to her lot. Sobs and shrieks have ever been regarded as unworthy of her. She was debarred from giving expression to sorrow, even if the heart, over-wrought with grief, should break. Verily she has her reward in the respect shown her by all, and in the adoration of her children. As I have said elsewhere, there is no more tender relation than that between the Japanese mother and her son.

Nothing is more erroneous than to regard the general character of our women as anything like that of the *geisha* type. The very *raison d'être* of the latter class lay in the fact that our wives and mothers were sedate and even stern "home-made bodies," with little tact for entertaining and much less for amusing, better versed in ancient poems than in the newest songs, more deft with needle and spear than with the guitar and the *samisen*. The presence of professional entertainers—dancers and singers—in our society has called forth much criticism both from our own people and from foreigners. The *geisha* are not necessarily "bad women," as you call them, not any worse professionally than the actresses and vaudeville artistes of America. There is little immodesty inherent in their vocation, but danger to feminine probity there certainly is. I am afraid, however, that they will continue to be in demand until our wives and daughters learn the art of entertaining their guests and appear more freely in society. The presence of the *geisha* does not of necessity argue immorality. As I have said in the early part of this lecture, there is a recognised margin of decorum in their deportment and treatment.

Plutarch tells us that the ambition of a Spartan woman was to be the wife of a great man and the mother of illustrious sons. *Bushido* set no lower ideal before our maidens; their whole bringing up was in accordance with this view. They were instructed in many martial practices for the sake of self-defence, that they might safeguard their person and their children; in the art of committing suicide, that in case no alternative opened to save them from disgrace, they might end their lives in due order and in comely fashion. That she might keep her honour spotless, upon leaving the threshold of her father's house, every maiden was given a dagger to use it upon herself in extremity. Such a dagger was called *goshin-to*, "the protector of one's person." She had already learned exactly where to cut her throat and how to bind her lower limbs, so that in the agony of death she might not throw them about indecently. Peaceful accomplishments—music, dancing, belles-lettres, the arranging of flowers, etc.—were not to be neglected, but readiness for emergency, housekeeping, and the education of children were considered by far the most weighty lessons to be learned.

If Stoicism is insisted upon for woman, much

more is it required of man; so that no sooner is the
heart stirred than the will is brought into reflex
action to subdue it.   Is a man angry?   It is bad
taste to rage; let him laugh out his indignation!
Has tribulation stricken him?   Let him bury his
tears in smiles.   If he must vary from an even
temperature—say seventy degrees!—in his demeanour, since· nature will never remain long in
equilibrium, let him be warm within and cold
without; but let him see to it that he freezes
nobody and throws a wet blanket upon none.   It
is a common remark that the Japanese are a light-
hearted, mirth-loving people and that the girls
are ever giggling dolls.   This is due to their idea
that cheerfulness is a part of politeness.

The idea of politeness is, *au fond*, to make your
company and companionship agreeable to others.
It is the first requisite of good society.   Bows and
courtesies are but a small part of good-breeding.
Etiquette is not an end in culture; it is one of the
many ways whereby man may foster his social
nature.   In drinking tea, it is a slight affair how
you handle your spoon, but it is never too slight
to show what you are. "Manners make the man."
Stoicism and politeness, apparently so far apart,
are in reality brother and sister: he bears all that
she may shine; without her, he is stolid; without
him, she is trivial.

Not infrequently have politeness and probity
been set in opposition, as though the two must at
times tread different paths.   Confucius himself

has said, "In pleasant countenance and gentle words there is little benevolence," and some of his followers have gone to the extent of desecrating pleasant manners and speech, indirectly encouraging brusqueness and boorishmess, forgetting that rusticity is just as likely to harbour vice as is urbanity.   If one is bent upon deceiving, manners set no barrier to this intent.   Sincerity has little connection with man's outward mien, and what etiquette requires does not always involve moral issues.   Etiquette stands between morals and art. She must combine in her person rectitude and charm.   Hence her behaviour must not be judged by either standard alone.   Is not this the reason why the so-called conventional lies of society are not condemned with the rigour which is meted to mendacity in general?   It is to this civil kind of falsehood that Byron's words may be applied;

> "And after all, what is a lie? 'T is but
> The truth in masquerade."

Now I have never studied lying—by which I do not mean that lying comes natural to me.   I mean that I have never devoted serious attention to the philosophy or history of mendacity; neither to its classification, characteristics, and different uses, nor to its effect upon man and woman.   It is a matter of surprise to me that no scientific treatise (unless it be the didactic dissertation by Amelia Opie) has been written on an intellectual feat so old and universal; a device so convenient and historically so important. Just at this moment what interests me most is its chromatic quality—the relation between light and lie. In Japan there is only one colour for a lie—viz., the red. But in this rich country, you have at least two species— the black and the white. Like the colours worn by different Hindu castes, the white is, I suppose, of a higher grade than the black. They correspond, I think, to the "lie direct" and the "lie circumstantial" of Mr. Touchstone in *"As You Like It."*

To our benighted souls the verbal denial of a disagreeable situation (such as the state of one's health) does not assume any hideous moral or immoral aspect. It scarcely deserves to be called a red lie. Perhaps you would call it a white lie; but impartial comparison will soon reveal in what respect it differs from a species of the same genus, not unknown in this country—feigning absence when one is at home. Of late, unfortunately for both countries, there seems to have developed the yellow lie of journalism. Referring to yellow journalism, I am reminded of a use of this adjective in our own language; for we have always spoken of a shrill excited voice as *ki-iro no koe*, voice of yellow color!

Speaking of Japanese lies, I ought not to forget to mention the American lie about Japanese lying, which has been widely circulated in this country, and is constantly confirmed by tourists. You

must have heard that in Japanese banks only
Chinese tellers and clerks are employed, because
our own people are too dishonest to be trusted by
each other.   In corroboration of this accusation,
those who have gone to banks in Yokohama or
Kobe swear to the startling fact.   "I have been
on the spot and have seen with my own eyes"—
carries great weight in the determination of any
question.   I myself have seen Chinese employed
in banks in Japan, but not in Japanese banks.
Tourists in the Far East, for obvious reason of
convenience, usually have their letters of credit
drawn on English banks.   Those who come to
Japan have them drawn either on the Chartered
Bank of Australia, India, and China, or on the
Banking Corporation of Honkong and Shanghai,
instead of on one of the two thousand three hundred
and thirty-seven Japanese banks in the country.
Where these British houses have their headquarters, is evident from their names.   Their agencies
in Japan are only a small part of their business,
and their transactions with the Japanese are quite
limited—their   chief   patrons   being   foreigners.
Naturally their staff is also British, and the
lower personnel is supplied by the Chinese, who
are sent from headquarters.   I do not believe
there are even Americans at work in these British
houses, but that does not prove the dishonesty
of Americans any more than does the absence of
Americans in a branch office of the Royal Bank of
Canada or of the Credit Lyonnais in New York or

Chicago. Suppose a Japanese comes to this country: he is provided with a letter of credit to the New York agency of the Specie Bank of Yokohama; so he wends his way for his money to No. 58 Wall Street, finds a big and busy place and sees many people, among whom, however, except the stenographers and messengers, he sees no Americans. Suppose, on his return home, he goes about saying, "In America the people are so dishonest that no American tellers are employed," should he not be believed? Believed? Why he was there and saw with his own eyes! I am sure he will thrill his audience if he closes his speech with the patriotic inference, "The honesty of our countrymen is so well established that in American banks only Japanese tellers are employed!"

There is no opprobrium cast on Japanese character more widely accepted than this fable of our employing Chinese in our banks. Before I left the country on my present trip, I made investigation as to whether a single Japanese bank employed Chinese as clerks, tellers or *compradores*. Since my arrival I have continued my inquiries, and here is the reply from our agent in Wall Street, explaining more fully than I have done, the real situation:

"China having for many years been a silver-using country, and there being no proper coin of fixed weight, size, and fineness, but silver bullion of every description as to the fineness and size being used as medium of exchange, the Chinese people have naturally become more or less experienced and trained not only to easily distinguish good silver from bad, but almost to tell its fineness by the ring of the metal when touched with a metal rod.

It is therefore quite natural that so-called silver experts are found among the Chinese. Considering the monetary system prevailing in China, these people are quite necessary for the banks that are carrying on business in that country.

Before Japan adopted the gold standard, as I previously explained, silver was fractionally the only circulating medium in Japan. Even trade dollars were used to supplement the Japanese coinage. Japan having had legal-tender notes and coins issued by the Government for generations, her people naturally lacked the acquaintance with, and consequently the knowledge of silver bullion, and were not so well fitted to detect the variation in fineness as the Chinese experts. This is the reason why a few Chinese silver experts were at one time employed even in Japan by the Yokohama Specie Bank, Limited, a Japanese concern engaged in international exchange, and in similar lines; but with the gold standard firmly established in Japan, there was no longer a reason for the employment of Chinese silver experts in that bank or in any foreign banking institution in Japan.

There is also a commercial reason for the employment of Chinese by the foreign (not Japanese) banks. According to commercial usage among the Chinese, the seller of a shipment of goods draws a clean bill of exchange upon the buyer, but not a documentary bill, *i. e.*, a bill of exchange with the shipping documents attached. In other words, they do not hypothecate the goods to the bank as security for the draft. It is, therefore, difficult for the bank to determine whether a clean draft which they are about to negotiate is actually commercial paper or not. To be able to act intelligently on this point, and also as there is no Chinese mercantile agency that can supply the desired information regarding the financial standing of Chinese merchants, as is practised in Japan and elsewhere, it has been considered advantageous for the bank to employ a reliable Chinese whose influence and financial responsibility may be sufficient to safeguard the interests of the banks. But, as I have stated before, the tendency to do away with any kind of middlemen, and to reach the objective directly and straight, seems to prevail also in this direction, and as far as Japan and Japanese institutions, whether banking or commercial, are concerned, there no longer exists any necessity for Chinese employment."

We have stayed long enough in the bank— longer perhaps than we are warranted in doing. When business is merely a matter of *yen* and *sen*, it is quickly despatched—but a question of credit and morality necessitates more deliberate transactions. *Bushido*, which furnished the nation at large with the canons of right conduct, was originally, as I have explained, intended only for the samurai, and the tradespeople were little thought of in its scheme, or, perhaps more accurately, the tradespeople little thought of it. The common, every-day, democratic virtues of honest dealing, prudence, cheerfulness, diligence, were held

secondary to the higher virtues of patriotism,
loyalty, friendship, benevolence, and rectitude.

As the traditions of *Bushido* decline with the
progress of democracy, hastened by the importations of the "new school" of popular thought—
Nietsche, Tolstoy, Ibsen, Bernard Shaw, and
others,—the old system of teaching must go, but
before any one of the new schools can obtain
ascendancy (and I cannot believe that any one of
them will, since acorns are much of the same size)
the transition must somehow be passed through.

As was the case during the French Revolution,
when ethical theories were propounded and religious systems *galore* were proposed, so in the intellectual revolution of modern Japan there has been
no lack of scientific theorists and religion-mongers
—all too eager to impose upon their countrymen
the wares of their own making. As a general
thing, the characteristic which runs through most
of them is their appeal to patriotism. If they
wish to arouse moral enthusiasm, they teach us to
be upright, in order to be faithful subjects of His
Majesty. If they desire us to grow in piety, we
must increase our faith in the mission of our nation.
Broad views of humanity, the recognition of a
world-standard of right and wrong, the deepening
of personal responsibility—irrespective of race or
nation—are too often sadly lacking in the systems
of ethics and in the religions proposed. Preposter-
ous notions have been encouraged in the name of
patriotism and loyalty. Their gospel gives an

impression that we are a special ethical creation with gifts peculiar to ourselves, and that we must, accordingly, be Japanese before we are men.

Any claim to moral peculiarity—much less to moral perfection—by any people, will be found futile. The *Völkergedanken* theory has been tried as a working hypothesis but found wanting. Human nature is much the same everywhere, and it is this one touch that makes "the whole world kin." There are no exotics in the domain of ethics. Propriety and impropriety may be climatic products like the colour of the skin, but right and wrong are concepts above the pale of meteorology. Social usages may vary with geographical limits, like the food we eat; but good and evil are not bound by them. The historical development of each nation has imposed modifications upon the outward manifestations of moral ideas, but they remain in their essence identical throughout the world, and eternal. At present, as never before, is universal standardisation displacing localism and nationalism, in every higher sphere of human activity. If in manners and customs, if in language and art, if in forms of government and society, East is East and West is West, moral law has no respect for points of the compass, demanding of both hemispheres equal obedience. As said an ancient writer:

" The world in all doth but two nations bear,—
The good and bad, and these mixed everywhere."

CHAPTER VII

EDUCATION AND EDUCATIONAL PROBLEMS

AS far as our system of education is concerned, it was founded on an elaborate basis as early as the eighth century, at the time when Buddhist and Confucian influences were fresh and vigorous. You can see from the date that it antedated Charlemagne's Ordinance of Education by nearly a century, and the founding of Oxford by nearly two hundred years.

How far the system was put in practice, it is not easy to say definitely. But judging by so many Chinese schemes that are beautifully conceived without hope of being born, one is inclined to imagine that the schools and universities largely remained on paper. Perhaps this is too severe a charge, since we are told of magnificent academic halls and of learned men who bore high-sounding titles. We will at least give credit to our forefathers, however, for their noble idea; for, after all, ideas are seeds—as long as they do not lose their vitality.

The history of education, like the life-history

of a plant, has its seasons of feebleness and of strength, of retrogression and of development. Under unfavourable conditions it simply remains buried, biding the time to germinate. Was it not so in Europe? I make this commonplace remark in order that we may remind ourselves how unfair is the saying that Asia is a land of arrested growth, that all great ideas seem there to be applied and carried up to a certain point and are then stopped. Who knows whether the seed that lay dormant for a season or two—and some seeds retain vitality for decades and centuries—was killed? An idea once conceived is indeed the hardest thing to slay. You beat it, and with each stroke it waxes stronger. You suppress it, and every pound of pressure helps to make it more buoyant. Only a forgotten idea weakens. Who can tell whether Asia's ideas, apparently long forgotten and weakened, may not still rise again—not, I hope, like hordes of Huns and Tartars to devastate mankind, but to fructify the earth hand in hand with European ideas. It seems to me that, in the providence of the Almighty, the Asiatic seed was made to wait until the European should catch up. Youth takes count of time in days, age in years. A cycle of Old Cathay is even as long as half a century of Europe. The plodding patience of the East is to be admired no less than the swift energy of the West. When the two meet, we may see some result—a result now beginning to be visible (pardon my egotism!) in the education of Japan.

The educational idea conceived of Buddhism and Confucianism in the Nara period, seemed for some time to give signs of vigour; then it was buried under a mass of other interests and for centuries practically forgotten. It was remembered and forgotten at odd intervals, and barely kept up a semblance of vitality in monasteries during the turbulent period of what I called the Late Mediæval Age. Only as peace was restored and maintained under the Tokugawas d d education come to receive its share of attention. The Seido (the Temple of the Sages), in Tokyo, and a number of local institutions of higher learning maintained by the munificence of the *daimyos*, were an embodiment of the earliest ideas of education. All these institutions laid stress only on the study of Chinese literature and Chinese history. Their aim was cultural and literary. The method pursued was largely memorising and interpretation of the classics, made more or less lively by disputation among students. The object was mainly to train men for the service of the State, and hence it was almost entirely confined to the higher classes. As to the lower orders of society, upon the Buddhist priests devolved the duty of imparting elementary knowledge, though they did not monopolise it.

Old samurai who had retired from active service, very often opened a school. To give a concrete example, I myself used to attend such a primitive school, which consisted of a couple

of rooms where some twenty or thirty boys (and
a very few girls), ranging in age from seven
to fourteen, spent the forenoon, each reading in
turn with the teacher for half an hour, some para-
graphs from Confucius and Mencius, and devot-
ing the rest of the time to caligraphy. Of the three
R's, 'riting demanded most time and reading but
little, 'rithmetic scarcely any, except in a school
attended by children of the common people as
distinct from those of the samurai. Sons of the
samurai class had other curricula than the three
R's. They began fencing, *jiujutsu*, spear-practice,
and horsemanship, when quite young, and usually
took these lessons in the early morning. As a child
of seven, I remember being roused by my mother
before dawn in the winter and reluctantly, often
in positively bad humour, picking my way bare-
footed through the snow. The idea was to accus-
tom children to hardihood and endurance. There
was little fun in the school-room, except such as
our ingenious minds devised behind our teacher's
back. With Puritanic austerity were children
treated—not like children but like men. How
could they be expected to grasp the Confucian
category of virtues! They just read and recited
by rote—with less comprehension than boys and
girls here learn Biblical texts. What effect such
mental training must have on the mind, I leave to
psychologists to discuss. This much is certain,
that we grew up with no idea of physical or
natural science, no idea of mathematics, except

the first four rules, no idea of geography—if I were
to go on enumerating the many things nowadays
taught in elementary schools we did not learn,
I should have to give the entire list—and thus is
evident the weakness of our old pedagogic scheme.
Its advantages over the modern system lay in its
cultural value, in its alliance with daily conduct,
in its solemn deontology—in one word, in its
character-building aspect.

I would by no persuasion exchange the present
system for the old; but let us do honour to the
latter for its efficiency in making the men who so
wonderfully paved the way for the former.   Only
men unselfish in character, strong in conviction,
and far-seeing in intellect, could have done what
they did in leading a nation of thirty-five millions
from mediæval darkness toward the light of the
promised land.   The nation has been on this jour-
ney over forty years, and if we have not been
seriously lost in the desert, we have had to encounter the Ammonites, Hittites, and other giants
during the march.

Let me now relate how we first made our exodus.

When the present Emperor, on the occasion of
his accession to the throne, announced his charter
oath of five articles, he made it clear that enlightened democracy was to be the great aim of his
reign, and that this could be secured only by diffusion of intelligence.   Men trained under the old
régime were able, wise, and noble; but they did not
know "things new and Western."   They had wis-

dom, but not knowledge. They did away with the shogunacy and with feudalism, but what should they give instead?

A comparatively small quantity of new wine so effervesced in the old wine-skin that it burst, and then came the question, "Where and how can we get a new wine-skin?" "At the same time," they said, "let us renew the wine itself." Therefore, in the first years of this new era, a plan for universal education was drafted, and as the new era was new in its conceptions and conditions, new ideas and new men were needed.

The plan suggested at this exigency was virtually a translation of the French educational system, which was naturally very soon found to be impracticable without modification. While revision was under discussion, the epoch-making embassy of 1871 left Japan to pay a visit to the treaty Powers.

Among the members of this embassy were two of the greatest men of modern Japan—Okubo and Kido. On their arrival in San Francisco nothing astonished them so much as the intelligence of the American people. Just at that time, some sort of election was going on. Our ambassadors noticed the widespread excitement, but could not believe that the hotel employes, waiters, and bellboys, really knew what they were doing at the polls. A few questions put to these men, however, very soon showed that they knew what they were talking about—why they were voting for this or for that candidate. This single experience was enough to convince Okubo and Kido that only by education could new Japan stand erect and keep pace with the Western world. Deserving of mention, too, is the attitude of these two men as regards the initiatory step to be taken in the cause of national education. Okubo said: "We must first educate leaders, train such young men as will fill high positions, and the rest will follow; or, if they do not follow, the leaders will pull them up." Kido said: "We must educate the masses; for unless the people are trained, they cannot follow their leaders, or if they follow, it will never do for them to follow blindly."

The inspiration which they incidentally received in San Francisco proved a pregnant factor in the progress of their country. In the cabinet, Kido took by preference the portfolio of the Department of Instruction, and though he soon after resigned, the work of general education steadily grew in influence and efficiency.

The first draft of the law under discussion was nothing more than a translation of Napoleon's *Law of Education*. That it could not work goes without saying. Revision after revision was attempted, until the whole code was given up. About this time American influences became pre-dominant through the employment by our government of Dr. David Murray and Professor M. M. Scott. Then, too, popular interest in liberal education was aroused among our people through Spencer's work on education. But no definite ste~

towards radical reform or organised reconstruction was undertaken until Viscount Mori assumed the task in 1885. An ardent admirer of Anglo-Saxon spirit and institutions, and a thorough student of the educational systems of the world, he was the one man fitted to do this, and it is chiefly to him that we owe our present system.

I shall begin with an outline of our primary instruction, which, by the way, is more like that of America than of any other country.

In the elementary schools, all the instruction imparted is in Japanese, and no foreign language is taught in them, if one excepts a few schools in large cities. The teachers are usually of both sexes. Over one hundred and forty-four thousand teachers (nearly forty thousand being women) are engaged in the schools, which are attended by about six million pupils. The proportion of children in attendance to the total number of children of school-age is 98.8 per cent. for boys and 97.2 per cent. for girls—a remarkably high percentage, which can bear comparison with that of any country. But the attendance of school is not an unerring criterion of educational efficiency, though it shows that the law of compulsory and universal education is well enforced. It gives no clue to the quality of instruction. Of course, among such large numbers there are many who are sent to school just a sufficient number of hours or days to conform to the letter of the law, and are engaged part of the year in swelling the army of child labourers. As to the effect of instruction obtained in schools, its value is greatly diminished by the use of Chinese characters. Children, during the eight years of their elementary schooling, are expected to master some two thousand of these characters—most of which they will not use frequently and which will naturally slip out of their memory in a short time. It is no wonder that by the time boys are called for army conscription at the age of twenty, many of them have forgotten the more complex characters. With all the drawbacks, inherent not so much in our educational system as in the language itself, our primary education—which, by the way, was largely modified after the American and later after the Belgian pattern, but now so changed from either that it may be called genuinely Japanese—is quite satisfactory. Teachers in these schools, in spite of a mere pittance of salary (a monthly average of sixteen *yen*), keep pretty well up-to-date by their attendance of summer schools, and their connection with educational societies. They are respected in the communities in which they live. On the whole, her primary education is a feature of which modern Japan has reason to be proud.

The same cannot be said of our secondary schools, corresponding to your high schools. These receive the children who have finished their primary education; but as there is no co-education (except in the elementary grades already mentioned), separate institutions are provided—those for boys being called *Chugakko*, Middle Schools, and those for girls, High Schools. Of this grade, there are three hundred schools for boys (118,000 in number), and one hundred and eighty for girls (52,000). They vary in capacity, seating from two hundred and fifty to four hundred, exceeding this last number only in exceptional cases.

In conformity with the "good-wife-and-wise-mother" principle of female education, the Government offers to young women very few opportunities for higher education than that afforded in high schools and normal schools. There are Normal Colleges for women; but, as their name indicates, they are for a very definite purpose. The Academy of Fine Arts and the Conservatory of Music are naturally open to both sexes. A curious fact, hard to account for in so progressive a Government as ours, is the chronic reluctance it has shown toward the higher education of women. Its function in this respect seems to have been confined to a tardy recognition of work done by private enterprise. At present, therefore, there are private institutions of excellent reputation—the so-called "Women's University" under Mr. Naruse, Miss Tsuda's English School, two or three well-equipped seminaries under missionary management—doing work such as the Government has failed to make possible by its own initiative and on its own responsibility.

A large majority of middle schools is maintained by local bodies—prefectural or municipal.

Whereas in elementary education, which is compulsory, no tuition is charged unless otherwise decided by the local bodies, and in no case exceeds five *sen* a month in the rural and ten *sen* in the municipal schools, the secondary schools charge usually about three *yen* a month. When there are dormitories, room and board cost about six to eight *yen* a month. The course of studies prescribed for intermediate education covers much the same ground as it does in this country with this difference—that no Greek or Latin is taught, nor is German or French. The cultural equivalents to your dead languages are Chinese and Yamato (old Japanese). English occupies the most prominent part in the curriculum, and as six hours a week are devoted to it during the entire course of five years, by the time boys finish the middle schools they have a fair reading knowledge of it, for they will have read as text-books such works as Gray's *Elegy*, Dickens's *Tale of Two Cities* and *Christmas Carol*, Irving's *Sketch Book*, Smiles's *Character*, Franklin's *Autobiography*. Their English is for reading and not for colloquial purposes. Thus, almost any one of any education can understand some English, even if he cannot follow a conversation and much less take part in it. In commercial schools, more "practical" English is taught.

It is through the channels of the English language that Anglo-Saxon ideas exert a tremendous influence intellectually, morally, politically, and socially. In this way are the great leaders of English thought made familiar to us, and being constantly quoted they are perused both in the original and in translations. Several works of Shakespeare can now be read in Japanese; Bacon, Emerson, George Eliot, Poe, Stevenson, Long-fellow, Wordsworth, Tennyson, are names on the lips of every one.

English does not occupy the same prominence in girls' high schools, except in such institutions as are under the auspices of Christian missions. A feature of girls' schools that may attract curious attention from outsiders as being unique, if not odd, is the course in etiquette, including ceremonial tea and flower arrangement. I have no time to go into their elaborate proceedings, and to an American a mere description of them would be tedious enough; but so much importance is attached to them in our pedagogical scheme that they are invariably taught. For this purpose every girls' school has a special building in Japanese style, with a room which may be called "a laboratory of manners." In all modern schools, children sit on benches; but at home they have to sit down *à la japonaise* with their limbs bent under them—hence the necessity of a special etiquette room. To avoid possible misunderstanding allow me a moment's digression.

The concocting and drinking of tea—tea-ism, shall I call it?—has long been elevated to the dignity of a fine art, an art of social intercourse.

Its votaries even go so far as to regard it with almost religious devotion. It has created canons of propriety and beauty. We speak of one who lacks refinement and taste as one who has "no tea" in him—"a-tea-istic." We speak of a rash, irrational action as *mu-cha*, "un-tea-ful" or "tea-less," and, conversely, of a quiet, sedate, unworldly man as *cha-jin*, "tea-ist." A future philologist may write a dissertation on the etymology of taste and tea-ist, or of Theism and Tea-ism! One of our best writers, in dramatising *Les Misérables*, japanised all its characters, and in doing so, the nearest approach of which he could conceive to Bishop Myriel was a tea-ist. Strange that tea should purify taste, that the austere simplicity— verging on asceticism—of ceremonial tea-drinking should dictate rules of æsthetic conduct! and yet that this is the case will account for the general quiet and Quaker-like sobriety of our taste, the absence of bright colours in our costume, and the severe plainness of our parlours.

In finishing my comments on the secondary school, I have lingered long enough over the tea-cups; for young boys have no fancy for it, and even after matriculating in institutions of higher learning, they remain un-tea-ful. As a matter of fact, graduates of secondary schools cannot afford money or time for *cha-no-yu*. Life is too strenuous for them. They cannot get out of the world; they must prepare themselves to plunge into it. A large number find it impossible to continue their education further. For those who can, there is a Rubicon to cross; for the great question must be decided,—"Shall I seek the highest that Japan can offer (namely, the university), or, shall I choose the next best (namely, technical schools or private institutions for medical or legal study)? He who decides upon the latter course has comparatively little difficulty in continuing his studies, but he who aspires to a university education must first enter the so-called *Koto-Gakko*, Higher Schools or National Colleges, whose standing is about the same as that of a good American undergraduate collegiate course or of the German Gymnasium.

According to the law on education, a certificate testifying to the completion of the middle-school course entitles its holder to enter these colleges without examination. But as there are only eight of them in the country, they cannot take in all who apply for admission. Hence a rigorous entrance examination is required. The college in Tokyo is the oldest and largest, and has had a history that makes every youth ambitious to enter it. It has over one thousand students, and every year can admit about three hundred freshmen, but the applicants always exceed this number by about seven or eight times. It is a very touching sight to watch some two thousand boys, the pick of our youth from all parts of the Empire, flocking to the college for examination—to watch them at their heavy task, all the time knowing that seven

out of every eight will be disappointed. Those
who fail one year can try again; a great many do
try three or four times, and in exceptional cases
seven or eight times, one instance of perseverance
being on record, where success crowned the four-
teenth attempt!

I believe there is nothing that chills the genial
current of the youthful soul more than the inadequate number of collegiate institutions in our
country. Thousands of young men in the most
ardent and aspiring period of life, feel the very
door of hope slammed in their face! Their sole
consolation lies in the healing power of youth
itself. Inability to accommodate all who are
desirous to pursue higher studies, is not by any
means confined to the *Koto-Gakko*. Each year
sees Government institutions—Commercial College, Naval Academy, School for Foreign Languages, School of Navigation, Academy of Fine
Arts, Conservatory of Music, Institute of Tech-
nology, etc.,—overcrowded with applicants for
admission. It hurts me to confess how sadly our
Government fails to meet the educational demands
of young Japan.

The average age of those who come to the *Koto-
Gakko* is between eighteen and nineteen. They
stay three years, during which their time is mostly
taken up with foreign languages—English and
German—a few of them, however, taking French.
Here again no dead languages are taught except
to those who expect to take up medicine or law—

the amount required being homœopathic in quantity, just about enough to read prescriptions or to
understand technical terms in Pandects. Fortunately for those who finish their studies in the
colleges, the universities admit them without examination, except such faculties in the University
of Tokyo as have more candidates than can be
accommodated.

There are four Imperial universities, of which
the one in Tokyo is the oldest and most complete,
being possessed of six faculties—Law, Medicine,
Literature, Science, Engineering, and Agriculture.
The University of Kyoto has four faculties—Law,
Medicine, Literature, Science and Engineering,
the last two being merged into one. The other two
universities are still too new to be complete. One
of them is in the south, at Fukuoka in Kyushu,
and has Medical and Engineering faculties. The
other in the north, has a well-equipped Agricultural faculty at Sapporo in Hokkaido, and a
Science department in Sendai.

The university course varies in length from three
to four years according to the faculty. The lectures are given in Japanese, though a few foreign
professors (about a half dozen in number) lecture
in English or French or German. The number of
students in the University of Tokyo is about six
thousand, that of Kyoto some two thousand. The
courses of study are very much as in other countries, and we think the standard is equally high.
Perhaps we have carried further than other coun-

tries one branch of study—Seismology, or Seismography—the Science of Earthquakes, for which we have no lack of raw material.

The academic atmosphere is *"ganz Deutsch"*— barring *Mensur und Kneipe*, and alas, minus *Gemüthlichkeit*. Our students are on the whole exceedingly studious in their habits—I dare say too studious; and though they might enjoy the pleasures of the German students, they have not the English and American zest for sports. Their most popular exercises are fencing and *jiujutsu*, neither of which, however, arouses such enthusiasm as do the imported games of baseball and boat-racing. The two private universities of Keio and Waseda send their teams now and then to this country.

As for fraternities or any other secret organisations, they are quite unknown among our students. There are no purer democracies than our institutions of learning. Distinction lies only in brains. Family pride is not tolerated; any show of wealth is despised; snobbishness is scorned. In a dormitory, for instance, a millionaire's son would never think of decorating his room. If a boy should come in a carriage, he would be looked upon with contempt. To be a *shosei* (student), is to be plain in habit and in taste. To be poor or to be careless of social conventionality is described by the word *shosei*-like. Dandyism is a heinous offence in the society of learning. This identification of simple habits with study, of plain living with high thinking, has come down as a tradition, and still exercises a wholesome effect upon the young. It will not be out of place to mention here a practice generally in vogue among the nobility and the wealthy class. To protect their children from the enervating influence of wealth and rank, to shield them from being spoiled by their caressing grandmothers, or by a train of flattering servants, a small, unpretentious establishment is provided for boys to live in with their tutor and a small company of select young men —perhaps class-mates of the boys and some older and more advanced students. Here they all share the same simple diet, such as they might get in ordinary boarding-houses or dormitories. The boys are allowed to visit their parents once or twice a week. This Lacedæmonian treatment, if it is hard on the boys as well as on the parents, especially on the mothers, has proved quite efficacious. I have myself witnessed admirable results accruing from it. Moreover, friendship—which is often a notably strong bond between our youths— formed under these conditions, is deep and lasting as love. I have spoken of our training as masculine.

An extension of the same system is also not at all uncommon. Men, usually teachers in active service or in retirement, offer to take a limited number—varying from half-a-dozen to fifty odd boys—under their own roofs, conversing with them at meal-time or spending some hours with them daily. In *jiuku*, as such a system is called, boys pay their own board and possibly a small sum for rent, but the fundamental idea is to live under the guidance of superior men.

It is a still more common custom for a man who can afford to do so (had I time I could give most touching examples of men of small means, such as school teachers and officials with a monthly salary no larger than thirty or forty *yen*) to offer a home to well-deserving students and take them in as members of his family. Such students are called *shokkaku*, "table-guests." A man of more or less prominence usually has several such in his house. I number among my own friends some who have no other hobby than that of helping poor students. No charge is made for their food and room; but they usually requite the kindness done them by little services, clerical or domestic, or, when there are children in the family, tutorial. Far from being parasitic, such an arrangement corresponds to what the biologists speak of as symbiotic. "House Communism" of this kind is but seldom detrimental to the family life of the patron or to the character of the clientele. Among those who now fill prominent positions in business circles or in public service, are many who spent their student days as *shokkaku*.

The expenses of university education amount to about four hundred *yen* for the whole year, inclusive of board, room, and books. This is a very respectable sum in Japan, where the cost of living is low, and it is an oft-mooted question

whether it pays to give a boy a university education, seeing that graduates usually begin their
career at forty *yen* a month, and many of them
obtain positions with difficulty. Still a university
diploma goes a long way in the struggle for life,
so much so that it is the ambition of all parents
to see their sons in possession of it. I could tell
you stories from actual life of the brave sacrifices
made by mothers for the sake of their sons' education, or tales of abject despair on the part of
young men who failed to enter college. Yet as
far as privileges are concerned a diploma avails
but little. If a graduate desire a Government
position, he must pass a severe civil-service examination. It is pitiful to see a promising boy beset
all along his path by examinations. Just think
of some exceptionally good schools taking children
of twelve by "exam" into the higher grade of
primary education, or of some middle schools, particularly well known, requiring entrance "exams"
of boys from fourteen to fifteen years of age.
When entering college at eighteen or nineteen, the
candidates have that awful examination of which
I have spoken. If the course they wish to
pursue in the university is crowded, they must
take another examination. They leave the university at twenty-five or twenty-six, and after this
they try the State examination for civil service.
When I see the heart-rending as well as head-
racking struggle, I am reminded of the dwarfing
features of French life that Monsieur Desmoulins

gives in his *Anglo-Saxon Superiority*. Yet, until we can devise some better system, we shall go on with the present; for certainly there are many advantages in it. Here again permit me to make a digression. By this series of "exams" the weaker minds are pretty thoroughly sifted out, and we can get the best in public service. Such young men, when they get their first appointment as clerks, receive, as I have said, about forty *yen* a month. If, instead of going into Government service, they should accept a place in a private corporation or firm, they can ordinarily command twice or three times as large a salary; but so honoured and so stable are Government positions that they would by far prefer them to more lucrative employment. This explains why paternalism and bureaucracy, carried as they are to a degree unbelievable in other countries, have not proved so onerous. It explains, too, why "socialism," so abhorred by officialdom, is really carried out in great measure by the State itself. I say this with no desire to defend bureaucracy. On the contrary, its defects—particularly its red-tape—are intolerable; but the remedies for them are most likely to come from the official classes themselves. But I am afraid that our educational plan and the system of competitive examination for every advancement have very cramping effect upon intellect and character. The value of education comes to be measured by the facility it gives to the attainment of success in examinations. People study not for the sake of knowledge, but to "answer examination questions." The men who can write the best examination papers are heroes among students. There is little encouragement to enjoy knowledge for its own sake; for every effort is exerted to cram. The opinions of members of the examining bodies are repeated, even when they may not be accepted. There is developing what might be termed a science of examinations; and as to an art of passing them —this has already advanced far. Under these circumstances it would have been a dire national calamity if corruption had crept into the examination system; but fortunately we are exempt from it—for the same reason that civil service takes the pick of our young men. It remains true, nevertheless, that cramming of mind means cramping of character.

My laudation of the personnel of our civil service implies the converse—that the worst do not come into civil service; but it does not imply the obverse —that the best men never enter other than official careers. Some of our best minds have adopted for their life career engineering, mercantile business, legal professions, and journalism. As for academic vocations, they are included in official callings, as all the principal institutions of the country are under governmental control. I ought to add, however, that there are in the country some important private institutions of higher learning. Among the most famous are the Keio University, founded as early as the year 1867 by Fukuzawa, one of the wise makers of new Japan; the Do-shisha, organised by the illustrious Christian, Joseph Neeshima; the Waseda, established and still patronised by the well-known statesman, Count Okuma. Besides these, we have several private law schools which bear the name of university. One of the chief reasons why institutions of this grade are so eagerly sought, lies in the privilege accorded (provided they conform to the regulations relating to accommodations, teaching staff, etc.) to their matriculated students of postponing military service while pursuing their studies.

From what has been said above, it may be seen that with us higher studies are pursued primarily for utilitarian purposes—to get positions, to earn bread. They are *Brodwissenschaften*. And it is this fact that strikes me as the lamentable feature of our present education. Culture, in a broad and lofty sense, is entirely neglected. In the universities and in higher or technical schools, there is but little moral influence exerted in any form. Personal intercourse between professors and students is as good as *nil*. During the collegiate period, students are most interested in moral problems; but ethics is chiefly studied as science—as something to discuss and to dissect rather than to believe and to be lived up to. In the secondary schools moral discipline is very much more stringent. Here, as in all other institutions maintained by public funds, religious teaching is carefully excluded. It is given only in schools supported by religious denominations, Buddhist or Christian.

The absence of moral factors in our educational system is a matter of serious concern. In our haste to construct the nation on a new basis, the political and material institutions of the West were largely adopted, because we believed, rightly or wrongly, that it was in these that the West excel us. But in course of time, it became evident that without emphasising the moral side of life, material progress was fraught with more danger than is adherence to old traditions. Should we, then, retrace our steps? Should we withdraw into the old shell? Some reactionary people began to raise their voices against occidentalisation. They appealed to so-called patriotism—the cheap resort of the blusterer!—invoking the passions of the semi-educated in exhorting them to be true to the traditions of their fathers, calling advanced thinkers traitors to the highest heritage of the nation. This reaction, though wholesome in a small way, set back our progress by several years. In the meantime, young Japan was bewildered in its judgment as to moral issues. The old system of things which was as good as dead, reactionary chauvinism could not resurrect with all its yellow shrieks. The new construction period has not yet come. In the meantime shall or can the nation suspend its moral judgment?

We are exceedingly fortunate in having for our ruler a man of unusual insight and power, who incorporates in his person the best intent of his subjects.   Himself true to the noblest teachings of his race, doing his daily round of tasks under the dictates of a rigid discipline, our Emperor is in a position to give out a code of morals which fills a great educational need.   In 1890, was issued what is known as the Imperial Rescript on Education.   It is perhaps the only document that has been made public without the signature of his ministers, and a glance at the instrument will show that no cabinet minister could take upon himself the responsibility of enforcing the precepts stated therein.   For instance, what minister could claim the power to make husband and wife live in harmony!   Here is a translation officially made, and I confess that no English rendering will do justice to the dignity of the original.   However, the general trend of the thought, if not the exact meaning of every clause, may be clear enough.

THE IMPERIAL RESCRIPT ON EDUCATION

KNOW YE, OUR SUBJECTS:

Our Imperial Ancestors have founded Our Empire on a basis broad and everlasting, and have deeply and firmly implanted virtue.   Our subjects, ever united in loyalty and filial piety, have from generation to generation illustrated the beauty thereof.   This is the glory and the fundamental character of Our Empire and herein also lies the source of Our education.   Ye,

Our subjects, be filial to your parents, affectionate to your brothers and sisters; as husbands and wives be harmonious, as friends true; bear yourselves in modesty and moderation; extend your benevolence to all; pursue learning and cultivate the arts, and thereby develop intellectual faculties and perfect moral powers; furthermore, advance public good and promote common interests; always respect the Constitution and observe the laws; should emergency arise, offer yourselves courageously to the State; and thus guard and maintain the prosperity of Our Imperial Throne, coeval with heaven and earth. So shall ye not only be Our good and faithful subjects, but render illustrious the best traditions of your Forefathers.

The way here set forth is indeed the teaching bequeathed by Our Imperial Ancestors to be observed alike by Their Descendants and the subjects, infallible for all ages and true in all places. It is Our wish to take it to heart in all reverence, in common with you, Our subjects, that we may all thus attain to the same virtue.

The 30th day of the 10th month of the 23rd year of *Meiji*

(*Imperial Sign Manual, Imperial Seal.*)

This document forms at present the basis of all moral teaching in schools. A printed copy with the Emperor's autograph, is kept as the sacred treasure of every educational institution. It is read with much ceremony on all state occasions. Text-books on ethics are usually commentaries on or expansions of it. You can see for yourselves what a comprehensive epitome of moral duties it presents. Its very comprehensive-ness allows ample room for liberal interpretation. As explained and taught in schools, I have often wondered how nearly its usual exposition ap-proaches the original idea of the Emperor himself. There is certainly a demand for a more universal —and not exclusively national—exegesis of the Rescript.

We must learn the fuller meaning of all the duties we have been wont to look upon as of solely worldly concern. Our loyalty must not end with our relations to our masters; our truthfulness must not be limited to our dealings with our neighbours; our benevolence must have no geographical limits. We are not merely subjects, but citizens, not only citizens of Japan but of the world-community. These are trite sayings; but a strange superstition has for some years been current in our country, that we are a "peculiar" people, that our history is different from—by which of course is meant better than—that of other peoples, and that our ethical ideas are unique and superior. In these strains have the chauvinists been preaching the moral apartness of our people, and in this strange wise has the spectre of old insular isolation cropped out again. But ghosts vanish with the coming of the morning!

As at the dawn of our pedagogic history, we sat at the feet of Hindu and Chinese sages, and as in course of time we imbibed their precepts and made of them the very fibre of our being; as at the commencement of the present régime, we placed ourselves under the tutelage of European and American teachers, and then gradually assimilated their thought,—so, in the future, when the period of fruition shall have come, we should show forth what may rightly be expected of the intellectual welding of two hemispheres, of the spiritual wedding of the East and the West.

CHAPTER VIII

ECONOMIC CONDITIONS

SO often has the saying, "Man doth not live by bread alone," been repeated, that it has been assigned a place among platitudes. Nevertheless the trend of our age is toward an undue emphasis of our physical wants. As a result, civilisation is measured largely by its success in fulfilling them; hence bread-winning has grown from a material necessity to a social, iron law.

Its rigour is, however, relentless only in the field of daily need, relaxing as the requirements of our living ascend in scale from articles of necessity to those of decency, and from these again to the demands of comfort; and when they reach the domain of luxury, the so-called bread-winning ceases to be a law of life, but becomes in very truth a cause of death.

Oriental teachers have always looked upon material well-being as a matter of subsidiary concern. They have taught more of life than of living. Mr Wrench in his recent work, *The Mastery of Life*, has called the attention of the

West to the fact that it is too much absorbed in
the means of life, while the East tastes life itself.
You speak of "Oriental luxury"; but is there not
more of an Oriental flavour in that part of the
Sermon on the Mount where the Master teaches:
"Therefore I say unto you, Be not anxious for
your life, what ye shall eat, or what ye shall drink;
nor yet for your body, what ye shall put on. Is
not the life more than food, and the body than
raiment?" The pagan Orientals live more the
life of "the birds of the heaven, which sow not,
neither reap nor gather into barns," or the life of
the "lilies of the field," which, without toiling
or spinning, grow and array themselves in the
glory that Solomon could not surpass. Wealth,
as such, has been discarded from all high thinking
and high teaching. Privation was even courted
among religious and literary men as a condition
under which one can best work out one's salvation. Men in public life were expected not to
look to filthy lucre for the reward of their service.
An ancient saying runs, "When civil servants
begin to covet riches and when military men begin
to love life, then is the beginning of an end."
Superiour men looked upon wealth as illth.

Poverty was not considered a disgrace. We
have an inelegant adage, *Bushi wa kuwa-ne-do
taka-yoji*—"As to the samurai, though he eats not,
he proudly picks his teeth,"—which is equivalent
to saying "How far above creature-comforts soars
the soul of the samurai!" There has thus been

a general feeling that wealth is something unworthy to be chased after.   Food and raiment and shelter, and medicine in sickness,—and beyond these the simplest demands of propriety; more than this cometh of evil.

If human happiness is the result obtained by dividing the good things of this life by our desires, our old masters taught us to increase the quotient not by increasing the numerator, or the supply of things, but by decreasing the denominator, our desires.   Infinity can be procured, as Carlyle taught, by reducing our covetousness. $\frac{1}{0} = \infty$.

Economic activity was held ever subservient to human and humane purpose.   Japanese thinkers of former days defined Political Economy much as Ruskin did, asserting that its main object is the production of souls of good quality.

To teachings and feelings like these, is to be largely attributed the comparatively backward economic condition of Japan.   Much of her dormant wealth was left undisturbed; her virgin lands untilled; her mines unexplored.   I do not mean that our economic advancement was checked solely by our ideal view of life.   There were other reasons for our slow progress; but above these reasons towers our mental attitude toward wealth. Make plain living honourable and display will take its flight to lodge among the tawdry; there will be less of a scramble for bread and for gold. Modern civilisation, however, does not tolerate old-time simplicity.   Bread!   Bread!!—sour **or**

sweet—leavened or unleavened—bread has become
the first and last cry in this modern age.

Owing to the onslaught of materialism upon
Japan, the samurai has put away his sword, the
statesman has taken up the abacus, and the new
gospel of "a good living" has come in vogue.
Callings hitherto despised have suddenly come to
be honoured. Merchants have become nobles,
shopkeepers have usurped such social positions as
knights enjoyed before. With this mental and
social transformation, the foremost energies of the
nation rush into money-making channels. With
a new value placed on the power of wealth, both
among the people and in the esteem of one nation
towards another, the moral concept of social progress passes through a radical change. As wrote
Shakespeare in *King John;*

> "Well, whiles I am a beggar, I will rail,
>   And say—there is no sin, but to be rich;
>   And being rich, my virtue then shall be,
>   To say—there is no vice but begging."

The logic of this sad cynicism leads to the universal adoption of a "gold standard" for all concerns of life. As at the devil's booth, all things
come to be sold or bartered for bread. Poverty,
despicable in our industrial age, as it was in the
religion of Mammonism, is the gravest of sins.
Gauged by the physical standard, Japan certainly
stands low among the nations.

It has been computed by competent statisticians

that the entire wealth of Japan amounts to some
24,000,000,000 *yen*, which will give at ten per cent.
an annual income of 2,400,000,000 *yen*. This in
turn gives *per capita* a yearly income of about
forty-six *yen* (the population being 52,000,000).
Out of this sum is to be paid 8.80 *yen* for taxes of
various kinds, leaving to each citizen, irrespective
of age or sex, an annual revenue of 37.20 *yen* or a
monthly quota of 3.10. As a family consists on
an average of five persons, its income is 15.50 *yen*
per month. With this meagre sum, a household
manages not only to sustain and to perpetuate
itself but to lead a cheerful life. This absurdly
low state of economic development does not pre-
clude the existence of millionaires, nor does it by
any means argue the prevalence of indigence.
Wealth is comparatively evenly distributed, and
the proletariat in the slums of Tokyo fare better
than does the "residuum" of New York, London,
or Paris. In the most wretched hovels we rarely
meet with the herding together of the sexes and
of families. The clothing of our poor being cotton,
it is oftener and more easily washed than the
woollen garments of your paupers. Their food
consisting largely of vegetables, putrefying grease
does not scent the air. The struggle for life is
bad enough, but has not reached the most acute
stage, and luxury has not yet made victims of the
unsophisticated peasants who form by far the
largest proportion of our population. For though
the urban population is increasing at a rapid rate

(twenty-five per cent. of our population living at present in towns of over ten thousand inhabitants) the bulk of our people are still engaged in rural pursuits, and agriculture is as yet our principal industry.

Whether considered as a food-producing occupation or as man-producing—inasmuch as no other vocation is more conducive to health and character,—agriculture has always been held in high esteem. In former days, the social classes were ranked, according to their callings, as samurai (knights or gentlemen), as tillers of the soil, as artisans, and as tradesmen. This recognition of the status of the peasantry is not to be wondered at when one remembers that Japan was, until forty years ago, what Thuenen calls an "Isolated State," her whole economic life being based on the principle of self-sufficiency and her political philosophy being physiocratic. Let me describe our system of husbandry.

Japan proper, which I single out as best representing our national life,—*i. e.*, Japan exclusive of her colonial acquisitions in Formosa, Korea, and Saghalien,—embraces an area of about 95,000,000 acres, of which the highest estimate rates some fourteen per cent., or 14,000,000 acres, as arable. The rest, or about eighty-six per cent., lies waste, or, if not strictly waste, waste as far as food-producing is concerned. No civilised country in the world has so small a proportion of agricultural land. If all these cultivated acres were put together into one big farm, and if you were to ride in an automobile at the speed of fifty miles an hour, you would be able to skirt the entire centre perimeter in less than twelve hours.

Yet from this limited area our peasants produce enough to feed and clothe themselves and the nation, and to furnish more than half the silk worn by American ladies.

It is evident that our agricultural method must be very intensive, intensive in the double sense of the liberal use of capital and labour, though, as we shall see, the intensivity is largely that of labour. Regarding the capitalistic side of our farming, it consists almost exclusively of the use of fertilisers and of water for irrigation. Possessed of scarcely any capital in the form of cash, the farmers know how to make the best use of water for irrigation and of the last scrap of refuse for fertilisation.

Poor as the peasants are, they apply yearly 85,000,000 *yen* worth of fertilisers, of which 20,000,000 *yen* are expended for imported fertilisers. A great French agriculturist, Monsieur Gasparin, has remarked that agriculture reaches its highest development, which he calls *culture hétérositique*, when it is forced to depend upon imported fertilisers for its successful operations. Our peasants have long practised rotation of crops and the renovation of soil by the cultivation of leguminous plants—of course empirically, having had no scientific knowledge of their usefulness.

One of the beautiful sights which greets foreign travellers in Japan is that of fields or valleys covered with a little pinkish-purple vetch—often called by them "Japanese clover." It has not been sown to please the eye, but merely to be ploughed under for manure.

Though Dean Swift's fame did not rest upon truth-telling, I believe the reverend gentleman's words may be taken literally, when he says that "he who makes two blades of grass grow where one grew before, is the true benefactor of mankind." In this sense our peasant deserves the highest niche in our shrine of gratitude.

I have at home a small brass image of a peasant in his straw rain-coat, holding in his hands a hat made of rushes. It is one of a number of images which a celebrated prince of Mito had made for the members of his household, and which he instructed them to place upon their trays (individual tables) at every meal, so that they might never forget the toil of those who provided them with food.

With surprising diligence, combined with intelligence, our peasants make two blades of grass grow where one grew before. From one field they get three and sometimes four successive crops in a year. Hence, like a dime which when used ten times is worth a dollar, one of our acres yields as much as three or four acres in America.

Our population of 52,000,000 (about one-half that of the United States) is thus fed and clothed by the labour of over 30,000,000 people—nearly sixty per cent. of our population being engaged in agriculture. As these 30,000,000 farmers, including women and children (5,500,000 families), cultivate 14,000,000 acres, it is evident that two farmers are occupied in tilling one acre of land, or, what amounts to the same thing, the proportion of arable land to the agricultural population is no more than one-half acre per head.

Seventy per cent. of the agricultural class own and cultivate farms of less than two and a half acres. Twelve acres are considered a very respectable holding. By assiduous labour an owner of such a lot can realise a goodly sum—say three or four hundred *yen*—after paying a heavy land tax of perhaps fifty *yen*, the rate of tax on agricultural land being 4.7 per cent. on its assessed value, which is in turn calculated at ten times its annual rental. In a land of *petite culture*, an area of twenty-five acres entitles its owner to the position of a local magnate.

You can easily understand that when land is so minutely divided, farming is carried on much as gardening, horticulture, and truck-farming are here. People work with their own hands with hoe and spade. Mr. Edwin Markham might well call them "brother to the ox," were he to see them wading through mud in the heat of the day or turning the sod in the winter twilight. Animals are not altogether wanting. From of old, we have had horses, cattle, fowls, dogs, and pigs in limited numbers. The sheep is a new creature to us, and flocks of them are still quite rare. Mutton chops are therefore a luxury! The horse is used for draught, but its flesh is seldom eaten. Here I might state that in recent years, since our wars with China and Russia, astounding improvement has been made in our cavalry mounts, and in horses generally, so that it is difficult nowadays to find a specimen of pure Japanese breed. This disappearance of a native breed is still more conspicuous in the case of the canine family. The kind of dogs that I used to play with in childhood is entirely extinct, except in remote mountain districts. Dog-flesh was never eaten by us; and even pork, which is a favourite food among our neighbours, the Chinese, has not been much relished. Chickens, eggs, and fish—most commonly salted herring, sole, sardine, salmon, or cod—furnish the principal meat supply of our diet.

Now that I have inadvertently taken up the subject of diet, I may proceed with the standard of our living. Though rice is considered the staff of life in Japan, it is not freely indulged in by the peasants who raise it. The proper ration of rice per head is calculated to be one-and-a-half pints of the uncooked grain per day, though hard-working labourers must have over one quart. The poorer people cannot afford to take unmixed rice; therefore they boil with it cheaper barley and millet. In some southern provinces, sweet potatoes form the chief part of daily food.

As rice requires for its cultivation land well irrigated, the prospective increase of paddy-fields in Japan is not likely to be very great. At the present rate of increase in population and of cultivation, we shall reach the margin of rice-culture in some thirty years. Hence it is a grave question how long we as a people can depend on the mono-culture of rice. Already the recent enormous rise in the price of this cereal indicates the necessity of a change in our dietary system.

Besides the grains named, a large quantity of beans—the so called soy-bean—is used in various forms. Fermented beans in the form of soup constitute an essential part of the standard breakfast for rich and poor alike. Indeed beans largely supply the protein of our food, and without this nitrogenous element of their diet, our peasants declare they cannot work. Among vegetables, the most important is a huge radish, which we term *daikon*, and which is often two or three feet long and four inches in diameter. It is served pickled in salt or grated or boiled, and science has recently proved it to be rich in diastase—another example of the empiric use of an unknown principle, as our people long ago found that unless they ate *daikon* pickles with their rice they could not consume the latter daily without suffering from indigestion. Carrots, burdock, cucumbers, melons, potatoes (sweet and white), yams, taro, lotus-roots, cabbage, squashes, egg-plants, and mushrooms are freely eaten, while many dainty

dishes unfamiliar to you are enjoyed,—such as
the young fronds of the brake, the tender sprouts
of the bamboo (taken just as they appear above
the surface of the ground in the spring), and the
bulb of the lily—the variety you know as the
"tiger lily." Now that we have seeds from England and America there is indeed scarcely a vegetable grown in these countries that we have not
made our own. I am thinking now of tomatoes,
Indian corn, asparagus, and celery, all of which are
welcomed in Japanese cuisine.

Wherever one is within reach of a city market,
a good supply of fruit is obtainable—and here again
the importation of foreign varieties is evidenced
by the peach, the pear, and the apple, and by
strawberries, gooseberries, and grapes, the indigenous stocks being generally inferior. When we
add to these our own delicious plums (not the
umé) and many kinds of native oranges, our *biwa*,
or loquat, and the luscious persimmon of the
autumn, you will see that we do not suffer for lack
of refreshing fruit.

The ordinary beverage is tea—what Emerson
calls the cordial of nations—of which there are
grades ranging in price from five cents to five
dollars a pound, so that the poor and the rich can
take their choice. Black tea is of comparatively
recent introduction and is but little used in Japanese households. When we simply speak of "tea,"
we mean our green tea, and by this is understood
a natural or pure, and not a coloured, tea, as is

so often mistakenly thought in this country,—
the colour being due to the process of curing.

The intoxicating drink of the country is *saké*,
brewed from rice and quite strong in alcoholic
content (fifteen or sixteen per cent.). Beer is
imported as well as brewed in Japan. The same
is true of wine, though a smaller quantity of this
is consumed. I may add that drunkenness is not
as apparent with us as it is in America, and that
with us, as with you, there is a movement against
all social drinking.

A labouring man can get his food for about
twenty *sen*[1] a day, and he can feed his family
(wife and a couple of children) on an additional
thirty *sen*. In fact, if he makes eighty *sen* and his
wife thirty *sen*, a sum total of a *yen* and ten *sen*
a day, they can keep a little house with a couple
of rooms, paying a rent of three *yen* per month,
read newspapers (for the humblest can read), take
daily baths (a racial necessity), send their children to school (for education is compulsory), and
put in the savings bank two or three *yen* a month.
Does this sound delectably Arcadian?—and yet of
families like these the duties of modern citizenship
are demanded—viz., the payment of taxes, service

---

[1] The *yen* is the standard of our monetary system and in
exchange is equal to about fifty cents in American money; but its
purchasing value in Japan is practically equivalent to that of the
dollar. You can readily see that it becomes only half as great
in the purchase of imported goods. As in your currency one
hundred cents make a dollar, so in ours one hundred *sen* make
one *yen*.

in the army, and attendance at school on the part of the children.

In such a cursory review of Japanese economy as I am giving, there is little space for a discussion of our national finance. Suffice it to say that our taxation and debt have increased heavily since our war with Russia. The latter now amounts to about 2,650,000,000 *yen*, an increase of 2,100,-000,000 as compared with the debt prior to the war. This increase is roughly the price we have paid or are still paying for victory. Whereas the *per capita* debt of our people was less than eleven *yen* in 1904, it is now about forty *yen*. Our taxes were 150,000,000 *yen* before the war; now they are 330,000,000. The chief sources of revenue are the taxes on liquors, land, and income. We get about 50,000,000 *yen* from the customs. A very important part of our revenue is derived from public undertakings and State property (about 126,000,000 *yen*), and from postal, telegraphic, and telephone service (about 50,000,000 *yen*); also from the profits of salt, camphor, and tobacco monopolies (about 50,000,000 *yen*). The total annual revenue of the Empire has lately been approximating the sum of 560,000,000 *yen*. How can the people bear such taxation? Are they simply crushed, so that they cannot raise their voice?

Heavy burdens of taxation and military service, without corresponding improvement in economic welfare and morals, may be fruitful of social danger. We are aware of this. Fortunately, thus

far, our country has been free from proletariat
revolts or labour trouble of any magnitude. Socialistic propaganda is feared, and only last year we
had the saddening sight of a band of anarchists
arrested and condemned on the charge of high
treason. They were called socialists, but not in
the sense that our Government itself may be
called State-socialistic—neither in the sense in
which Professor Hart in his recent book, *The
Obvious Orient*, says: "Never was there such a
socialistic community, such an ant-hill of human
beings, busy, contented, and all interested in each
other's affairs. Socialism," he adds, "is realised
in Japan."

This blunder in designating the worst class of
destructive anarchists "socialists," has done no
little harm. The very term "socialism" has been
dragged into ill repute, even when it is used in
its noblest and most scientific sense, and has
also given a false impression to the outside
world regarding the justice of our courts in imposing what was naturally thought to be excessive
punishment.

With the increasing concentration of population
in cities, with the development of the modern mill
system, labour questions will become more and
more serious. Whether we can progress from our
still prevailing feudalistic and artistic stage of
economy to its modern form, without undergoing
the throes of democratic upheavals, it is impossible
to say.

In the meantime the population is growing rapidly. In 1907 it was 49,000,000. At present (1912) it is about 52,000,000. Fifty years hence it should reach the dignity of nine ciphers. Can the land support so many? Certainly more intensive agriculture will yield more food. With the rise of prices, the margin of cultivation will extend to land as yet entirely neglected. A rough estimate points to the possibility of doubling our present arable area. Another source of relief will come from emigration into our new dominions— Formosa, Saghalien, and Korea, and the leased territory of Manchuria. The success we have realised in the administration of Formosa will be recounted elsewhere. I will simply say that in eight years, under the guidance of the late Viscount Kodama as Governor-General and his colleague Baron Goto as Civil Governor, that island was brought from a state of wide-spread disturbance created by the bandits and of economic inefficiency, to a condition of stable government and self-supporting finance. Korea, despite some mistakes which every colonial power makes at first in dealing with a subjugated people, any impartial critic will admit, is now better governed than it ever was. We are bent upon making our rule there, economically as well as politically, successful and praiseworthy. Since 1906 the Imperial treasury has spent nearly 200,000,000 *yen* in the tranquilisation of that peninsula, but it will not be long before the land will be made self-supporting financially, and it will also afford homes for our overflowing population. Both Korea and Formosa can raise enough rice to feed the whole Japanese nation. They are both possessed of mineral resources—coal, oil, iron, gold—which await further development. Still another source of relief is destined to come from industries. We are driven into manufacturing channels by force of circumstances. The time-honoured respect for agriculture must give way to the adoption of twentieth-century industries. In the abundance of water, we are assured a cheap source of power; in the growth of population, an ample supply of labour. Some nations are looking askance upon the industrialisation of Japan—slow as it is (how slow!)—and condemn it as another instance of "accursed Japanese competition in the East." On the whole, however, the present commercial treaties do not lay any serious hindrance in the way of our progress, and if we cannot accelerate its speed, we must not blame others. How smoothly we can effect, in a few years, a transition which it has taken Europe several decades to accomplish, is just now a very grave social problem.

While, by means of education in agriculture, of co-operative popular banks, of young men's associations, of the consolidation of small, scattered plots into larger farms, of the construction of irrigation canals and roads, we are solving, in part, the vexed problems of country-life, at the same time by old-age pensions, compensation for

injuries in factories, universal insurance, and labour
laws, we will try to mitigate the suffering of the
transition.

It is too early to predict with any approach to
accuracy how far our new legislation and our
effort to maintain the old moral relations between
employer and the employé, between landlord and
tenant, will avert the evil that has worked havoc
in other lands. I am afraid, however, that our
endeavour will not accomplish much, unless we
take the question more seriously, and the reason
why it is not more seriously discussed is because
modern industry is still a new thing with us,
whereas the older industries are largely of the
nature of art-crafts, and labour as such plays but
a subordinate part.

A bare enumeration of our well-known industries—such as pottery, cloisonné, embroidery,
lacquer, ivory and wood-carving, inlaying and
hammer-work—will be sufficient to show you
that they are handwork executed by individuals.

The arts and crafts are pursued not by mere
artisans but by artists, and usually on a small scale,
i. e., under the direct control of the masters. You
have heard of the porcelain-maker, Seifu. His
workshop is his private house, where he and his
family live and share with his half-dozen pupils
food and lodging. You look in vain for large
kilns; but see only two or three small ones under
which the master himself may be building the fire.
His products are not turned out *en masse*. Every

imperfect article is discarded, and those that pass
inspection bear his name and the impress of his
personality.   The same is true of the productions
of other master workmen.   Labour—especially
mechanical labour and drudgery—forms only a
small fraction of their exertion, and even in the
execution of inferior artisans, labour is not degraded into a mechanical process.   It is for this
artistic element of our manual work that Japanese
manufacture is most admired by the West, and I
assure you it will not be lost; but will be kept up as
a sacred inheritance of the race, in spite of commercial production on a large scale.   Yet, of the
rank and file of our handicraftsmen, it is not fair to
demand, in this age of search for gold and struggle
for bread, that they alone remain uncontaminated.
We cannot ask martyrdom of others for our own
enjoyment.

As for manufacturing and other industrial enterprises, I am glad to say these are growing steadily
and on the whole sanely.   Near the close of the
war with China and of that with Russia, there were
those usual indications of industrial expansion
which always work disaster in the social economy of a victorious nation.   The Government,
well aware that this danger was imminent, took
every pains to prevent it by cautioning the public
through the press, educating them in the general
principles of *post-bellum* finance by pointing to
the experiences of other countries.   Had it not
been for this precaution, calamity might have

ensued in our business circles. As it was, we came
out better, perhaps, than most of those nations who
have passed through a similar experience. Naturally there was a sudden rise in industrial activity
after each war, amounting to a boom, in 1907, but
followed by two-and-a-half years of depression,
after which normal conditions again prevailed.

The field for financial investments during those
years lay, and still largely lies, in banking, cotton
mills, electric works, mines, fisheries, manufactures,
and shipping, and also in smaller trades.

Roughly, one may say some 400,000,000 *yen*
represent the annual capital invested in the country—equivalent perhaps to about one-eighth of
the amount invested by the United States, a fourth
or fifth of that of Great Britain, France, or Germany. Small as is our gross investment, if we compare it with the estimated wealth of the country—
24,000,000,000 *yen* in round numbers—it forms
over one and six-tenths per cent. as against one
and four-tenths per cent. in the United States.

Of our large industries, conducted in mills, I
shall give three features which may strike you as
different from yours: (1) the unfortunate absence
of iron, (2) lack of skilled labour, (3) predominance of female labour.

As an indication of the insignificance of our iron
industry, there is only one steel foundry in the
whole country, and that managed at a loss by the
Government. Of some 450,000 tons of pig-iron
used in the country, two-thirds are imported.

Regarding skilled labour, factory-work being new to the people, we have not yet had time to train first-rate operatives. Compared with the output, experience in shipyards, arsenals, and steel foundries shows that it takes two or three Japanese to do the work of one European in a European factory. Careful experiments in cotton mills have shown that three hundred Japanese operatives are required where two hundred English are sufficient, and where one hundred Americans do the same work. As yet, there seems to be no immediate fear of an industrial Yellow Peril!

As respects female labour, its efficiency as compared with that of Western countries is very much in our favour. Especially is this true in the case of silk-culture, silk-reeling, weaving, tea-picking, straw-braiding, etc. Among some 10,500 factories employing not less than ten operatives each, thirty-eight per cent. of the employés are males, the remaining sixty-two per cent. are women. These operatives constitute an industrial army of eight hundred thousand, of which five hundred thousand are of the weaker sex.

Child labour is disproportionately large. In some mills twenty per cent. of the labour is done by children under fourteen years of age, but this is an extreme case, though the proportion of five per cent. is not unusual. In some kinds of work, infants under ten years of age are employed. Though as many as ninety-eight per cent. of the children of school age (six to fourteen years) are actually attending schools, a considerable portion of these do so just long enough to follow the letter of the compulsory education law, coming to school the minimum number of hours.

The conditions of labour in the factories are far from satisfactory—in many of them they are positively disgraceful. Here, again, the Government has made quite a careful study of the question and has repeatedly submitted to the Parliament a draft of factory legislation. Only last winter (1911) a law was enacted, with emendations, however, which waive some vital provisions. It was thought by the legislators that a rigid enforcement of a stringent factory law might kill our infant industries; for, be it remembered, our industrial system is about a century behind that of England. The spirit of the said law is gradually to prepare our industries during the coming fifteen years, for the complete adoption of all the requirements of hygiene and education. Any seed of reform, however, is better than no seed, and this enactment will lead to closer inspection and encourage further improvement in our mills. As the new law forbids the employment of children under nine in factories, and the working of women at night, a starting point is provided for a better condition of things.

Industrial progress is so intimately connected with foreign trade that, without understanding the state of the one, it is impossible to comprehend that of the other. A generation ago (1876), our total foreign trade (exports and imports together) was slightly over 50,000,000 *yen*, or one and one-half *yen* per head of population, and by 1910 it had risen to over 922,000,000 or over eighteen *yen* per capita. Of late the amount of imports has been steadily exceeding that of exports, owing to large purchases made abroad during the war. The excess of imports, necessitating the payment of the balance in gold, together with the need of sending about seventy-eight millions as interest on our foreign loans—public, municipal, and company— has been draining the country of gold specie, and one of the most serious questions with which we must cope is how to make good its possible deficiency in the near future.

When the country was opened to foreign trade, sixty years ago, it was naturally carried on entirely by foreigners. That tradition lasted long enough, and so of late years, in the natural course of development, the Japanese have been gradually taking the export and import trade into their own hands,—much to the chagrin of those who were accustomed to look upon it as their prerogative. Whereas, in 1906, forty-six per cent. of the foreign trade was transacted by the Japanese themselves, in 1910 the proportion rose to fifty-four per cent., and every year will and must see its progression. We think it only proper to designate this progress, but in the English language, which is in current use among foreign merchants in Japan, it is described as "the Japs stealing our business,"—a curious use of the verb unknown to

Johnson or even Webster when they wrote their dictionaries.

To return from etymology to commerce, the chief articles of import are cotton and wool, iron and steel, sugar, grain, machinery, chemicals, and oils. The United States supply us with nearly all of our imported flour (wheat), sole leather, kerosene oil, and a large amount of raw cotton, as well as iron and steel.

Among the items of our export, the principal are silk, cotton goods, copper, coal, tea, marine products, grain, drugs, chemicals, and matches. The United States is by far our largest customer. Nearly all our tea finds its way thither, and I can testify that the Government enforces stringent laws against artificially colouring or adulterating it. Then, yearly, about three million dollars' worth of porcelain is brought to the United States, together with a similar amount of straw-braids. But beyond comparison the greatest product of our land exported to America is silk, of which nearly a hundred million dollars' worth is annually bought by your country, supplying over sixty per cent. of all your silken demands.

Among the countries from which we make our purchases, British India holds the first place with its supply of raw cotton, then follow Great Britain and China; the United States stands as fourth in the list, with Germany steadily catching up. It has been said the Kaiser's subjects will prove the keenest competitors of America, in the Far East.

As for the countries which buy of us, by far the most important is the United States, she being the only customer whose purchases have regularly been above one hundred and twenty million *yen*, whereas China comes next with eighty or ninety millions, followed by France, which trails far behind.

Unfortunately and often unjustly, but alas sometimes justly!—our commercial morality, especially in dealings with foreigners, has been assailed. The articles sent out by our merchants have often fallen short of the standard of the sample, their weight has proved lighter than stated in the invoice, or their length less; then, too, they have lacked uniformity in workmanship. I believe there may too frequently have been intentional dishonesty; but it has far oftener been true that uniformity of standard was impracticable, since many of our export goods are products of hand-labour and therefore inevitably subject to variation—a fact well understood and allowed for in the transactions of our home-trade, but not sufficiently considered by foreign importers accustomed to machine-made goods.

To avert further discredit of our commercial morality, and to prevent dishonest practices, guilds have been formed in all parts of the country and in all trades. Their main function is to examine manufactured goods destined for export, and to condemn such as are found lacking in quality, weight, or length. Such goods are even publicly turned. Of these industrial guilds there are at present about six thousand. There is a special conditioning house in Yokohama, where all silk intended for export must be examined before being shipped abroad.

Commercial dishonesty, so often branded by foreign merchants as peculiarly Japanese, is but a passing phase. Experience teaches that "Honesty is the best policy," and this kind of morality is a virtue easily learned. As a burnt child has a wholesome fear of fire, so does a tradesman find that it does not pay to cheat. Moreover, what nation can throw the first stone at another for breach of honesty? In a recent issue of the *Century Magazine* (April, 1912), a well-known American writer gives his countrymen's disregard of the observance of the terms of contract as a reason why the United States does not make greater advance in its trade with Italy. The impotence of American insurance companies to meet their obligations after the earthquake and fire in San Francisco, is a notorious illustration of business immorality. Examples like these may be multiplied, but they do not convince us that Americans as a nation are deficient in moral sense —neither does the immoral practice of some individual Japanese merchants prove that honesty is foreign to our soil. The truth is that all are alike sinners, but we all find comfort in believing that we are rising upward, making stepping-stones of our own dead selves.

Commerce, apparently sordid and selfish, is evidently the handmaid of a higher principle. The time has passed of which Goldsmith sang that "honour sinks when commerce long prevails." On the contrary, it is raising the international standard of morality, teaching fair play and a square deal, uniting nations and peoples, and bridging space. As, with the growth of a nation's commerce, its monetary system comes to be changed and expanded, so will its concept of moral values and its media of mental exchange be modified and enlarged and brought into unity with world standards. The empire of trade encompasses the globe, and men through gainful effort are learning that by argosies of merchandise, and not by Dreadnoughts, will be decided the final victory on the race-course of nations. As all roads, primarily military, led to Rome, so all trade routes now lead to Peace. The economic interests of our people are in themselves a strong argument for the maintenance of peace in the Far East, and notably with our large creditor and chief customer, the United States.

CHAPTER IX

JAPAN AS COLONISER

HISTORY has repeatedly shown "how wide the limits stand between a splendid and a happy land." As with individuals, so with nations, greatness and happiness lie, alas! too often at opposite poles. What belongs to the one may be shared by the other; but, as a rule, he who plucks the flower must forego the fruit. Falsely or truly (it is not now my purpose to discuss the moral or political issues involved in colonial enterprise), modern nations vie with one another to express their greatness and splendour in territorial expansion, or else in ethnic colonisation.

With the acquisition of the small island of Formosa in 1895, Japan joined the ranks of colonial powers. Since then, she has added the southern half of the island of Saghalien by the treaty of Portsmouth in 1905 and the kingdom of Korea, now officially called Chôsen, by annexation in 1911. Besides these territories, Japan holds the small province of Kwang-tung in the Liao Tung peninsula, as well as a long and narrow strip of land along the South Manchurian railroad. These last two were leased from China in continuation of the contract which that nation had made with Russia before the war.

In recounting what Japan has done as a coloniser, I shall for several reasons devote my time to a review of what she has achieved in Formosa. In the first place, because it is the first, and may be called the only colony with which we have had experience of any length; in the second place, because it has served the purpose of educating us in the art of colonisation; and in the third place, because the administration of this island forms a precedent for the government of later acquisitions. To these three reasons may be appended one other—namely, that I can speak of Formosa from a long and personal connection with it; and to me the last is here the strongest and the best reason.

Before proceeding further, let us refresh our memory regarding geography.

Scattered over a wide surface of the globe are about a dozen places christened with the Portuguese term Formosa—"Beautiful." It is needless to add that the word is of Latin origin, despite the fact that it is not to be found in the ancient or in the mediæval list of *nomina geographica*. Among the modern places bearing the name, some are so small that many gazetteers do not condescend to notice their existence.

There is an immense territory of the name of

Formosa covering 42,000 square miles, in the north of Argentine. Then there is a little town of the same name on the north-eastern coast of Brazil, as well as one on the southern coast of South Africa. Among the group of the Bissagos islands, is a Formosa. In the interior of Europe, too, on the Russian border, near the Danube, is a village of the same name. On a map of Asia, we find Mount Formosa, Formosa River, Formosa Strait, Formosa Banks, etc. On the American continent, in Bruce County, Ontario, there is a settlement called Formosa. In the slightly modified form of Formoso, there is a banking and post village in Kansas (Jewell Co.), and in the still more modified Spanish form of Hermosa, one meets with the same name in New Mexico (Sierra Co.), in South Dakota (Custer Co.), and in California.

Thus, in Europe, Asia, Africa, North and South America are found Formosas. But the Formosa which is the subject of my discourse, is, I suppose, the best known of them all. It is an island, lying a short distance off the eastern coast of China. Its area is 14,000 square miles, being about 240 miles in length, with the Tropic of Cancer crossing through its centre. Of volcanic formation, ranges of slaty and schistose mountains, mainly of the Tertiary age, run through its length, some of their peaks towering as high as 13,000 feet. The eastern coast is rocky and steep, affording very few landing places; but the western coast consists of flat, fertile, alluvial plains, where are raised rice, sugar cane, tea, ramie, bananas, oranges, and sweet potatoes. Among the mountains grow gigantic trees of various kinds, the most important being camphor and *hinoki* (*Thuya obtusa.*)

The island is as beautiful as it is fertile. The Portuguese navigators, as they sailed along the eastern coast, were so charmed by its precipitous but wooded mountains, its fantastic rocks and the foaming billows which dash against them, that they put down in their log-book their favorite name of "Ihla Formosa." From the other side, the Chinese, who can quite easily reach the western coast in their junks—the distance from Foochow to a Formosan port is only a little over a hundred miles—were struck with its beauty, as from their anchorage they saw hillsides inhabited and cultivated, and they called it Taiwan, the "Terraced Bay," which is still the official designation of the island. The Japanese, too, had long known of it, and in times past venturesome spirits used to frequent it, but in later days only the poetical name "Takasago" (The High Sandy Tract) remained, suggesting in popular fancy a land of lotus-eaters.

Our knowledge of Takasago was as fanciful as the account given of the island by that famous literary impostor, George Psalmanazar. A Frenchman by birth (born about 1679), he was taken from Holland to England by the chaplain of a Scotch regiment, and was there received with much curiosity and honour because of his well-maintained pretension of being a native of Formosa. His amusing treatise on *A History and Description of the Island of Formosa off the Coast of China*, published in London in 1704, still remains an amazing document of fabrication. The man evidently showed no lack of intellectual ingenuity when he constructed an entire linguistic system including grammar and vocabulary. It is only to be expected that his description did not tally with facts. Our acquaintance with Formosa, however, was not much better. But it came quite forcibly and unpleasantly upon us in 1874, when the report spread that the savages of Southern Formosa had slaughtered some Japanese sailors who were wrecked on its coast. China at that time held sway over the island. For the murder of her subjects, Japan demanded satisfaction of China, but, as the Celestial Government evaded responsibility, we sent an army to the island itself. It is interesting to notice that a number of American officers at first joined in this expedition; but, being warned by their Government to observe strict neutrality, they reluctantly left our service. After subjugating the hostile tribe, our army left the island, China in the meantime offering to pay for damages. Our interest in Formosa then ceased, and nothing was done towards its conquest or even towards securing its trade.

More than twenty years later, when the war between China and Japan came to an end, Formosa was most unexpectedly brought into prominence. When Japan proposed that China should cede the island, we were not at all sure that the suggestion would be regarded with favour. But the Chinese plenipotentiary, Li Hung-Chang, took up the proposition, as though it were wise on the part of his country to be freed from an encumbrance, and he even commiserated Japan for acquiring it. He pointed out that the island was not amenable to good government: (1) that brigandage could never be exterminated; (2) that the practice of smoking opium was too deep-rooted and wide-spread among the people to eradicate; (3) that the climate was not salubrious; and (4) that the presence of head-hunting tribes was a constant menace to economic development. The island, somewhat like Sicily, had, in the course of its history, been subject to the flags of various nations. Holland, Spain, and China ruled it at different times; a Hungarian nobleman once dominated it; and at one time Japanese pirates had practically usurped supreme power over it. In 1884, the French under the celebrated Admiral Courbet planted the tricolor on its shores, where it waved for eight months. Such instability in government is enough to demoralise any people; but among the inhabitants themselves there were elements which put law and order to naught.

If these were the main causes of chronic misrule or absence of any rule in Formosa, let us see what Japan has done.

In accordance with the stipulation of the treaty

of Shimonoseki, one of our generals, Count Kabayama, was dispatched as Governor-General of
Formosa.   In that capacity, he was about to land
on the island with a large army, when he was met
by the Chinese plenipotentiary at the port of
Kelung, and in an interview which took place on
board the steamer *Yokohama Maru*, the 17th of
April, 1895, it was arranged that a landing should
be effected without opposition.   This marked the
first occupation of the island by our troops.
There were at that time some Imperial Chinese
soldiers still remaining in the island, and they
were ordered to disarm and leave the country.
Many did so, but a few remained to oppose our
advance; there were also a few patriots who did
not feel ready to accept our terms—not prepared
to accept alien rule,—and these either went from
the island or took up arms against us.   The so-
called patriots proclaimed a republic, one of the
very few republics ever started in Asia.   Tang
Ching-Sung was elected president.   The republic
of Formosa lasted three weeks, during which
mobocracy and deviltry in all its forms reigned supreme, leaving behind no evidence of its existence
other than some postage stamps valuable for
collectors!   At this time the professional brigands
took advantage of the general disturbance to ply
their trade. Peaceful citizens suffered more from the
hands of their own countrymen—that is, from
Chinese troops and brigands—than they did from
us.   Evidence of this lies in the fact that, as our

army approached the different towns, it was everywhere received with open arms as a deliverer from
robbery and slaughter.   As for Tang Ching-Sung,
he fled to China, as did also some of the wealthiest
inhabitants, although many of these, learning of
the security enjoyed under Japanese rule, have
since returned.

Though the island was pacified, no one knew
what would happen next.   We did not understand
the character of the people.   Very few Japanese
could speak Formosan, and fewer Formosans
could speak Japanese.   There was naturally
mutual distrust and suspicion.   The bandits
abounded everywhere.   Under these conditions
military rule was the only form of government that
could be adopted until better assurance could be
obtained of the disposition of the people.   To
carry out a military régime, it was calculated
that some ten million *yen* (five million dollars)
would be needed yearly.   Out of this necessary
sum only three million *yen* could be obtained in
the island by taxation and from other sources of
revenue.   The balance had to be defrayed by
the Imperial, that is by the Japanese, exchequer.
Now, in those years, an annual appropriation of
six or seven million *yen*, to be spent in an island
far from home, with no immediate prospect of
return, was a heavy burden for the rather limited
finances of Japan.   We know how land values are
rising everywhere.   Even in Africa, England had
to pay very much more than she expected she

would have to, in getting land in the south; and I think Italy has by this time found Tripoli rather more expensive than she at first anticipated. A colony that looks at a distance like the goose that lays the golden egg, on nearer approach, and especially when you have to pay the bills, often proves to be a white elephant. So among us, impatient people, infatuated with *gloire politique*, who had expected great things and great benefits to come from Formosa, began to clamour for greater thrift, and some of the very best publicists went even so far as to propose that the island should be sold back to China or to some other Power. To remedy this state of affairs, in the course of some thirty months governors were changed no less than three times.

The first Governor-General was Count Kabayama, known as a hero of the Chino-Japanese War; the second was no less a man than Prince Katsura, of international fame as our Prime-Minister during the war with Russia; and the third was General Nogi, of Port Arthur renown. Finding that the country could ill afford such a luxury as a colony, the Parliament of Japan cut down its appropriation of six or seven million *yen* payable from the national treasury by about one-third, thus reducing the subsidy to only four millions. Now who would accept a position held by such a galaxy of talents, but now reduced financially to two-thirds of its former prestige? Only a man of unbounded resource, of keen per-

ception and quick decision—or else only a second
or third-rate man—would accept such a place.
Japan is forever to be congratulated on finding the
right man at the right time for the right place.
Viscount Kodama, who, as a member of the General Staff, had made a study of the Formosan problem, was ready to accept the governorship and the
task of putting to rights the bankrupt housekeeping of the colony.   I am afraid that this name, so
well known among us, is much less familiar in
America.   Perhaps you can best remember it, if I
tell you that he was the real brains of the Russo-
Japanese War.   In the choice of his assistant, the
civil governor, he made the discovery, as he called
it, of a man who proved himself a true right hand,
and who in efficiency actually exceeded his most
sanguine expectations.   I refer to Baron Goto,
who in the last cabinet held the post of Minister of
Communications and was President of the Railway
Board.   Until he was made civil governor of
Formosa under Kodama, he had been known as
an expert on hygiene, having been a physician.
The advent of these two men in Formosa marked
a new era in our colonial administration.   Upon
entering their new duties early in 1898, the first
thing they did was to bring about a practical sus-
pension of military rule; at least, it was made subservient to civil administration.   Military rule is
apt to become harsh, and to the Chinese especially,
who are not accustomed to respect the army, it is
doubly harsh.

Kodama and Goto, to whom English colonial service was an inspiring example, surprised the official world by a summary discharge of over one thousand public servants of high and low degree. They collected about them men known and tried for their knowledge and integrity. They used often to say: "It is the man who rules and not red tape." In an old and well-settled country "red tape" may be convenient, but in a new colony great latitude of power and initiative must be left to individual men. I emphasise this point because these men, I mean the Governor-General and the civil governor, attributed their success largely to the selection and use of right men.

When General Kodama went to Formosa, he found brigandage still rampant, and with military rule in abeyance there was some likelihood of its becoming worse. To offset this, the constabulary department was organised and made efficient by proper care in choosing men for the police and by educating them in the rudiments of law and industries, to prepare them for their difficult and delicate tasks. Exceedingly arduous are their callings, for these policemen are required not only to represent law and order but are expected to be teachers as well. They keep account, for instance, of every resident of the island, and they watch over every man and woman who smokes opium; they must become acquainted with children of school-age and know which children go to school and which do not. Our Formosan police are expected to instruct the people how to take care of themselves, especially in regard to pests and about disinfection. They perform many duties that would scarcely be required even of the Trooper Police of Australia. They often live in villages where there are no Japanese other than the members of their own families. Of course, they must know the Formosan language and speak it.

Now, under civil administration, armies were not mobilised against brigands, and if there was any trouble, it was the policemen who had to go cope with the situation. The brigands were first invited to subject themselves to law, and if they surrendered their arms, they were assured not only of protection but of means of subsistence. Not a few leaders took the hint and were given special privileges. Those who resisted to the end were necessarily treated as disturbers and as criminals. Twelve years ago the brigands were so powerful that the capital of Formosa, Taihoku (Taipeh), was assaulted by them; but in the last ten years we have scarcely heard of them. I went to Taihoku ten years ago, and, whenever I went a few miles out of the city, half-a-dozen policemen armed with rifles used to accompany me for my protection. For the last five or six years a young girl could travel unmolested from one end of the island to the other—of course, outside of savage or aboriginal districts, of which I shall speak later.

Thus, what Li Hung-Chang said in the conference of Shimonoseki turned out to be of little

consequence. According to him, brigandage was
something inherent in the social structure of Formosa. He said it was something that could not be
uprooted in the island; yet here is Formosa to-day
with not a trace of it. That is one of the first
things which was accomplished by Japan as a
coloniser.

Then, another great evil in the island, to which
Li Hung-Chang alluded, was the smoking of
opium. When the island was taken over, this
subject was much discussed by our people. Some
said opium-smoking must be summarily and
unconditionally abolished by law. Others said:
"No, no, let it alone; it is something from which
the Chinese cannot free themselves; let them
smoke and smoke themselves to death." What
took Baron Goto for the first time to Formosa was
the mission of studying this question from a medical standpoint, and the plan he drew up was for
the gradual suppression of the evil. The *modus
operandi* was the control of the production by the
Government; because, if the Government mono-
polises the production and manufacture of opium,
it can restrict the quantity as well as improve the
quality so as to make it less harmful. Smuggling
was watched and punished. A long list of all
those who were addicted to this habit was compiled, and only those who were confirmed smokers
were given permission to buy the drug. Children
and those who had never smoked were not
allowed to buy, much less to begin the use of,

opium, and strict surveillance was instituted by the police, who, as I mentioned before, know every man in the villages to which they are appointed. The annual returns made of confirmed smokers and of the quantity consumed in the island, show a distinct and gradual decrease. In 1900 those addicted to the habit numbered in round figures 170,000, or 6.3 per cent. of the population. As the older smokers die off, younger ones do not come to take their place; so there is a constant diminution. In five years the number decreased to 130,000 or 3.5 per cent. of the population. We think this is the only right way to deal with this vice. It may interest you, perhaps, to know that American commissioners from the Philippine Islands came to study our system, and that they expressed much satisfaction with its results. Thus, the second evil which Li Hung-Chang said was ineradicable in Formosa, has been greatly weakened and seems destined to disappear.

What man has built up, man can destroy. The artificial habit of opium-smoking can be discouraged by law. But there are formidable natural enemies which confront the sound economic development of the island. I mean its sanitary disadvantages, especially some prevalent forms of disease—above all, malaria and bubonic plague and tropical dysentery.

What money and the spirit of enterprise have undertaken has so often been largely nullified by a small mosquito. There are no less than eight kinds of Anopheles, responsible yearly for at least twenty per cent. of all cases of sickness, many of which end in death.

Chiefly owing, directly or indirectly, to malaria, the population of Formosa has never been very great. It appears that in pre-Japanese days, the population of the island was recruited by immigrants from China. Only lately is the birth-rate slowly showing a net increase over and above the death-rate. The mortality from malaria has been roughly estimated at three-and-a-half per thousand of population. Among the Japanese, this rate is diminishing, but not among the Chinese. The fact that new-comers from Japan are so easily attacked, is the greatest drawback to colonising the island. Sugar-mills, for want of sufficient labour, have imported Japanese; but usually one-third of them cannot be depended upon—that is to say, the efficiency of labour may be said to be diminished by one-third on account of malaria. When I went to Panama last winter, nothing commanded my respect for the American work conducted there more than Colonel Goethals's system of sanitation. As I meditated upon the careful detail of medical supervision in the Canal Zone, I naturally compared the results with the situation in Formosa, and thought if we could afford to spend as much money as the Canal Commission does, if Taiwan were smaller in size, if it could be brought under military administration, and if there were no rice-fields—then we might succeed better in our crusade against the insect. Even under present conditions every effort is made to drive out malaria; and in the meantime an army of scientists is advancing against the Anopheles in biological, physiological, and chemical columns, with clearly visible results. In the barracks outside of Taihoku, there is little malaria. In the town itself, the improved drainage—a sewerage system having been constructed of the stones of which, in Chinese days, the city walls were built—has evidently contributed toward the same end. So, also, has the good water supply, which has taken the place of wells and cisterns. Then, too, new building regulations enforce better ventilation and access to sunlight. In the principal cities, large portions of the town have been entirely rebuilt. I have heard it said by medical men that if the Japanese coming to Taiwan make their domicile in the capital (Taihoku) and remain there, they are quite free from malaria. Other cities, notably Tainan in the south, are making sanitary improvements, so that they will probably show a similar immunity within a few years. As for the island at large, owing to the fact that irrigation is the very life of rice-culture, there are necessarily unlimited breeding-places for mosquitoes. Consequently, general hygienic progress, such as Dr. Boyce describes with just pride in writing of the West Indies, will not be so easy to accomplish in Formosa.

Smallpox and cholera have been practically eliminated from the list of prevalent diseases.

With the bubonic plague, the Government has had
a pretty hard fight. Dr. Takaki, who has been
chief of sanitation for some years, has devoted his
energy and scientific knowledge to the eradication
of it by every possible means, so that there has
been a steady and regular decrease of pest since
1906.

To give an idea of the decline and fall of the
sway of the Black Death, I will state in round
numbers the death-rates for the following years:

1905	4,500
1906	3,350
1907	3,250
1908	2,700
1909	1,300
1910	1,030
1911	20

Though we still suffer from its sporadic appearance, we have every promise of its near extinction.
At present, the most troublesome disease is tropical dysentery, which, if not usually fatal, is extremely persistent and enervating.

Allow me to insert here a remark about the
rinderpest. Some ten years ago, its ravages were
so great that we feared we might lose all our water
buffaloes and bullocks; but, thanks to vigilance and
inoculation, we have for the last five years been
having only a few hundred deaths annually,
whereas they used to be counted by thousands.

Thus the third great impediment which **Li Hung-Chang** thought would prohibit progress in Taiwan is being steadily overcome, and now I reach the fourth and last obstruction,—namely the presence of head-hunting tribes, allied to the head-hunters of Borneo made familiar by the pen of Professor Haddon. These Malay people are the oldest known inhabitants of the island. That they are not autochthonous is evident from the tradition, current among many tribes, that their ancestors arrived in a boat from some distant quarter. At present they number about one hundred and fifteen thousand. They are in a very primitive state of social life. The only art with which they are acquainted is agriculture, and that of a very rude sort—what in Europe is called spade-culture, or what scientific men dub "Hack-Kultur" (hoe culture), as opposed to agriculture proper,—a kind of farming which Mr. Morgan in his *Primitive Society* first explained as a precursor of real agriculture, in which the plough is used. They raise upland rice, millet, peas, beans, and some common vegetables, such as pumpkins and radishes. They do not know the art of fertilising land, and they look upon manuring as an act of contamination.

They have scarcely any clothing; a few tribes wear none. Their houses are usually built of wood and bamboo and are roofed with slate or straw. Scrupulously clean in their personal habits, bathing frequently, they keep their huts very

neat. In character, they are brave and fierce
when roused to ire; otherwise, friendly and child-
like. They must have occupied the alluvial
plains of the coast in years gone by, but were
driven upward by the Chinese immigrants, Hakkas
and Haklos, until they now dwell among almost
inaccessible heights.

What concerns us most nearly in their manner
of life, is their much venerated custom of conse-
crating any auspicious occasion by obtaining a
human head. If there is a wedding in prospect,
the young man cannot marry unless he brings in
a head, and the susceptibility of the human heart
being much the same in savagery as in civilisation,
this is a tremendous spur to head-hunting. A
funeral cannot be observed without a head.
Indeed all celebrations of any importance must be
graced with it. Where a bouquet would be used
by you, a grim human head, freshly cut, is the
essential decoration at their banquet. Moreover, a man's courage is tested by the number of
heads he takes, and respect for him grows with his
achievements. Thus the gruesome objects adorn
the so-called skull-shelf, for the same reason that
lions' and stags' heads are the pride of a gentleman's hall. One sometimes comes across a hut,
near which is placed a tier of shelves ornamented
with heads in all stages of decay—the trophies of
some brave head-hunter!

The district where they roam is marked off by
outposts, which I shall soon describe. Like the

"Forbidden Territory" or *boma* in British East Africa, no one is allowed to enter the "Savage Boundary" without permit from the authorities. The importance of this decree will be obvious if I state that its area covers more than half of the island, and when the savages want a head, they steal down, hide themselves among the underbrush or among the branches of trees, and shoot the first unlucky man who passes by. I was told of one savage who had his rifle so placed on a support that he could shoot any person who happened to walk past a certain fixed distance and at a certain height. There he waited for days for somebody to come within range; and he succeeded in getting a head! With such people it is practically impossible to do anything. We have made repeated attempts to subjugate them; but so far we have not succeeded in doing as much damage to them as they have done to us.

During Chinese ascendency the Government built a line of military posts, somewhat like the *trocha*, of which one still sees remains in Cuba. But after we had tried different methods, we came at last to the use of electrically charged wire fences. At a safe distance from savage assaults, generally along the ridge of mountain ranges, posts about five feet high are planted at intervals of six or seven feet, and on them are strung four strong wires. On each side of the fence a space of some thirty feet or so is cleared of brush, so that any one approaching may be detected at once. All along the fence are block-houses, perhaps three, four or five in a mile, guarded by armed sentinels (usually Chinese trained as police), who are semi-volunteers. The most important feature of the fence is that the lowest wire has a strong electric current running through it. Such a wire fence stretches a distance of some three hundred miles. It costs thousands of dollars to keep it in order; yet every year we extend some miles farther into the savage district, so that their dominion is being more and more restricted to the tops of the mountains. When they are practically caged, we make overtures to them. We say, "If you come down and don't indulge in head-hunting, we will welcome you as brothers,"—because they are brothers. These Malay tribes resemble the Japanese more than they do the Chinese, and they themselves say of the Japanese that we are their kin and that the Chinese are their enemies. Because the Chinese wear queues, they think that their heads are especially made to be hunted. And now every year, as I say, we are getting better control over them by constantly advancing the fence, and owing to the fact that they are in want of salt, cut off as they are from the sea. Then we say, "We will give you salt if you will come down and give up your weapons." Thus tribe after tribe has recognised our power through the instrumentality of salt, and has submitted itself to Japanese rule. Here I may say, to the credit of these primitive men, that when once their promise of good behaviour is made, it is kept. When they submit themselves, we build them houses, give them agricultural tools and implements, give them land, and let them continue their means of livelihood in peace.

Thus I have dwelt in a very sketchy manner on the four points to which Li Hung-Chang, in the conference at Shimonoseki, alluded as great obstacles in the way of governing Formosa. What, now, is the result? At first we could not manage the colony with the money that we could raise in the island; every year we had to get some subsidy from the national treasury. It was thought that such a subsidy would be necessary until 1910. But by the development of Formosan industries—the better cultivation of rice, the improved production of Oolong tea, for which you are the best customer, the control of the camphor industry (for nearly all the camphor that you use, if not artificial, is produced in Formosa), the successful encouragement of cane culture, which has increased the output of sugar sixfold in the last ten years—by developing these industries, we can get money enough in the island to do all the work that is needed to be done there. An accurate cadastral survey made landed property secure, enhanced its value, and added indirectly to its taxpaying capacity. The consumption tax placed on sugar alone brings in more than one-third of the public revenue. The growth of Formosa's foreign trade has been such that the customs now return no mean sum. The administration of the Island has been so successful that it attained financial independence two years before the expiration of the term fixed for it.

There still remains much to be done. Irrigation work, for instance, is being carried out on a large scale. Then, there is the improvement of the harbours. Both in the north, at Kelung, and in the south, at Takao, commodious and deep harbours are now being constructed or improved. We have built a railroad from one end of the island to the other, but there is demand for further extention. Schools and hospitals are to be met with in every village and town, but more are needed. In all these things we think that we have succeeded quite well, especially when we compare our colony of Formosa with the experiments that other nations are making.

In giving this very rough sketch, I have only tried to show the general lines of policy pursued in the development of Formosa. Though the colony was at first thought to be a luxury, it is now a necessity to us. And the example that we have set for ourselves will be followed in our other colonies.

I may say that the general principle of our colonial policy in Formosa was, first of all, the defence of the island. Much is said about our increased navy. Some people in America think that we are enlarging our navy prompted by a dubious motive; but with the acquisition of Formosa, of the island of Saghalien, and of Korea, our coast-line has been greatly increased, and still the augmentation of our fleet is not sufficient for the proper defence of all our shores.

The second principle is the protection of property and life, and the dissemination of legal institutions—the rudimentary functions of a well ordered state. People unaccustomed to the protection of law feel as though it were despotism. But they will soon find that, after all, good government and good laws are the safeguard of social well-being, and we have to teach in Korea as well as in Formosa, what government is and what laws are.

You read now and then in the newspapers of arrests in Korea, and forthwith Japan is charged with being a cruel master. Let the world remember that a change of masters is rarely made without friction. It takes some time for a people to know that a jural state means enforcement of justice, and that this does not imply encroachment upon personal liberty, which under the old régime Korean courtiers identified with royal favour. Without law, no real liberty is conceivable, and lawlessness must suffer its own consequences.

Then the third point is the protection of health. I have spoken to you of what we have done in Formosa. A similar policy will be pursued in Korea. In an interview with Prince Ito in Seoul, when I said that the population in Korea had not increased in the last hundred years and that per-

haps the Korean race was destined to disappear,
he replied: "Well, I am not sure. I wish to see
whether good laws will increase the fecundity of
the Korean people."

The fourth consideration is the encouragement
of industries and means of communication. In
Formosa we have seen how much the Government
has done to improve the quality as well as the
quantity of rice, salt, camphor, and sugar. Nearly
all the improvements in these industries have
been initiated or suggested by the Government.
As to means of communication, the prefectures vie
with each other in building new roads or in making
old ones better.

The fifth point in our policy is that of education. In Formosa we have just reached the stage
where we are taking up educational problems seriously. We could not do it sooner, because our
idea was first of all to give to our new fellow-sub-
jects something that would satisfy their hunger
and thirst; their bodies had to be nourished before
their minds. Now that economic conditions are
so much better, schools are being started in all the
villages.

These, then, are some of the broad lines of
colonial policy which we have practised with good
results in Taiwan, and which will be carried out in
Chôsen. In writing of the Japanese rule in Formosa, Mr. MacKay, the British consul there, con-
cludes his article by expressing two doubts: one
in regard to the commingling of races, Japanese

and Formosans; the other, in regard to the Japanisation of the Formosans. He seems to doubt whether either will take place. As far as the Japanese are concerned, they do not trouble themselves about these questions, any more than do the English in their colonies. I think assimilation will be found easier in Korea, for the reason that the Korean race is very much allied to our own. In Formosa, assimilation will be out of the question for long years to come, and we shall not try to force it. We put no pressure upon the people to effect assimilation or Japanisation. Our idea is to provide a Japanese *milieu*, so to speak, and if the Formosans adapt themselves to our ways of their own accord, well and good. Social usages must not be laid upon an unwilling people. An ancient saying has it: "He who flees must not be pursued, but he who comes must not be repulsed." If the Formosans or the Koreans approach us in customs and manners, we will not repulse them. We will receive them with open arms and we will hold them as our brothers; but if they do not desire to adopt our way of living, we will not pursue them. We leave their customs and manners just as they are disposed to have them, as long as they are law-abiding. Our principle is firmness in government and freedom in society. Firmness in government is something which they did not have before, and that is what we offer to them. If they look upon it as they used to look upon court intrigue and family vendetta, they

must learn at their own cost what modern nomoc-
racy means. At the same time, Japan must know
that the secret of colonial success is justice sea-
soned with mercy. Should she fail to recognise
this ancient truth, she will but add another illustration of the poet's words cited at the beginning
of this chapter.

CHAPTER X

WITH the Declaration of Independence, the trade of the United States with her quondam mother-country naturally declined without showing any appreciable increase in commerce with other nations, and her shipping was diverted from accustomed lines on account of English navigation laws. Discouraging commercial conditions like these, aggravated by small returns from their agricultural pursuits, turned the attention of the New England people to adventures in the Far East very early in the history of this country. Already in 1784, within a year after the definitive Treaty of Peace was signed, a bark flying the flag of the Stars and Stripes made a bold cruise into Oriental waters, where in those days the English Union Jack overawed all other national ensigns. As the bark approached the coast of China, it was unexpectedly hailed by two French men-of-war, and, escorted by these, entered the port of Canton. The bark carried but little

merchandise, but the business transacted was
exceedingly lucrative. Especially were furs disposed of at a good price. Next year the voyage
was repeated, and in three years as many as fifteen
American vessels visited this port, largely with
seal-skins, otter and other furs from the South
Seas and the north-west coast of this continent.
These vessels brought a cargo of tea, silks, and
other Chinese produce.

In those days, Japan was apparently passed over
or passed by, as impossible of access. It is true
that in 1797, an American ship, the *Eliza* of New
York, Captain Stewart, made a voyage to Nagasaki. This was perhaps the first time that the
American flag was seen in our waters. The *Eliza*
repeated her voyages for several years following,
but on no occasion except the last did she come
on her own initiative. She was hired by the
Dutch in Batavia, who, afraid of the English navy
in the Indian seas in the days when Holland was
under Napoleon's rule, dared not make their regular visit to Japan. When Captain Stewart made
his last voyage in 1803, he attempted to open trade
on his own responsibility, but was not successful.

In 1798, an American ship, the *Franklyn*, Captain James Devereux, made its way to Japan,
sailing under Dutch colours. The next year there
came, also under the charter of the East India
Company, a Salem ship, Captain John Derby. It
is recorded that these men came and left their
footprints on the sands, soon to be washed away,

however. Individually they left no trace, but they counted as landmarks in the development of American-Japanese intercourse; for not a "black ship," as a foreign vessel was then called, was sighted, without being watched and studied and discussed—thus contributing a blow, however slight, to the final overthrow of Exclusivism.

As the China trade developed, the skippers discovered the new importance of the Hawaiian Islands, known on their charts ever since the time of Captain Cook (1792). Situated in mid-ocean, they afforded a most convenient stopping-place for replenishing the supply of water, for making repairs, and for avoiding occasional storms. It was not long before they found that sandal-wood, which fetched an exorbitant price in China, grew in abundance in these islands. This wood gave a fresh impetus to Oriental trade. However, commerce founded upon sheer exploitation is not guaranteed a long lease of life. Fur-bearing animals decreased year by year, owing to the ruthlessness with which they were hunted. The sandal-wood forests were felled, and this without scruple. In the first two decades of the nineteenth century, the foundations of trade with China were in jeopardy, and, with them, American interests in the Pacific.

The Pacific coast was not yet connected with the Atlantic, and the first city founded there, Astoria, suffered heavily during the War of 1812. The American merchant marine in the Pacific also underwent severe loss, together with the navy, at the hand of the Britishers. Nevertheless, during this "War of Paradoxes," American commerce showed a wonderful power of growth, especially in the New England States, and when peace was concluded the New England merchants sought a new field of investment. What their fathers lost in the Gulf of St. Lawrence and on the coast of Newfoundland, they attempted to regain in the Pacific. Fishing had been practically wiped out during the Revolution; but in the first quarter of the nineteenth century, whaling became a profitable outlet for investment. It was not a new industry, having been carried on prior to the Revolution; but its importance grew rapidly after the War of 1812. In eager pursuit of prey, the American whalers soon rounded Cape Horn and their black ships could be counted by scores—in a few years by hundreds—between the Hawaiian Islands and Japan.

As yet, however, they were exposed to dangers of manifold kinds, notably to the depredations of their English rivals and to the mercy of storms and waves. The danger resulting from the latter source could not well be avoided unless they had friendly havens, but such there was none, as Japan, far from affording shelter, carried the logic of exclusion to its extreme conclusion, by treating as criminals whomsoever drifted by misfortune to her shores. As for the former danger, the United States had despatched a few gunboats to cruise in the whaling districts for the protection of her citizens. Commodore Porter was one of the officers who were sent out for this purpose, and he could recommend no better means of security to American whalers than that of bringing Japan into amicable relations with his country. To this end, he addressed a letter to Secretary Monroe in 1815. This was the year that a squadron under Decatur was sent to the Mediterranean and a treaty was signed with Algiers. Why should not another squadron be sent westward to Japan? The proposal seemed about to be put into effect, and the Commodore was to be sent as envoy, with a frigate and two sloops of war. In the meantime the whaling industry made steady progress. In 1822, as many as twenty-four whaling vessels anchored at one time in the harbour of Honolulu. About this time, not only on the seas, but also on land, the United States was expanding with great strides, and it is no wonder that John Quincy Adams should urge that it was the duty of Christian nations to open Japan, and that it was the duty of Japan to respond to the demands of the world, as no nation had a right to withhold its quota to the general progress of mankind. Still no official step was taken, indeed nothing definite was planned until 1832—under his successor, Andrew Jackson—when it was suggested that Mr. Edmund Roberts should be appointed as a special agent to negotiate treaties with Oriental courts. But again nothing came of the plan. Mean-

while interest in Japan was awakened in some influential quarters and for unexpected reasons.

The Black Current, the Kuro-Shiwo, flows from
the tropics along the eastern coast of Japan, and
continues to flow northward beyond the limits of
that Empire, then turns in a large curve and joins
with a current that washes the western shores of
America. Many a shipwrecked sailor and fisher-
man of Japan must, in the course of centuries,
have drifted on these currents and been cast ashore
on the American continent. Mr. Charles Wolcott
Brooks enumerates a large number of well authen-
ticated cases of this kind, in his monograph on
*Japanese Wrecks, Early Maritime Intercourse of
Ancient Western Nations*, as well as in his pamphlet on the *Origin of the Chinese Race*.

Now about the middle of the third decade of the
last century, a band of fishermen who were wrecked
on our coast were carried away by the Kuro-Shiwo
and were picked up near Astoria. As curious
specimens of humanity, they were cared for, and,
after being sent from place to place in the United
States, they were taken to Macao, China, where
there were American houses, in the hope that they
could be more easily shipped from there back to
their home. An American merchant residing
here, C. W. King by name, saw in the return of
these men, seven altogether, an opportunity to
begin negotiations for the opening of trade with
Japan.

Mr. King equipped at his own expense a merchantman, the *Morrison*, for this errand of mercy. To avoid every possible cause for suspicion, he removed all guns and armament, which sailing-craft of all descriptions used to carry at that time.

To further emphasise the peaceful character of the undertaking, he took with him his wife. They were accompanied by three clergymen who have since made their names famous in the history of Christian missions—Peter Parker, Charles Gutzlaff, and S. Wells Williams. Dr. Williams had learned some Japanese from the shipwrecked sailors who were to be sent home by the *Morrison*. I may mention here that it was Dr. Williams who was the chief interpreter during subsequent negotiations with Perry. Mr. King took with him a number of presents—such as books, instruments, etc., with the view of impressing the Japanese with the greatness of his country and of the triumphs of Christian civilisation. While the preparations for departure were being made, Dutch traders brought the news to the Japanese authorities that a "Morrison" might visit their harbours at any time. Hereupon forts were repaired, cannons were put in prime order, sentinels were multiplied at all the main points of defence on the coast. Thus by the time the *Morrison* entered the Bay of Yedo in 1837 with every manifestation of good will, she was so mercilessly fired upon that she had to weigh anchor and flee. She attempted landing a few days later in the southern port of Kagoshima, but here, too, she received no more hospitable reception. For all his good intentions, Mr. King reaped nothing but hostile feeling. As Dr. Williams writes: "Commercially speaking, the voyage cost about $2000 without any returns; and the immediate effects, in a missionary or scientific way, were nil."

For the students of Japanese history of this period, unusual interest and pathos are attached to this voyage of Mr. King's. For, in the thirties or forties of the last century, while Japan was still under the strictest régime of seclusion, there was working in certain small circles a powerful leaven of Western knowledge, which was soon to leaven the whole Empire. Among the pioneers of European culture may here be mentioned two of the most prominent—Noboru Watanabe and Choyei Takano. They were tireless in gathering information about the West and in their effort to convince the authorities of the futility and folly of exclusion.

A few months after the unhappy episode of King's enterprise had transpired, the rumour reached the ears of Watanabe and Takano that a "Morrison" was coming to Japan, whereupon the latter published a booklet entitled *The Story of a Dream*. This zealous exponent of Western learning was naturally opposed to the policy of resorting to force, should a "black ship" approach our dominion. In his pamphlet he ridiculed the idea of defending our territory against a foreign navy by relying upon old-fashioned rifles and wooden barracks and cotton curtains. He grows still more sarcastic when he exposes, as he thinks, the utter ignorance of the authorities about things Western. "The idea of taking the name of Morrison for that of a ship is simply absurd. Why, it is the name of a man, a great scholar, who is well versed in Oriental lore, familiar with all the classics of China. Should a man of his eminence honour our land with a visit, we should receive him with due respect and hospitality." Takano was himself mistaken as to the bearer of the name Morrison. He was thinking of the Rev. Robert Morrison, who, however, had been dead since 1834. Such an error on the part of so well-meaning and progressive a student of Occidental affairs is in itself touching; but the climax of pathos is reached when for his *Story of a Dream* he was sentenced to perpetual imprisonment, and though he fled from the execution of the law for a little while, hiding himself or wandering about under different assumed names, so closely was he pursued that, in order to escape an ignominious death, he put an end to himself. His colleague, Watanabe, a great scholar as well as painter, whose works adorn the literature and art of our nation, did not fare much better.

To return to the *Morrison*, Mr. King, upon coming back from the fruitless expedition, made public his experience and his reflections on it in a book, *The Claims of Malayasia or the Voyage of the "Morrison,"* the first book published in America on Japan. In the most earnest tone, he appeals to "the champions of his country's benevolence," not to despair about opening the sealed portals of Japan. He argues that Great Britain and America divide the maritime influence of the world, and that "America is the hope of Asia beyond the Malay Peninsula, that her noblest effort will find a becoming theatre there." He tells his country- men "that Japan will more readily yield to and repay their efforts, and that China can be more easily reached through Japan." He calls upon all the best instincts of the American public—its Christian sympathies, its commercial interests, its republican glories—to exert themselves in this heaven-appointed task lying before it.

Mr. King's appeal was evidently little heeded. American interests in the Pacific were not ap- preciated enough to call forth response from the Government or the people. Meanwhile Ameri- can trade with China was increasing and the whaling industry was constantly assuming greater magnitude.

In 1839, out of some 555 American ships engaged in whale-fishery, the overwhelming majority cruised in the Pacific. Professor Coolidge says that in 1845, according to the local records, 497 whalers, manned by 14,905 sailors, visited the Hawaiian Islands, and of the total, three-fourths flew the flag of the United States. Two years later, the number of vessels rose to 729, and the capital invested in the enterprise was calculated at $20,000,000. By 1848, the New Bedford men passed through Behring Straits into the Arctic Ocean, and of the whole American fleet, no less than 278 were in North Pacific waters.

It was chiefly in the interest of whaling that the Hon. Zadoc Pratt of Prattsville, Orange County, N. Y., member of Congress and chairman of the Select Committee on Statistics, laid before the House a report, in 1845, concerning the advisability of taking prompt action by sending an embassy to Japan and Korea. The next year, Commodore Biddle was appointed to head an expedition and embark with a fleet consisting of the *Columbus* and the *Vincennes*. He was provided with a letter from President Polk to the Emperor of Japan. The object of this expedition was to ascertain whether the ports of Japan were accessible. The Commodore arrived safe and well in the Bay of Yedo, and opened communications which continued for ten tedious days, at the end of which, on receipt of the following anonymous note, he left.

The object of this communication is to explain the reasons why we refuse to trade with foreigners who come to this country across the ocean for that purpose. This has been the habit of our nation from time immemorial. In all cases of a similar kind that have occurred, we have positively refused to trade. Foreigners have come to us from various quarters, but have always been received in the same way. In taking this course with regard to you, we only pursue our accustomed policy. We can make no distinction between different foreign nations—we treat them all alike; and you, as Americans, must receive the same answer with the rest. It will be of no use to renew the attempt, as all applications of the kind, however numerous they may be, will be steadily rejected.

We are aware that our customs are in this respect different from those of some other countries, but every nation has a right to manage its affairs in its own way.

The trade carried on with the Dutch at Nagasaki is not to be regarded as furnishing a precedent for trade with other foreign nations. The place is one of few inhabitants and very little business is transacted, and the whole affair is of no importance.

In conclusion, we have to say that the Emperor positively refuses the permission you desire. He earnestly advises you to depart immediately, and to consult your own safety by not appearing again upon our coast.

Commodore Biddle's mission was worse than a mere failure. It had the effect of lowering the dignity of his country in the mind of the Oriental. The defiant and haughty tone running through the foregoing note was, I dare say, the result of his having accepted insult without strong demonstration. It may be, he meant only to be cautious and courteous, and that his caution and courtesy were sadly misconstrued. I refer to an unpleasant incident which occurred during his interview with certain Japanese officers. He describes it as follows: "I went alongside the junk in the ship's boat, in my uniform; at the moment that I was stepping on board, a Japanese on the deck of the junk, gave me a blow or push, which threw me back into the boat." He says that the conduct of the man was inexplicable; but after assurance had been obtained from the officials that the man would be severely punished, nothing further was asked or demanded by the Commodore. A stronger attitude on his part might have ended in his reaping the glory of opening Japan, or, at least, in relieving the sufferings of many of his countrymen; because, with the growth of whaling in Japanese waters, the ship-wrecked sailors and deserters landing on our coast increased in number. Only two months before Commodore Biddle appeared, the *Lawrence*, under Captain Baker, who had sailed from Poughkeepsie the previous summer, was wrecked on the coast of one of the Kurile Islands. Seven of the crew survived. At first they were treated kindly, but no sooner had their presence been reported to the authorities than they were placed in close confinement, subject to privation and ill-treatment which lasted for seventeen months, so that all the while that Biddle was negotiating in the Bay of Yedo these poor creatures were in dire distress. They were finally liberated and sent to Batavia by a Dutch ship.

Two years later, the crew of another whaler, the *Ladoga*, on account of bad treatment, deserted the ship in five boats, two of which were soon swamped. The surviving three parties, consisting of fifteen men—nine of whom were Sandwich Islanders—drifted upon an islet near the town of

Matsumaé (now Fukushima). Suspected of being
spies, they were put in jail in Matsumeé and after-
ward in Nagasaki. Their repeated attempts to
break away from the prison only seemed to con-
firm the Japanese in their suspicion, and the rigours
of confinement were doubled. One Maury, a
Hawaiian, hung himself in the prison; Ezra Gold-
thwait died of disease, or, as was charged, of
medicine prescribed by a quack. Suffering from
brutal treatment one day, "on being taken out of
our stocks," so narrates one of the prisoners, "we
told the Japanese guards that their cruelty to us
would be told the Americans, who would come
here and take vengeance on them. Our guards
replied, sneeringly, that they knew better, and
that the Americans did not care how poor sailors
were treated; if they did, then they should have
come and punished the Japanese at Yedo, when
a Japanese had insulted an American Chief."
The last allusion was to the incident which we have
already related concerning Commodore Biddle.

With nothing to break the monotony of their
irksome captivity, except growls and threats from
the guards, the poor sailors of the *Ladoga* were on
the verge of despair, when one evening the report
of a distant gun, a sure signal of the approach of a
foreign ship, reached their ears. A foreign ship
it was. James Glynn, Commander of the U. S.
Ship *Preble*, was dispatched by Commodore D.
Geisinger upon the advice of John W. Davis, U. S.
Commissioner to China, to whom the news of the

captivity of the *Ladoga's* crew had been communi-
cated by J. H. Levyssohn, Superintendent oi
Dutch trade in Deshima.   The *Preble* entered the
harbour of Nagasaki on the 17th of April, 1849.
After a week's conference, it was arranged that
the ship-wrecked mariners, who had been suffering
so long from the effect of their misfortune, should
be delivered up immediately.   Accordingly, on
the 26th, they were all carried to the town-house,
where, for the first time, they unexpectedly met
another of their countrymen, McDonald, who had
been lodged in another part of the town.   They
were all taken away by Commander Glynn.

The story of the above-mentioned Ronald
McDonald is so unique as to be worthy of further
notice.   His life and character-sketch have been
penned by a number of writers.   (R. E. Lewis,
Educational Conquest of the Far East, 1903; also
Mrs. Eva Emery Dye, *McDonald of Oregon*, 1906.)
Born in Astoria, Oregon, this son of a Chinook
princess and a Scotch employé of the Hudson Bay
Company had in his childhood probably heard
the country of Japan frequently mentioned, or
had in all likelihood seen the Japanese who in 1831
were drifted ashore at the mouth of the Columbia
River.   In 1845, when in his twenties, he shipped
at Sag Harbour in a whale-boat, the *Plymouth*.   He
made an arrangement with the captain that, when
they neared the coast of Japan, he should be left
alone in a small boat, so contrived that he could
capsize it himself.   It was his intention to cast

himself ashore and obtain some knowledge of the
land and the people of this *terra incognita*. He
was accordingly set adrift, and coasted along the
shore for a day or two, when he discerned some
fishermen at a distance. He beckoned to them,
and, as they approached, he jumped into their
boat and landed with them about twenty-five
miles from Soya in Hokkaido. During the eight
days that he remained under the roof of the fishermen, he was treated most kindly; but the good
people, fearing that they were disloyal to the law
in harbouring a foreigner, notified an officer of his
presence, and, when he came, poor McDonald was
taken to Matsumaé and afterwards transferred to
Nagasaki. In each of these places, he received
reasonable attention. Lodging was provided for
him in a temple, and, though narrowly watched,
he was not treated like a prisoner but was allowed
to occupy himself in teaching English.

The very year (1848) that the crew of the *Ladoga*
were wrecked and McDonald of the *Plymouth*
succeeded in landing (both of these ships were on
whaling voyages), three American sailors belong-
ing to another whaler—the *Trident*—were wrecked
on one of the Kurile Islands. They, together with
some twenty-seven English seamen who had also
been wrecked while out whaling, were returned
home through the Dutch factory.

That the narrow cleft in the sealed door of
Japan, into which Perry drove his wedge of diplomacy, was the rescue of American whalers, Mr.

18

Fillmore implies in his address before the Buffalo Historical Society: "The proceedings which resulted in the opening of Japan sprang from a wrong perpetrated by that nation and which, like many other wrongs, seems to have resulted in a great good."

There were causes other than the mere safety of whalers which led to the inception of the American expedition to Japan. On the one hand, the rise of industrial and commercial commonwealths on the Pacific, the discovery of gold in California, the increasing trade with China, the development of steam navigation—necessitating coal depots and ports for shelter,—the opening of highways across the isthmus of Central America, the missionary enterprises on the Asiatic continent, the rise of the Hawaiian Islands; on the other hand, the awakening knowledge of foreign nations among the ruling class in Japan, the news of the British victory in China, the growth of European settlements in the Pacific, the dissemination of Western science among a progressive class of scholars, the advice from the Dutch Government to discontinue the antiquated policy of exclusion—all these testified that the fulness of time was at hand for Japan to turn a new page in her history.

Intelligent interest was now aroused on this side of the Pacific in the question of opening Japan. We must remember that the middle of the last century was the era of American clippers. In the year 1848, Robert J. Walker, then Secretary of the Treasury, called public attention to " Japan, highly advanced in civilisation, containing fifty millions of people, separated but two weeks by steam from our western coast. . . . Its commerce," he continues, "can be secured to us by persevering and peaceful efforts."

During the next year, Aaron Haight Palmer of New York, who accumulated what was at that time a vast amount of information respecting Oriental nations, in his capacity as Director of the American and Foreign Agency of New York (1830–47), saw the great necessity of establishing commercial relations with the East, and sent memorials upon the subject to the President and the Secretary of State. He was backed by memorials from the principal merchants of New York and Baltimore. In his letter to Secretary Clayton, on the plan of opening Japan, he recommends four measures to be followed: (1) to demand full and ample indemnity for the ship-wrecked American seamen who had been unjustly treated; (2) to insist upon the proper care for any American who might from any misfortune repair to the coast of Japan: (3) to enforce the opening of ports for commerce and for the establishment of consulates; (4) to claim the privilege of establishing coaling stations, and also the right of whaling without molestation. Mr. Palmer says that, in the event of non-compliance with the above on the part of the Shogun, a strict blockade of Yedo Bay should be established.

James Glynn, who had for two years been

cruising about the North Pacific Ocean, and who, as we have seen, had had opportunity to learn something of the Japanese people, writing in 1851 of the prospect of Chinese trade, speaks of the absolute necessity for a coal depot on the coast of Japan; and in his letter expresses a strong belief in the possibility of securing such a depot by proper negotiation, and of eventually opening the whole Empire.

About this time a newspaper article concerning some Japanese waifs who had been picked up at sea by the bark *Auckland*, Captain Jennings, and brought to San Francisco, attracted the attention of Commodore Aulick.   He submitted a proposal to the Government that it should take advantage of this incident to open commercial relations with the Empire, or at least to manifest the friendly feelings of this country.   This proposal was made on the ninth of May, 1851.   Daniel Webster was then Secretary of State, and in him Aulick found a ready friend.   The opinions of Commander Glynn and Mr. Palmer as authorities on questions connected with Japan, were asked. Their letters on this occasion evince keen diplomatic sagacity.

Clothed with full power to negotiate and sign treaties, and furnished with a letter from President Fillmore to the Emperor, Commodore Aulick was on the eve of departure when, for some reason, he was prevented.   Thus the project which was set on foot at his suggestion was obstructed just as it was about to be accomplished and another man, perhaps better fitted for the undertaking, entered into his labours.

But by relating the achievement of Perry, I shall trespass beyond the limit I have set to this narrative, which is to concern itself with American-Japanese intercourse prior to Perry's advent.

CHAPTER XI

THE RELATIONS BETWEEN THE UNITED STATES AND JAPAN

THE well-known French historian Michelet, speaking of great geographical explorations and discoveries, ends one of his perorations with these words:

"Who opened to men the great distant navigation? Who revealed the great ocean and marked out its zones and its liquid highways? Who discovered the secrets of the globe?" And he answers: "The whale and the whaler. . . . It was the whale that emancipated the fishermen and led them afar. It led them onward and onward still, until they found it, after having almost unconsciously passed from one world to the other."

President Fillmore, in whose administration Commodore Perry was dispatched to Japan, confirms this rhetorical statement of Michelet's.

Let me briefly recapitulate the events that led up to the oft-repeated story of Perry's expedition.

That whaling was a great industry during a

substantial portion of the last two centuries, especially among the New England people, is well known. Then again, those who were unfortunate enough to be wrecked had no hospitable shores upon which to land.

To succour the whalers and to help and protect their industry, was the main motive of the United States Government in initiating an expedition to Japan. Before any official step was taken in this direction, some private American citizens had visited Japan in the service of the Dutch East India Company. The first suggestion of sending an official envoy emanated from Commodore Porter, but without tangible result. When, in 1846, Commodore Biddle was accredited by President Polk to the Shogunal Court at Yedo, to ascertain how far her ports were accessible,—the interest in Japan obviously marked an advance from talk among whalers to grave counsel in Washington. The acquisition of California, its sudden development upon the discovery of gold, and the constantly increasing trade with China, almost eclipsed the importance of the whaling industry, but brought into prominence the need of opening up intercourse with our country.

Five years elapsed before any definite plan was formulated. In 1851, as we have seen, Commodore Matthew Calbraith Perry was appointed to undertake the mission. He was the younger brother of the more celebrated Admiral Perry, the hero of the Lake War of 1812.

I have often wished and tried to find where "public opinion" stood when the United States Government decided to send forth Perry's expedition. A Washington correspondent writes in a Philadelphia paper: "There is no money in the treasury for the *conquest* [mark the term, if you please] of the Japanese Empire, and the administration will hardly be disposed to pursue such a romantic notion." Only two days before the expedition sailed, the Baltimore *Sun* correspondent wrote from Washington: "It will sail about the same time with Rufus Porter's aërial ship," and even after it had sailed, he advises "abandoning this humbug, for it has become a matter of ridicule abroad and at home."

Not less sarcastic are the English comments. The London *Times* doubts "whether the Emperor of Japan would receive Commodore Perry with most indignation or most contempt," and omniscient *Punch* insisted that "Perry must open the Japanese ports, even if he has to open his own." "For ourselves," says the London *Sun*, "we look forward to that result with some such interest as we might suppose would be awakened among the generality, were a balloon to soar off to one of the planets under the direction of some experienced aëronaut." Another London contemporary "cannot agree with an American journalist in thinking such a small force (two thousand men) will be sufficient to coerce a vain, ignorant, semi-barbarous, and sanguinary nation of

thirty millions of people." In his queer and
quaint *Almanac* for 1852, the so-called Prophet
Zadkiel notes: "A total eclipse of the Sun, visible
chiefly in the eastern and northern parts of Asia.
The greatest eclipse at 3 h. 24 m. A.M., December
11th, Greenwich time. . . . It will produce great
mortality among camels and horses in the East,
also much fighting and warlike doings, and I judge
that it will carry war into the peaceful vales of
Japan, for there, too, do the men of the West follow
the track of gain, seeking the bubble reputation,
even in the cannon's mouth."

Looking through a number of newspapers and
periodicals of the time, I am struck with the
absence of public sympathy concerning an enterprise of which the United States can so nobly and
so justly boast.

If history is philosophy teaching by example,
certainly examples were not lacking to show that
the newspaper fear of conquest or war did not
materialise—and may we not compare Zadkiel's
prophecy with a recent pamphlet by one Johndro
of Rochester (which I mentioned in a former
chapter) purporting to be an astrological evidence
of war with Japan, and which commands our respect for its copious illustrations and diagrams,
but above all for the profuse use of capital letters!

For some of us, history has written more clearly
than the stars that Perry's mission was conceived
in peace and concluded in peace. When I say
this, I mean peace between the two nations

concerned. In another sense, peace there was none. When the treaty of peace was signed, there was great excitement throughout our country, followed by the assassination of those who took a responsible part in the negotiations, and, later on, by civil war.

On the part of America, Perry's treaty brought no satisfaction. Naval officers laughed at his haughty demeanour during the negotiations; commercial men complained that trade did not develop at once. And no wonder, when we read that, as early as 1852, a direct annual trade of two hundred million dollars was expected,—an amount which is six times the sum which America exports to Japan at present!

It must be admitted that the treaty made by Perry was not a commercial agreement. The main object at which he aimed was the establishment of a coaling station. The consummation of a commercial treaty was reserved for a man who was sent out to put into effect the articles proposed by Perry. This country is to be congratulated upon having sent the right men to Japan. Seldom have your representatives been good diplomats, if we confine the calling of diplomats to Wotton's definition of them as "honest men sent out to other countries to tell lies." They were greater as men than as diplomats, if Wotton's definition be accepted. Townsend Harris in particular was a man of whom this country may well be proud. A man of sterling qualities, of honesty of purpose, and withal of kindly disposition, he proved himself the best friend, adviser and teacher of Japan, in the early and stormy days of her foreign intercourse.

During the period immediately following the opening of the country to foreign trade, the rise in prices was tremendous. In two years, some things rose three hundred per cent. Gold, which used to be exchanged for four times its weight in silver, suddenly rose to eight, ten, sixteen times its former value. Naturally, only people greedy of sudden gain flocked to the ports; respectable houses even refused the request of the Government to deal with foreign merchants. Such a state of affairs did not tend to convince the Japanese nation of the blessings of Western civilisation— especially as many of the foreign representatives behaved in a way quite at variance with our ideas of justice or good-will. But, through all the vicissitudes of anti-foreign demonstration, Townsend Harris stood an unwavering friend to Japan.

At one time, when all his diplomatic colleagues left Tokyo (then Yedo), being warned by our authorities of plots of assassination and incendiarism, Townsend Harris alone remained, and without a single American guard at that, placing his reliance upon only a few Japanese sentinels. When his own secretary was killed on the street and he was requested not to go out of his house, he paced the wooden verandah where he took exercise until it was worn by his steps.

It was during this anti-foreign period (1862–64)

that the feudal lord of Choshiu fired upon an American steamer that passed through the strait of Shimonoseki, which was within his province. Later on, a French and a Dutch man-of-war were similarly treated. Then naturally followed an alliance of these Powers to bombard the town. The Lord of Choshiu was badly beaten. All this ended in Japan's paying an indemnity of three million dollars. The share for the United States was nearly eight hundred thousand dollars. This sum was about forty times greater than the damages which she sustained, which really amounted to some twenty thousand dollars. One might think this transaction was a profitable bargain. So far the dealing does not seem fair; but there is a sequel to the story. A few years later, educators in this country began to agitate for the return of this sum to Japan. Men like Dr. Northrop of Yale wrote, lectured, and preached regarding this course. Men like Secretary Seward warmly approved of it, and the Committee on Foreign Affairs in the House of Representatives reported that the remittance of this indemnity would result in the establishment of more intimate relations between the two countries and would ultimately prove of great benefit.

If you ask me how this money was spent when it came back to us, I assure you that it was not all blown off in the form of gunpowder. "Cast thy bread upon the waters and thou shalt find it after many days." If you visit our country, the first port at which you anchor is the exposed harbour of Yokohama, and, as you begin to wonder how a ship can anchor there, you will notice a long stretch of breakwater, within which you will soon find a haven of safety. After long deliberation, it was decided by our people that the money you returned to us should be expended in some work that would perpetuate in lasting, useful, and visible form the good-will of this country, and to this end, the breakwater in the harbour of Yokohama testifies.

The spirit which actuated the United States to return the indemnity of Shimonoseki dictated all its dealings with Japan under successive presidencies. General Grant proved himself an unfailing friend; not only during his tenure of office, but even after he retired to private life, his friendship never flagged. When making his tour around the world in 1880, he made a long sojourn in Japan. In the repeated interviews he had with our Emperor, he won the absolute confidence of our Sovereign, and the advice Grant then gave has made a deep impression upon the Emperor's policy. A man of the camp and the battle-field, President Grant served the cause of peace when he mediated between China and Japan on the question of the Loo-Choo Islands.

To further illustrate this cordial relationship, take the cases of consular jurisdiction and of tariff autonomy—two questions which harassed our nation for a long time. Let me explain. When the treaty was first signed, Townsend Harris was averse to depriving Japan of the power of enforcing its own laws upon foreigners; but, as our laws were at the time crude in the extreme, he proposed extra-territorial rights for his country-men.   This example was naturally followed by all European Powers.   As for the second question, the tariff—having had no foreign trade regulations prior to the Commercial Treaty with the United States, we were ignorant of the means of raising a revenue by tariff, much more of protecting native indus-tries.   Commerce with the Chinese and the Dutch had been conducted upon a basis of fair trade. Townsend Harris first taught us to impose cus-toms duties.   Instead of taking advantage of our ignorance, he carefully compiled a tariff-schedule, more with the interest of Japan in view than with that of America,—again showing a remarkable sense of equity.   These tariff regulations were altered when the anti-foreign movement gave to the Treaty Powers an opportunity to further their claims for more advantages.

To recover her judicial autonomy by the sum-mary abolition of foreign jurisdiction and to regain the power of fixing her own tariff-rates, were the fundamental objects of our treaty revision in the eighties of the last century.   Without these powers, no country can be said to be on an equal footing with the rest of the world.   Indeed, she can never aspire to belong to the "family of great nations" and will forever be treated as an inferior and a stranger.

Japan decided to frame all her laws on Western

principles; so that the Treaty Powers might recognise the equity of her legislation. After every preparation had been made to claim legal and tariff autonomy, when we proposed to the Powers that the treaties should be revised, it was the United States that most readily acceded to our desires, and though the revised treaty was first signed with England, everybody concerned knew that the consent and the backing of the United States were a powerful factor. Mr. Cleveland, in 1884, expressed entire willingness to revise whatever was detrimental to the integrity and interests of Japan in the treaties then existing.

Nor was Japan always the passive recipient of American good-will. In Korea, in the last two decades of the past century, how often did American citizens have to take shelter under the roof of our Legation, for protection from mobs!

Such an act implies more than mere international courtesy, or at least it can be made a tie of more than rigid formality. So it was during the war between China and Japan. Japan asked the United States to look after our interests in China, and China asked the same of the United States in Japan.

More than once has the United States performed the good office of aiding us to solve intricate international problems. Of General Grant's service, I have spoken. Even before his time, in 1871, when a complication arose between China and Japan regarding Formosa, and we were obliged to send out an armed expedition to that island, General Le Gendre, the American Consul in Amoy, rendered valuable aid in making clear to the world, so to speak, our real intentions and attitude.

At the close of the Japan-China War, the presence of the Honorable John W. Foster, in the capacity of adviser to Li Hung-Chang, served the cause of Japan as much as that of China, in bringing about a satisfactory solution of the differences between the two nations.

As for the attitude of America in the Russo-Japanese War, the event is still so fresh in your memories that it is needless to review it. It was in 1905 that this great war ended and peace was concluded at Portsmouth through the good offices of President Roosevelt.

Only six years have passed since America crowned her traditional friendship of half a century towards Japan, with her unstinted sympathy during the Russo-Japanese War! Only six years! —a short period in a nation's history, even in these days of steam and electricity. If Rome was not built in a day, a Nero or a Vandal can destroy it in a day. Are there not Neros and Vandals in the twentieth century, who delight in working havoc among friendly nations? In the brief interval, mischief has been brewing in some quarters to bring about disruption of our historic relations. Some ominous prophecies have been uttered that a war between Japan and America is inevitable in a few years. "The best of prophets of the future is the past" (Byron), and looking back upon the past, who has cause to fear? Which of the parties has wronged the other? Those who know nothing of the past, strain their eyes to discover the slightest possible cause for trouble. They represent Japan as harbouring territorial ambition, of casting an evil eye upon Hawaii and the Philippines,—or nearer, upon Magdalena Bay!

We have a proverb, "Fear creates hobgoblins out of shadows." The most unsophisticated Japanese labourers, toiling in the sugar plantations of Hawaii or in the tobacco fields of Luzon, are elevated in the eyes of the doubting to the dignity of military spies. Not a single gunboat is built in Japan but is constructed as an evidence that preparations are in train for the bombardment of San Francisco or the seizure of Manila. If we buy rice from China—which we annually do—in quantities greater than the usual amount, because of floods in our interior, that, too, is distorted into an indication of victualing the navy. Certainly Japan is flattered beyond her deserts when the world thinks that she can lightly go into war with a foreign Power or take Hawaii and the Philippines, in spite of all that she has to carry on in Korea, Manchuria, and Saghalien! The American public has forgotten the agreement between this country and Japan, signed only four years ago, November 31, 1908, by which instrument each Government promises to respect the territorial possessions of the other on the Pacific.

This document fully implies community of purpose and practical co-operation in Far Eastern affairs. The agreement further pledges that the two Governments, in case anything should occur to menace the *status quo* of either, will communicate with each other, in order to arrive at a mutual understanding regarding the measures to be taken.

So much for the terror of Japan's territorial aggression upon American dominions!

What other possible cause is there for rupture between us?

The California question ! Much ado was made about nothing. When facts are all carefully sifted, we shall be forcibly reminded of an old Latin proverb—*Parturiunt montes; nascetur ridiculus mus.* (The mountains are in labour; a ridiculous mouse will be brought forth.)

The so-called anti-Japanese crusade was started and organised by a certain Tveitmoe, who, when still in his native country, Norway, served it by working in prison as a convict and who is at present serving his adopted country in the same capacity. His habit of spending much time in a penitentiary seems to have been contagious. Anyhow, it is a striking coincidence—let it be said in honour of the American judiciary!—that three or four other people who took prominent part in the anti-Japanese movement in 1906 and 1907 are all serving their term in jail—and this despite the fact that Japanese laws are not in force in California! Another agitator, one Fowler, who distinguished himself as Secretary of the Japanese-Korean Exclusive League, had not been long on the stage before he was adjudged insane by Judge Kellogg (who, it may also be remarked, is not a Japanese justice) and was committed to an asylum. These "martyrs" are not the only mice that were brought forth from the mountains of the Golden State, when they were in labour. With a fund supplied from some mischief-making source, they went about declaring impending danger to American civilisation from the incoming of the Japanese; but I wish to make it clear that their imprisonment has nothing to do with their attitude against our people. I must state in justice to the great fairness of mind shown by these men that they did not attribute to Japanese importation or machinations the San Francisco earthquake! Even now, anti-Japanese sentiment sometimes makes its appearance to adorn the platform of some office-seekers in times of local election, or when work is slack and propagandists are well paid. Otherwise all is quiet along the Pacific Coast, and the American orchardists and the farmers, as Mr. Mackenzie in his official capacity as Labor Commissioner of that State has reported, are regretting the decreasing supply of Japanese labour.

Viewed not only as a California problem but as a matter of national significance, the immigration question is certainly more serious; but its serious feature is largely of an abstract and not of a

concrete character. Our labourers began to come to
California in 1886, and their immigration steadily
increased until they numbered thirty thousand in
1907. Thirty thousand is not in itself a small
number, and might have given anxiety if the
labourers had settled in one place; but we must
remember that thirty thousand is no more than
one four-hundredth part of about one million two-
hundred thousand immigrants of all nationalities
who came to the United States in that one year
of 1907. In no year has Japanese immigration
reached two per cent. of the total, whereas Austro-
Hungarians, Italians, and Russians usually exceed
twenty per cent. of it. If it is feared that our
people confine themselves to the Pacific Coast,
official returns should comfort you with the
assurance that those who remain there are only
about one-sixth or one-seventh of the number of
the European immigrants who reach these Western
shores. As to their character, the majority of
them are farmers and farm-labourers, just what
California orchards and farms are most in need of.
Then there are a considerable number of professional men. As to financial competence, the
official returns show that the average sum of
money brought by each Japanese (the figure is for
1906, which was by no means an exceptional year)
is thirty-one dollars,—smaller than the fifty-eight
dollars of the English or the forty-one dollars of
the Germans, but larger than the sum brought by
the Russians, Italians, Irish, Scandinavians, Poles,

and some others. As to our labourers becoming public charges, here again we turn to the official report of the Immigration Bureau and read with some surprise that in 1906 there was one Japanese received into the hospital for treatment, as against two thousand one hundred and twenty-two Italians, two thousand four hundred and ninety-five Hebrews, or one thousand Poles. If our people do not (cannot!) compete with members of other nationalities in the field of public relief, neither do they compete with American labourers in the field of employment. They are mostly engaged in work which American labourers shun— agriculture.

I have inflicted upon you some dry figures, hoping that they will reveal to unprejudiced minds how much alarm has been created for so little cause! Let it be far from me to make any attempt to show that our immigrants are better than those of other nationalities,—though a close study of the Immigration Commissioner's Reports and the Reports of the State Labour Commissioner of California may point that way. I am not here to advocate their cause. If I can only make it clear that they are not worse than European immigrants and that they are not a menace to American institutions—that is all I care to prove, or at least to intimate.

As to restrictions to be imposed on the free entrance of foreigners, Japan recognises that America or any other country has a right to frame its own laws concerning immigration into its own territory, and, recognising this, she offered to restrict on her side the departure of an undesirable element of her labouring population to this country. She has kept to the letter the terms of the so-called gentlemen's agreement on this matter. The most prejudiced opponent of Japanese immigration has no reason for complaint, for more of our people are leaving the Pacific Coast than are arriving there. Many an American has expressed the opinion that our Government is carrying out its word too rigorously and scrupulously. At any rate the immigration question is practically solved.

For want of a plausible cause for alienation between the two nations, ingenious minds have tried to find one in China and Manchuria. They claim American interests clash with those of Japan. I fail to see what American interests are meant. If they refer to trade, I only wish that America had trade there large enough to make it worth while for us to compete with. Our trade in Manchuria totals about twenty million dollars per annum, and that of all other countries put together (excepting the trade of China) amounts to only seven millions. If by interest is meant American capital, I should like to know how much of real American capital is invested there. When it is understood that the loan forced upon China by the Four Powers is in a precarious state, American capital will be glad to find investment elsewhere— nearer home in South America—where Germans are pushing on, the while Americans are talking of the Far East. If interests mean Americans resident in Manchuria, the whole American population there can be put in a couple of Pullman cars, fifty-two Americans as against forty thousand Japanese.

Reports have been current in newspapers and periodicals, to the effect that the commercial advance of Japanese in Manchuria was made under selfish discrimination and in flagrant violation of "Open Door" promises. It is a remarkable fact that those who make this charge against us never cite a concrete case, never give the exact date or data, to substantiate their accusation. It is always by deductive or rather seductive logic that they try to prove it. They state that Japanese merchants are making headway there, whereas the accusers themselves (all honourable men, of course) made a failure of their own enterprises—therefore the Japanese must have resorted to clandestine methods; the same argument that was used against Othello's success. Our answer must necessarily be very much like his. The truth is that our present advance—and we also expect reverses, according to the natural course of commerce—is so simple and plain that it may well serve for the school-room illustration of a principle in political economy. It is this: Manchuria produces an abundance of soy beans. Until a few years ago, they were not used in Europe or America, and Japan was almost the only purchaser of them. A good deal of the trade in the interior of Manchuria is transacted through barter, or, if with money, by the use of small silver coins, and, buying most, we sold most. There is in the whole transaction no further mystery than this, that in all exchange he who takes most, gives most. There might indeed be mystery if we should buy Manchuria's beans without selling anything in return. The Mitsui firm, who conduct the bean trade, naturally, and wisely too, as they imagined, tried to open a new market for it in Europe, and succeeded so well that the oil-seed crushers of England found the soy beans excellent for their purpose, as well as for cattle feed. As the demand for these beans increased year by year, British firms began to deal directly with Manchurian farmers after the manner of the Japanese—with the result that beans form a considerable portion of Hull imports, and that English trade is now making its way farther and farther into the interior of Manchuria, at the expense of ours. The door is wide open; there is no reason why American trade should not enter,—the more so, as flour and kerosene oil (just the articles we ourselves purchase from this country) are in great demand there. No, there is no infernal magic or underhand discrimination in our trade in Manchuria. Our methods are such as any other people can adopt, and when they adopt them and succeed, we shall perhaps appear less villainous.

If evil reports regarding our advance in Man-

churia should reach their ears, it will pay lovers
of peace and of justice to take the trouble of tracing
them to their sources; for I myself have heard them
emanating from those who failed through their own
incapacity or miscalculation. There is nothing so
illuminating in historical research of any kind as
to go straight to the *Quellen!*

At present, at least, as far as commercial rivalry
is concerned, one will seek in vain in Manchuria for
a cause important enough to cause a rupture of
friendship between the United States and Japan.

A rather childish belief prevails among some
credulous people that simply because Japan has
distinguished herself twice in two decades as a
military power, she may engage in war at any
time upon the slightest provocation.

Why we went to war with China and why with
Russia are matters of history so well established
as to leave no doubt regarding the motive of
Japan. But even in undertaking these wars, just
and justifiable as they were, we did not act hastily.
In the good old Book, it is written: "What king,
as he goes to encounter another king in war, will
not sit down first and take counsel whether he is
able with ten thousand to meet him that cometh
against him with twenty thousand?"

We believe we are sufficiently sane to count the
cost of a war. What can we gain by mobilising
our army or our navy, as some people delight in
prophesying, against the United States?—send a
whole fleet across the Pacific or concentrate our

battle-ships in the Philippines, unmindful that we shall thereby expose our back naked, as it were, to China and Russia; unmindful of the most important trade we have—the trade with this country; unmindful of the enormous debt we already have and of the still greater financial strain which would accrue; unmindful of all the cordial relations of the past, even though these may be largely a matter of sentiment, but none the less a strong sentiment?

Our statesmen and our populace know better than to take such a rash step. They know full well that what they want is peace.

I cannot more fitly describe the sentiment of our nation or more appropriately close this chapter than by relating my last conversation with our leading statesman and recent Premier—Prince Katsura. A fortnight before I left Japan on the present mission, I spent some hours with him, and when I asked his opinion regarding the rumours of war with America, he answered by saying:

"You know, Mr. Nitobe, more or less of my career. In my teens, I fought in the war of the Restoration as a private, in the old feudal fashion. As I grew up, I studied military science and art in Germany, and in our war with China I led an army as a general. Then later on, in the Russo-Japanese War, I led the whole nation as Prime Minister. I say this not to brag, but to remind you that I am not a novice in the matter of wars. I know them well—too well. I know all the horrors of war and the worse horrors of its after-effects. It is largely people who have never seen war who talk glibly of it. I wonder if the newspaper men who write of it really know what it means, what it involves. As for myself, I cannot advocate it. As long as I am in office—and even after leaving office, as long as I have any influence in national affairs—I assure you, there shall be no war with America."

CHAPTER XII

AMERICAN INFLUENCE IN THE FAR EAST

PRIOR to the advent of Cushing to China (1884) and of Perry to Japan (1852), while the British in the Far East were engrossed with their policy of forcing the opium trade on the Celestial Kingdom, an American merchant of Macao, Mr. C. W. King, was engaged, as we have seen in a previous lecture, on his own initiative and responsibility in an attempt to unlock the doubly-barred portals of the Japanese Empire so that foreign commerce might find entrance. This he was bent upon accomplishing by peaceful means, indeed by the most humane of means—by taking with him in his own ship, the *Morrison*, seven ship-wrecked Japanese subjects, who had been thrown ashore on the Pacific Coast of the American continent.

Like a few previous attempts made by his countrymen, Mr. King's mission ended in failure—a failure, which was, as it were, but the repulse of a lesser wave in the ever-swelling tide of the ocean of history. On his return, he appealed to "the

champions of his country's benevolence" not to
despair of opening up intercourse with Japan,
adding, in the most earnest tone, that Great
Britain and the United States divide the maritime
influence of the world and that "America is the
hope of Asia beyond the Malay Peninsula, that
her noblest effort will find a becoming theatre
there." In his mind's eye, he could already discern, rising at the gateways of the sun, a grand
scene of human probation, the vast colosseum of
the moral world, as he called it. He predicted the
time when Japan would more readily yield to and
repay the efforts of America than China, and that
the latter could best be reached through the
channels of the former.

Such was the first audible utterance—albeit
not so clearly recognised as it deserved—of an
American citizen, and for aught I know it voiced
the sentiment of his people as the avantcourier of
Western progress.

A whole generation, as measured by the royal
psalmist, has since passed away, and in these
three-score years and ten, the sun has witnessed
marvellous changes, such as it never before
witnessed in its career around this planet—
changes that have transformed the face and the
spirit of the Far East. True to the traditions
of their fathers and pressed by the necessity of
self-preservation, both China and Japan have in
that interval reverted more than once to the
tactics of exclusivism and resorted to weapons

of violence in order to close the doors they once opened.

No cannon-balls have done more effective work in the history of civilisation than those fired by the combined fleet of Great Britain, Holland, France, and the United States upon the forts and batteries of Shimonoseki, in the autumn days of 1863. That they did not fail to strike the defences of this harbour, is a matter of small concern. The balls pierced farther than the bulwarks of stone. They penetrated the very walls of exclusivism. Henceforth, there were apertures through which Western influence could find entrance. Civilisation is like a fluid that follows the law of osmosis. Cultures of different densities, when separated by a porous partition, flow each into the other for final equable diffusion. Inequalities in culture are not tolerated in modern civilisation. "America is not civil," says Emerson, "while Africa is barbarous."

Through the apertures made by the Shimonoseki bombardment, there flowed into Japan the ideas and ideals of the Occident. In China, owing to the magnitude of her territory and population, the process was not so simple. The more redoubtable walls of Chinese exclusion had to suffer repeated assaults, starting with the Opium War, through the vicissitudes of the Taiping Rebellion and the war with Japan and ending with the Boxer movement, before perforations were made large enough for osmosis freely to begin. Indeed, in the case of our great neighbour, instead of the steady influx of a regenerating stream effecting her deliverance, we see that her moss-grown ramparts are crumbling before the sudden and devastating torrent of a republican deluge.

The soul of Japan, quickly responding to the impulse from the West and rising to the consciousness of her destiny, adjusted her institutions, social and political, to the demands of the age, and set forth on a new career of what sociologists like to call telic progress. China is now fast following in the same path, though with more painful steps, paying higher toll for her long delay. She has but newly learned what Japan learned fifty years ago, that contact and communion with the West under external pressure bring no guarantee of safety or growth.

What part in this epochal interchange between the East and the West, between the Pacific and the Atlantic—the moulding influence of knowledge, ideas, and institutions—does the United States play? Are the conditions in the Far East so radically changed that the words of Mr. King no longer voice the attitude of the American people? Has the phenomenal growth of its Pacific Coast so estranged the higher interests of China and Japan from the heart of this nation, that it now throws stones instead of offering bread? Has the acquisition of the Sandwich Islands so turned the thoughts of America that she now looks upon us as possible intruders and enemies? Has the entrée of this country into the sphere of Asiatic politics brought about a deviation in public opinion from the viewpoint of a King to that of a Hobson? Is the Panama Canal, to the opening of which the Japanese and the Chinese are looking forward with great anticipations of trade—I ask, is the Panama Canal intended for a war-path or a trade route?

There are voices heard on the American side of the Pacific, shrill and alarming, that a conflict, and an armed one at that, is inevitable between the East and the West. The "Yellow Peril" scare, started by the Kaiser and the Czar, leaped over the British Islands, crossed the Atlantic, and found some adherents here. Managed by a paid propaganda, it has been preached and proclaimed by a host of minor prophets.

What a far cry from the time when King made his appeal to "the champions of his country's benevolence"; from the later time when Dr. Samuel Wells Williams concluded his account of the Perry expedition in these words: "In the higher benefits likely to flow to the Japanese by their introduction into the family of civilised nations, I see a hundred-fold return for all the expenses of this expedition to the American Government," and from the still later day when Townsend Harris, Minister Bingham, Secretary Seward, Minister Burlinghame, and General Grant enunciated in no uncertain words the ethical principles which should guide their country in its dealings with the Far East. No, I cannot believe that this nation, still in the prime of manhood, could so easily forget the pledges and ideals of youth. Its assurances of friendship and of good will were not uttered as idle words of diplomacy.

In 1851, at the time that Perry's expedition was still under contemplation, the English historian, Creasy, declared that American diplomacy in the East would be "bold, intrusive, and unscrupulous and that America would scarcely imitate the forbearance shown by England at the end of her war with the Celestial Empire." Of the prophet, Zadkiel's quaint *Almanac*, vaticinating dire misfortunes for Japan in the year 1852, we have already spoken. But the foreboding of historian and prophet alike, proved false. That its early spirit of justice and equity still guides this nation in its Oriental policy, is evidenced by the words of so recent and authoritative a writer as Captain Mahan. Speaking particularly of China, he says: "Our influence, we believe—and have a right to believe—is for good; it is the influence of a nation which respects the right of peoples to shape their own destinies, pushing even to exaggeration its belief in their ability to do so."

American influence in Asia cannot be otherwise than wholesome as long as it is exercised in infusing the vast mass of humanity there with the consciousness of their own dignity and mission—a task which Europe not only neglected, but positively refused to perform on every occasion. Great and real progress must work from within, though its first impulse may come from without. Unless it can intensify the inner impulse, external pressure only ends in making for a while a shallow dent on the surface.

A culture that is forced upon an unwilling nation belongs to things of time "that have voices, speak and vanish." China knows this only too well. Spiritual power comes only through our own choosing. We are free to prefer a stone to bread, or a serpent to a fish. Men and nations are judged by the choice they make. The real difference between the culture-grades of individuals as of ethnic groups is the one difference between their voluntary and their involuntary activities,— between compulsory adoption and reflective choice, between mechanical imitation and judicious selection, between bondage and freedom. It has been said that *Die Weltgeschichte ist das Weltgericht,—* equally truly, though in a different sense of the term, may we not say that a nation's history is a nation's judgment?

Any outside influence, to be permanent, must strike at the root of inner consciousness—the very bottom of sentient existence; at the core of personality where man divests himself of every race distinction and stands on the ground common to the White and the Yellow, the Black and the Brown, and where there is "nor border, breed nor birth, though they come from the ends of the earth."

It is by awakening in the Far Eastern mind,

the sense of personal and national, responsibility, that America has imparted energy to its inertness —by suggesting to it that power which so eminently characterises the American people and which Professor Münsterberg calls "the spirit of self-direction." It was this spirit of self-reliance and self-development which early passed through cannon holes into Oriental communities, and there leavening the leaders and the masses emancipated Japan from the iron shackles of convention and conformity, and which promises to put an end to the sleeping cycle of Cathay and lead that hoary nation to a new heaven and a new earth.

In so doing America has only acted in a manner true to her love of fair play, which among her sons is, as one of their exponents very happily puts it, "a kind of religion." It is a spirit of tolerance, or recognition of others' rights, which imposes on each the duty of regarding his fellow-men with impartiality and of taking the view, to borrow Dr. Henry Van Dyke's words again, that "any human system or order which interferes with this impartiality is contrary to the will of the Supreme Wisdom and Love."

Diplomacy, conducted in consonance with these high principles, shed radiance at once far-reaching and benignant. This great feat America has achieved and can achieve to a still greater degree. Her noblest labour in the Far East lay in the new evaluation of the individual, arousing self-respect and teaching personal as well as political liberty, with the result of the growth of national consciousness.

It is a well-known fact that their acquaintance with the Declaration of Independence of the United States, was the disclosure of a new mine of thought to the makers of new Japan. The idea of the present Chinese Revolution is a republic after the pattern of the United States.

In the light of the preceding statement, it is not difficult to perceive why European nations have found so little response among Eastern peoples. No wonder Mr. Meredith Townsend despairs of any lasting foothold of the West in the East. How many Christians would turn their left cheek when their right is struck! What people would willingly kiss the feet that tread upon them, be they never so beautifully shod!

The Roman god Terminus, in his palmiest days, drew a sacred circle around the Mediterranean, and its northern periphery touched the Black Forests; but in the course of a few centuries its charm was broken, and the august rule of divine Cæsars left behind traces which are now of interest chiefly to archæologists. When we compare the ruins of the Roman dominion, imposing as they are, with the immortal influence of Athens, which is carved deep upon the memory of Europe and is still exhibited in its noblest form, "wherever," to quote from the famous eulogy of Macaulay, "literature consoles sorrow and assuages pain, wherever it brings gladness to eyes which fail with wakefulness and tears, and ache for the dark house and the long sleep," we see that the influence won and exercised by the sword is destined to fade away as "the captains and the kings depart." Territorial domination upheld by the sword is guaranteed no long lease of life.

The best credential of American diplomacy in its early days in the Far East was the unsullied record of the United States in respect to territorial designs. In his day, Townsend Harris assured our Government in the following words:

"The policy of the United States is different from that of other countries. She has no territory in the East, neither does she desire to acquire any there. Her Government forbids obtaining possession in other parts of the world, and we have refused all the requests of distant countries to join our nation."

Though these words sound strange in view of the insular possessions of the United States, nevertheless, they were honest words then and true. China, Japan, and Siam felt perfectly safe in their dealings with the United States. While they had ample reason to suspect all the approachments of European Powers only as steps to ultimate encroachment, their offers of help as baits—a nation possessed of no greed for an inch of land, no thought for intervention in the internal order of a native community, was a pleasing discovery in Oriental eyes. Here lay the secret of the marvellous success of American diplomacy, and an Oriental Lothario could on his part exclaim: "Here or nowhere is America."

The disinterested position which the United States holds or has held in foreign politics, her freedom from European entanglements and complications, has placed her in an attitude of supreme independence in diplomacy. She can initiate a policy and act with little reference to European balance of power. The very possibility of the free exercise of will, sanctioned by a history which shows that she has never abused it, gives to her a preponderating moral advantage. Having deservedly gained a reputation for fair play, her judgment is summoned on occasions involving great issues. By the magic of her name, she can rally behind her a large following of European nations. We may recall in this connection names such as Seward, Grant, Cleveland, Hay, Foster, and Roosevelt. Mankind is always willing to follow a man or a nation in whose eyes there is no mud. America will continue to exercise this power as long as her eyes and her hands are clean; but the instant she stoops for a clod of earth, virtue will go out of her.

Has then her prestige waned with her début into the Eastern Hemisphere? Has she sold her birthright of world-moderatorship and of Asiatic guardianship for a pottage of tropical islands? God forbid that a taste of new territory should infect her with the lust of milomania. Mr. Roosevelt set an example of a novel American principle of colonial policy in San Domingo, and the Filipinos, now passing through the American school for self-government, may, in the fulness of time, rejoice in the completion of their tutelage and celebrate the day of their graduation by a grand convocation.

With such a vision before us, we welcome the presence of the United States in Asiatic waters. We welcome her as she emerges from behind the rising sun and marches to her new seat under the mid-day sky. As far as China and Japan are concerned, they would rather see the Stars and Stripes float over those isles of fronded palms she now rules than any other flag. European nations are still trying to discover and devise suitable methods of administering their Asiatic possessions, and while none of them are satisfied with their own schemes and plans, it will be a valuable contribution to the science of politics and the art of government, if the United States should succeed with her "Holy Experiment" in the Philippines.

The United States may by her mere presence exercise a salutary influence on the Far Eastern situation. Her position as an Asiatic Power entitles her more than ever to a voice in the parliament of Asia. She may do nothing; but her mere presence will have a catalytic action for wholesome activity. It has latterly been broached in irresponsible quarters that Japan looks with jealousy upon the naval growth of the United States. Why should we—as long as you have no designs upon us—and why should you have any?   It has been suggested that Japan fears to lose control of the Chinese market and of the Pacific Ocean.   Why should we be jealous of American trade in the Far East when it forms but a bagatelle of the whole amount of some two billion dollars, of which Great Britain's share is no less than a fourth?   If our ambition were to monopolise the Celestial or any other Eastern market, as we are suspected of wishing to do, we would contest with more important rivals than the Americans.

Control of the Pacific!   What does this high-sounding phrase mean, anyhow?   May we not say with Professor Coolidge that the grandiloquent expressions "dominion of the seas," "mastery of the Pacific," and the like, are mere claptrap?   If the control of an ocean means as much as was implied in the boastful message of Kaiser Wilhelm to Emperor Nicholas, in which he calls himself the Admiral of the Atlantic and the Czar the Admiral of the Pacific,—that phrase may be dispensed with as an empty bit of rhetoric.   Who is the lord of the Atlantic?   Who controls it, and who are debarred from its area of 35,000,000 square miles?   What national flag or flags can attain so gigantic a size as to cover the vast expanse of the Pacific, which is twice as large as the Atlantic?   Our school children are as familiar as are yours with the story of King Canute vainly commanding the waves to retire.   Let the United States increase her navy to a size commensurate with her greatness,—it will accentuate her presence in Asia. Let her steamships plough the ocean lengthwise and crosswise, it will make possible a swifter and larger exchange not only of trade but of cultural influences between the East and the West. Let the Stars and Stripes dot the Ocean of Peace as constellations strew the firmament above,—and I assure you that they harmonise well with the sun-flags of Japan. Never will the sun and stars collide in their orbits.

The six hundred million souls, comprising one-third of the human race, living on the borders of this great Ocean, will hail the ensign of the Union— as long as it is unfurled in the cause of human freedom and universal justice and individual development,—in one word, of the moral principles for which America stands; for I believe, that, paradoxical as it may seem at first sight, it is through the young civilisation of the United States that the old East will receive the freshest moral impetus.

At present one perceives in the Orient two currents of thought flowing from the Occident, moulding the rising generation. One is derived from the continent of Europe, especially from Slavic and Romance literature and art, making for skepticism and decadence, often pessimistic, negative, and destructive; the other, derived from the indefatigable spirit of the Anglo-Saxon race, constructive, robust, forever ready to be up and doing with a "heart within and God o'erhead."

Nor are the introduction and spread of the moral sentiments of the Anglo-Saxon race in the Far East like "the grafting of a bamboo shoot upon the stock of a pine," as we term incongruities. Psychology shows, and experience demonstrates, that the theory of race antipodalism is untenable. There is a tie of brotherhood between an English gentleman and a Japanese samurai. By the introduction or adoption of an Occidental standard of ethics, is not meant a blind acceptance of alien culture. Its purport is to express in the more modern and universal terms of the West, the thoughts and feelings that have been the heritage of the Orient for centuries past.

A man of high reputation for scholarship and character, in summing up impressions of his recent travels in the East, stated his belief that neither China nor Japan will be Westernised. Professor Hart, when he so expressed himself, had chiefly in mind outward manners and customs and social institutions, and I concur largely in his judgment. But it is none the less true that even in these exterior manifestations of culture, the East can no longer defy the ascendency of the West, notably of America. How can it be otherwise? The perforations made in the walls of Asiatic exclusivism have been deliberately, carefully, and constantly enlarged from within. The very men who reared the ramparts have razed them with their own hands for the more rapid and voluminous inflow of the streams of Western culture. Osmosis on a gigantic scale has set in, and even though as Professor Hart says, the East and the West may never realise uniformity of social customs and institutions, they can and will attain to unity of purpose and unanimity of thought.

If until the advent of Cushing to China, and of Perry to Japan, the American advance in the East had been repulsed like a wavelet that dashes in vain against a rock, the great tide of Western civilisation has since then, "without rest, without haste," been rolling on, laving the shores of Asia, surging over her rocks, filling her rivers and creeks with the eternal freshness and irresistible force of the swelling sea. As in a few years the waters of the Atlantic will mingle with the waters of the Pacific, the civilisation conceived in the womb of Asia, born on the shores of the Mediterranean and brought to maturity by the denizens of the Atlantic coasts, will soon enrich the venerable civilisation of its primal home, and thus make complete its circuit.

The Pacific awaits with open arms the coming of the Atlantic. We shall greet her with the words of Byron:

" Thou glorious mirror, where the Almighty's form
    Glasses itself in tempests; in all time,
    Calm or convulsed,—in breeze, or gale, or storm,
    Icing the pole, or in the torrid clime
    Dark-heaving; boundless, endless, and sublime,
    The image of Eternity,—the throne
    Of the Invisible!"

APPENDIX

PEACE OVER THE PACIFIC

[Delivered at the Leland Stanford, Jr., Uuiversity, September, 1911]

I CONSIDER it a great kindness on your part to invite me to this institution, whose fame as a contributor to knowledge has reached all quarters of the globe. I am conscious of the rare honour you have conferred upon me by so doing. I have accepted the invitation, however, not simply because I feel it an honour to do so, but because I feel myself under double obligation to this distinguished academic body. There is no institution of learning outside of our native country which has so many of my compatriots studying under such favourable circumstances as those I see around me. If in some parts of California you build your gates too narrow for our people to enter, here, at least, I see the portals wide open to welcome mankind irrespective of colour. Here, at least, the American flag flies over every race of man, to assure equal justice and equal opportunity. It is certainly a pleasure to stand in your midst and to thank you in person for the generous welcome you have extended to my fellow countrymen. But there is still another circumstance which puts me under obligation to you. Three weeks ago, I had the privilege of having your honoured and beloved president under my own roof. I had not had the pleasure of meeting him before, and I was

delighted to make the acquaintance of this man,
whose scientific achievements have placed him upon
a pedestal of immortal fame, and who, nevertheless,
has not lost a childlike simplicity of nature, whose
arms are ever extended to unite the world in the
bonds of peace.

America has done much in educating Japan; but
if there is any one message which you must send to
us just at this juncture, it is the one which Dr. Jordan
is carrying to my country; for, owing to one reason or
another, there seems to be afloat in the air the most
mischievous and the most unfortunate of rumours regarding a possible estrangement between the United
States and Japan. I know that you, as members of
the Leland Stanford Jr. University, have imbibed the
spirit of peace and a general love of mankind. Why,
these very walls preach peace and good-will to men,
and do not make it incumbent upon a stranger to
repeat what you have always heard; but in the world
outside the rumours are wild and loud. Many interests are involved in keeping them alive. "Most
of them," very rightly said Dr. Brown in the Lake
Mohonk conference last year, "most of them belong
in the category of thoughts which are fathered by a
wish. Men who fear and dislike the Japanese are
eager to see some nation fight them." There are not
a few business concerns which profit by agitation
about war; there are not a few individuals who utilise
the falsest reports for their own promotion or profit;
and there are not a few nations that would derive
benefit from an outbreak betwixt your country and
ours. I do not like to indulge in suspicion, but my
suspicions are well grounded that many an individual,
many a business concern, and many a nation is bent

upon stirring up strife between the two countries, solely from selfish motives. I do not charge any particular company with this crime; but many a company can get good orders for ship-building materials and armament and provisions, simply by inciting a war-scare.

While the peace-loving community is alarmed and distressed at the prospect of any rupture, the interested parties grow fat at their expense. A scarecrow in a melon-patch may frighten away innocent birds, but a thief may be hiding himself under the scarecrow itself. When I reflect that the general public is so easily swayed by the fabrications and machinations of scare-mongers, the infinite credulity of the human mind strikes me as appalling. You and I, however, who enjoy the advantages of a higher education than is allotted to the average citizen, certainly ought to know better. Sift all this empty talk of war, and what have you left? Air-bubbles cannot be sifted, nor can mere froth and foam. Not a grain of reason is left that can be given as a just occasion for war, whereas there is every reason to believe that the two nations which border the Pacific are united by bonds of friendship stronger than those that bind any other two nations. You may say, that sounds all very well, but what about racial differences? Is there not already a *Rassen-Kampf* (race struggle)? Furthermore, there is no legal instrument that unites the two nations in permanent peace; no alliance, no arbitration treaty. But, my friends, there are ties that bind more closely than blood. There are words that join us more strongly than treaties and documents. If you doubt this, cast your glance upon the history of American–Japanese intercourse from its very beginning, or, if you can afford more time, study it page by page, and you can draw a conclusion for yourself that the *alpha* and *omega* of this history is exhausted in the one word— Peace.

In the whole course of this history, you have always taken the active side; we have always maintained the passive. You have helped us in our *début* into the society of nations; you have always chaperoned us in our youthful career; and though gratitude is outside the category of political virtues, our national memory keeps alive the good-will that America has always manifested in her dealings with us. I am not so unsophisticated as to believe that Commodore Perry's expedition was prompted by an impulse of unalloyed Christian charity. I know that its motive was the advantage to be derived from possessing a coaling station, a refuge for the American sailors and waifs, and from the extension of commerce; but I also believe that it was the desire of the United States Government to effect its purpose in the kindliest manner. From his own account, we are aware that Commodore Perry was not always peacefully disposed. More than once did he ask his Government whether he might resort to arms, should diplomacy prove unavailing. As often was he told to refrain from using force. Because Perry succeeded in what was at that time regarded as an impossible task, by luckily avoiding bloodshed, he is called the benefactor of our country. From what he himself stated about his real attitude of mind, it seems that peaceful means were imposed upon him by his Government. We have erected a monument to his memory on the spot where he first landed, and it is far from me to detract one *iota* from the honour due his name, but we can call him the benefactor of our country only by a rhetorical stretching of the term. That term is more deservedly applied to the man and to the Government that stayed his hand from possible violence, and as long as the United States Government is a government of the people, by the people, and for the people, the gentle feeling of gratitude ought to go out, as it does, to you as a nation. And this incident in the life of Perry ought to teach us that whatever military and naval men may say, as long as public opinion, as long as you—men, women, and children—keep up the peaceful tradition of your fathers, the waters of the Pacific will remain calm and unbroken.

The American who came after Perry was indeed the type and in very deed the representative of Americans, of just and true Americans.

Townsend Harris, a merchant of New York, was dispatched to Japan, the first Minister representing the United States. A man of stern rectitude and gentlest powers of persuasion, he, indeed, more than any other, deserves the epithet of benefactor; because in all his dealings with us, the weaker party, he never took advantage of our ignorance, but formulated a treaty with the strictest sense of justice. He did not hesitate to sacrifice the many advantages which his country would gain by apparently honest means, if he saw that there would be undue loss for Japan. After him there were many representatives of this country, and a large majority did credit both to their people and to the cause of justice and humanity at large. Names such as Bingham, Hubbard, and Buck are still remembered, as will be that of your last Ambassador, Mr. O'Brien, with deep respect and affection. As I have said, you have been the active party in our diplomatic relations and it was fortunate, not only for us and for the other countries of the Far East, but for every friend of peace and justice, that your envoys did not represent merely their Government in Washington, but the cause of humanity as well. We are nowadays prone to forget, in our enthusiasm for nationality, that there is a cause higher and nobler than nationality. It is said that the Americans and the Japanese are the two most patriotic nations on the face of the globe; that they are most sensitive to national honour and interest; that they are most easily moved by any appeal to their patriotism; and it is no wonder that we are alike in this respect, for we are the youngest of nations. No other peoples feel as keenly as do we that we have made our respective countries what they are.

It is the bounden duty of every individual who looks upon national responsibility as though it were a personal one, to maintain the amicable relation that has existed between us. Sometimes suspicion creeps in between us, and sometimes arguments threaten to rend us apart. So-called scientists declare from the platform that races so diverse as the White and the Yellow cannot live under the same sky, apparently forgetting that there is no race known under the sun which has not enjoyed citizenship under the Stars and Stripes. It has been one of the grandest and most exalting sights that can be witnessed, to see thousands of immigrants, representing more than fifty distinct nationalities, pouring into America, and to see those streams of varied hues merging in a short time into one current of republican citizenship. To exclude a race on account of racial difference is to admit the incapacity

21

of American institutions to assimilate all races—
as was once the boast of the country. I cannot believe that the present generation of Americans has
lost the power which its forefathers possessed and
exercised, under conditions more strenuous.

One of the greatest sons of California, Mr Burbank,
has intimated in his *Training of the Human Plant*,
that, the wider the field for selection or for sports to
grow and the more chances there are for the crossing
of species, the greater is the probability of evolving
a plant of importance; and Mr. Kidd states that as
yet no scientific standard has been discovered to
gauge the superiority of one race over another. Every
race has traits which, when contributed, make the
human plant richer and higher.

Then there are economists who whisper to you that
cheap labour must be excluded, who forget that
labour is only one of the many factors of production.
If it is true that, the cheaper the labour, the greater
is the necessity for its exclusion, why not, as Bastiat
would say, burn all the latest inventions in machinery?

Then, again, there are moralists who are anxious
lest the good manners of their own people should
be spoiled by lower, alien standards of morality. This
is an old argument, which was current as far back as
the Middle Ages, and while examples are not wanting
to give colour to this solicitude, proofs are on record
that a strong nation exercises beneficent influence not
only upon those who come thither from afar, but
upon neighbouring nations. And certainly America,
in the prime of its national manhood, can exert a superior influence upon other peoples.

Of all the reasons which are given for the alienation of Japan from America, the one which has

seemed most disturbing to the American people at large is the assertion that the Japanese are incapable of assimilation. Lafcadio Hearn has given currency to the term "race antipodalism," the belief that the Japanese are psychologically so far removed that, the more you educate them even in Western knowledge, the farther they will diverge from you in thought. Hearn with all his wonderful insight into Japanese nature, or perhaps because of his enthusiasm for things Japanese, may have thought that he was serving the cause of our people by making them appear as a unique nation, and his opinion is echoed by many who fling it into our very face. Unfortunately, there are rampant Chauvinists among us, as there are everywhere else, who pride themselves upon being different from the rest of the world; who exaggerate small differences, and who insist upon diverging from the path the Western nations pursue; who identify idiopathy with native strength, and who, in so doing, exalt national foibles into national virtues, and purposely keep themselves aloof.

I myself have no patience with those whose mental vision never reaches beyond their limited horizon. They have failed to read in history that the peoples who called themselves special favourites of their Creator, who prided themselves upon what they possessed and upon what they did not possess, fell easy victims to the barbarians, Gentiles, and the heretics whom they were wont to despise. The time has long passed when a nation could live in seclusion and isolation. The modern age does not tolerate apartness. It grinds down peculiarities and will even coerce nations to surrender their characteristics until they learn to associate with others on a common, equal basis of right and wrong, of good and bad. I confess that the two great wars in which we came out triumphant have turned the head of some of our weaker brethren. They believe that our success was due expressly to the spirit of *Bushido*, the remnant of that excellent teaching which formed the samurai's code of honour. I myself feel partly responsible for disseminating this idea. I do not regret that I wrote regarding it and in behalf of it, and what I have written and spoken about it I have no mind to take back; but I do not share the views of the Chauvinists that the spirit of *Bushido* is the peculiar monopoly of our people; neither do I share the view that it is the highest system of morality that man can conceive or construct. I know its weakness. I know all its temptations to misinterpretation and degeneration, and I should feel a regret too deep for words, if my people failed to see that the new wine requires a new wine-skin. I should be most sorry if the noble ethics of *Bushido* were converted by bigots into an anti-foreign instrument. I know that I am exposing myself to grave suspicion and misunderstanding on the part of my countrymen, as though I were catering to the anti-Japanese effusions of some Americans by dilating upon the seamy side of what usually passes as patriotism; but patriotism itself is a word so grossly abused! Doctor Samuel Johnson said long ago that this word is the resort of the scoundrel. Especially among Chauvinists is it freely used as a substitute for reason and argument. Crimes, robbery, and slaughter are committed under the spell of its name. What common sense and morality cannot justify is exonerated under its sanction. Greed of territory and wars ensuing therefrom are vindicated by an appeal to it. So much

so, that some one has recently defined it not as love of
land but as "love of more land." Two such patriotic
nations as Japan and America, unless they are on their
guard, can easily deceive themselves into believing
that in some territory which they covet, whether
mutually or separately, they may come into conflict.
We were highly amused at the strict surveillance of
American authorities over the Japanese in the Philippines. It is too soon to forget the agreement signed
November, 1908, between the two countries, through
which instrument we mutually disclaimed all aggressive designs, in consequence of which each Government
respects the territorial possessions of the other on the
Pacific. This should be a sufficient guarantee that
Japan entertains no ambition to acquire the Philippines or Hawaii. Equally amusing sound to our ears
such articles as often appear in different magazines in
regard to Japanese artifice in China. Now and then
appears a book from the American press by some so-
called authority on Manchuria: full of suspicions but
with no facts to substantiate them, yet always wind-
ing up with the hackneyed conclusion—Japan is stealing American trade in China.

Americans ought to know by this time that, however
mistaken it may be in some directions, our patriotism
is not love for more land. My contention is, on the
contrary, that our patriotism is confined too narrowly
within the home land and feeds itself upon the insular
spirit, which does not see that there are regions
untouched by man where, if they but work, our
people will be welcome. Just as nature abhors a
vacuum, social economy abhors a dearth of labour
when land and capital can be had in abundance.
Look at those orchard hills and valleys where the

fruits are ripe for the hand of the picker; look at those plains where the sugar beets are ready for the weeder and the thousands of acres grown with grain and vegetables, all waiting for the labour of men; certainly California needs more labour. The State has indeed been for years in the condition of "chronic labour famine." A great state of over 165,000 square miles, larger than the area of Japan itself by some 10,000 square miles, and provided with only two and one-third million of population, equal to one-twenty-second part of our own, with a density of only fifteen per square mile, must depend upon foreign labour for the proper cultivation of its soil. Mr. McKenzie's report says that Japanese labour is responsible for nearly $30,000,000 worth of produce in this State. It is depressing to think of the vast wealth lying unexplored and unexploited in this great State, so abundantly blessed by nature, simply because of lack of labour. I wish some Stanford man would take up for scientific treatment,—perhaps under direction of such an authority as Professor Miller, the subject of the economic loss sustained by California on account of Orientophobia. Some new facts may come to light, as was the case in the study of a former member of your university, Miss Mary Roberts Coolidge, whose impartial researches made clear many points pertaining to Chinese labour. I shall not be at all surprised if in the near future, when prejudice shall have exhausted its breath in vociferation, and when the Orientophobic scales shall have fallen from the eyes of labour rings—California may once more open its doors for our people. I know too well the awful power of prejudice, but I also know that economic law is stronger than prejudice. What California lacks can be supplied by Japan, and what the super-abundant population of Japan, the density of which is three hundred and thirty-six per square mile, lacks—namely, field for employment—California can offer in abundance. Far from there being any conflict, there is actually harmony of interests, and a little concession on both sides will surely do away with the few obstacles that may be imposed. Amicable solution of any questions arising from these obstacles is certainly possible, if only the minds of both parties are open to it.

We have already gone a long way toward the solution of the problem, having adopted a method which is clear and summary. To put it concisely, we have taken upon ourselves the duty of restricting immigration to your shores. Without any treaty or convention, purely by a gentlemen's agreement, this has been accomplished. The result is patent to all. I have just come across the Pacific on one of our largest steamers. She was laden to her fullest capacity with silk and tea; but the steerage was almost empty, and the few Japanese passengers in it were bound to a French island of the Lesser Antilles. The rest consisted of a number of labourers from the Philippines, new American subjects who were, of course, admitted free of conditions. But to return to my Japanese immigration problem, though a practical solution has been reached for the time being, there is some doubt as to the permanency of the present arrangement, for a proviso regarding immigration at the end of Act II. of the old treaty was omitted in the new treaty made public last spring. Thus the whole situation depends upon the spirit of concession on the side of Japan, upon her magnanimity, as Professor Coolidge of Harvard puts it. "The arrangement," he says, "which will give the United States the protection it demands, will rest not on the efficiency of its own laws, but on the fulfilment of obligations voluntarily assumed by a foreign state." However willing Japan may be to continue the same course of restriction, America "cannot depend indefinitely on the generosity, real or presumed, of a neighbour."

Professor Coolidge is certainly right, speaking as a jurist,—just as Professor Von Holst was right in speaking as a publicist, of the dangers threatening the United States through what its Constitution has not provided for. At the same time, if a *bona fide* check to emigration is scrupulously carried out in Japan, it will in a few years become, as our Minister of Foreign Affairs said during the last session of our Parliament, the established policy of the Empire; then, the question will bother neither you nor us, for then there will be no question. Good-will can put to rights the confusion which an appeal to law can only make more confused. I believe there is not a single case that cannot be settled by friendly means better than by legal procedure. I think it was Mr. Rowell who expressed his solicitude lest, in the absence of a treaty stipulation, the act of a rowdy boy who might feel like smashing a Japanese window should lead to international complications, or at least jeopardise amity between the two Powers. If the authorities in California are as genuinely disposed as are the Japanese to settle such difficulties amicably, the police and the Court of Justice ought to be able to do so in five minutes. It is also feared that a demagogue may arise in Japan and make of a trifling incident an issue of international magnitude. I am sorry to own that

there are demagogues in my country as in yours,
and fire-spitting journalists, too, and hair-splitting
jurists as well; but a foreign policy, such as the policy
of restriction, once established and efficiently carried
out, is hardly likely to be upset by them. If I may
be allowed to express my private opinion, that policy
is too vigorously and too conscientiously put into
practice; so that some of our most promising students
are debarred from the advantage of American education and some of the most intelligent working-men
are lost to American economy. I may add this opinion of mine is shared by many American residents in
Japan.

But, pardon me, I have sojourned too long on
the California coast, because my mind is full of
California impressions. Though I landed here only
last Saturday, such strange sights and sounds as I did
not perceive twenty-eight years ago, when I first
passed through San Francisco on my way to Baltimore, overwhelmed my senses. There was then no talk
of war; no word of ill-will was heard, no sound of ship-
wrights working on a Dreadnaught, no sound of ma-
sons building a fort, no din of trumpet or of drum; all
was peace along the Pacific. I can scarcely believe my
own eyes and ears, so stupendously changed is the
tone of American life. I wonder if this is progress.
For myself, I cannot believe so. I live in a land
famed for its soldiers and sailors; but I cannot free
my mind from the thought that armament and mili-
tarism and what they bring in their train, will ultimately spell the ruin of the nations that play with
them.

So, as a son of Japan, and as a well-wisher of
America, it is my sincere hope that all these rumours

of war may prove but a transient dream, a horrible nightmare that passes with the coming of the dawn. May we earnestly pray, and diligently work toward the end, that, wherever else war-clouds may darken this earth, lasting peace shall reign over the Pacific.

INDEX

A

Adams, John Quincy, 262
Agnosticism, 119
Agriculture, 209–213; animals,
212–213; arable land, 35,
209, 219; capital, 210; colleges of, 191; staples, 213–
214; taxation, 212
Agricultural College, 191
Ainus (aborigines), 86
American-Japanese intercourse,
258–277; effect of whaling
on, 262, 278–279; unsuc-
cessful attempts to open
Japan, 263–265, 268–270
American-Japanese relations,
278–299; anti-foreign period,
283–284; Prince Katsura on,
298–299; services to Japan,
284–288
American influence, 300–315;
in education, 182, 184
Anglo-Saxon influence, 183,
186, 313
Army conscription, 78
Art: Oriental and Greek, 5;
Seiho (painter), 10; of Heian
period, 61; of Kamakura
period, 63; attitude of Japanese towards, 108–109
Asia. *See* East

B

Banks, 170–173
Bathing, 28, 153
Biddle, Commodore, 268–270
Black Current (Kuro-Shiwo),
263

Brown, Dr., 317
Buddhism: absorbs Shinto,
142; adopted, 56–57; doc-
trines, 145–148; history, 138–
139; influence, 58–59, 62,
140; sects, 139, 141
Bushido, 155–157, 166, 173–
174; author's valuation of,
324; and martyrdom, 69

C

Calendar, 80
California, 44, 290–291, 326
Character of Japanese, 107,
114-115
China: early communication,
55; influence, 56; in Formosa
235–236; regeneration of,
302–303, 308; trade with
Japan, 228
Chinese Bank clerks, 170–171
Chosen. *See* Korea.
Christianity: 16th and 17th
century, 68–71; present sta-
tus, 120
Civil Service, 195–197
Classes, Social, 209; abolished,
78
Climate: Japan, 28–30; Tokyo,
38; Hokkaido, 38
Colleges: Agricultural, 191;
Commercial, 190; National
(*Koto-Gakko*), 189; Normal,
185
Confucius and Confucianism:
Analects introduced, 55; in-
fluence, 73, 158; not a
religion, 119
Creation, Mythical, 51